Performance Drivers in the Australian Banking and Financial Industry

Talent management is a way banks acquire competitive advantage. Practices such as personality profiling with effective knowledge-based productivity and the application of high-performance work systems help to set a company apart from its competition and maintain this competitive advantage.

This book provides an in-depth look at the relationship between personality types and individual-level performance in knowledge-based environments, through cases in Australia's banking and finance sector. This book also examines how high-performance workplace systems influence individual performance in relation to productivity through a multi-level analysis of micro- and meso-level factors.

The findings in this book have relevant implications not only for the Australian system but also for other banking and financial service contexts outside of Australia.

Ami-Lee Kelly is a Senior Manager working in the Australian banking and finance industry.

Ashish Malik is an Associate Professor at the Newcastle Business School, University of Newcastle, Australia.

Philip J. Rosenberger III is a Lecturer at the Newcastle Business School, University of Newcastle, Australia.

Routledge Advances in Management and Business Studies
Green Human Resource Management in Chinese Enterprises

For more information about this series, please visit: www.routledge.com/Routledge-Advances-in-Management-and-Business-Studies/book-series/SE0305

Performance Drivers in the Australian Banking and Financial Industry

Ami-Lee Kelly, Ashish Malik and Philip J. Rosenberger III

Routledge
Taylor & Francis Group
LONDON AND NEW YORK

First published 2022
by Routledge
2 Park Square, Milton Park, Abingdon, Oxon OX14 4RN

and by Routledge
605 Third Avenue, New York, NY 10158

Routledge is an imprint of the Taylor & Francis Group, an informa business

British Library Cataloguing-in-Publication Data
A catalogue record for this book is available from the British Library

Library of Congress Cataloging-in-Publication Data
A catalog record for this book has been requested

ISBN: 978-0-367-50318-5 (hbk)
ISBN: 978-0-367-50319-2 (pbk)
ISBN: 978-1-003-04946-3 (ebk)

Typeset in Galliard
by codeMantra

Contents

Figures

Tables

Foreword I

In my seminar on Performance Management, I almost always start by asking participants to prepare two lists – the things that they are good at and things that they are not good at. Invariably, the first list is much, much, longer than the second one. Over the years, I have noticed that the little variance in the lists has to do with age and experience. The more experience the students have, the fewer the things they list as things they can do – however, the second list seems to stay more or less constant.

I then proceed to list a whole bunch of things that I cannot do – trust me, this list is rather long and gets longer as I get older! Nonetheless, I offer them a couple of examples to make the point – I am 6'2" but cannot play basketball to save my life, I would love to but cannot play the guitar, and I will not be jumping out of an airplane anytime soon, or ever. This helps some of them add a few things to the list on the right side (things they can't do). I then go on to tell them that I taught accounting and finance for ten years at the graduate level even though I had taken barely two courses in my life prior to being asked to teach this course. One was in the eighth grade – called double-entry bookkeeping, and the other was during my MBA, called capital budgeting. Of course, it took me six months of preparing day in and day out to give the first lecture, where I was extremely nervous, and literally stumbled through the three-hour session. With each successive iteration, I got better and more comfortable.

I use these examples to explain the importance of the AMO framework, and emphasise why individuals need the necessary skills, the appropriate motivation, and be afforded the opportunity to express discretionary effort. Of course, our personalities help determine how aware we are of our own limitations, motivations, and interest in a task, and how we approach each situation. My first reaction on being asked to teach the course was utter surprise (OK, shock), followed by excitement at the challenge, which led to the request for substantial time to prepare.

This book by Kelly, Malik, and Rosenberger III reports the results of a comprehensive examination of the impact of the AMO framework on employee attitudes and performance outcomes. Their treatise is based on analysing over

400 responses of productivity experts and in addition to measuring employee attitudes and performance outcomes; they also analyse the moderating effects of personality type, using the MBTI framework.

As someone who has studied, researched and taught Performance Management for almost three decades, I am pleased to see this book, which addresses a very key determinant of final performance – employee attitudes. As much as managers may want to keep individual attitudes out of the equation, the fact remains that you can no more separate individual attitudes from their performance than separate water from the oceans. Indeed, individuals are complex combinations of attitudes and personalities (and a lot more), and understanding this complex mix can go a long way in assisting managers get the best out of their people, whatever instrument they might use to measure these two critical factors.

If organisations are to achieve sustainable competitive advantage, they need to do a much better job of understanding the antecedents and consequences of individual performance – and, if managers want to manage their team members' performance better, they need to understand individuals' personality and attitudes.

The findings of this book have wider implications for the overall human resource department. First, organisations need to hire individuals who have the required skills for the job – easier said than done. Of course, since jobs evolve and individuals evolve, the individual's skills may not match the job skills down the road. This is where training becomes critical, in order to ensure that any gap in the individual's skills and the job requirements is reduced or eliminated on a continuous basis. Next, having the ability to do the job does not automatically mean that the individual will exert the effort. As such, it is critical that the manager and the organisation provide an environment that is conducive to individual effort – where individuals are motivated to work towards the assigned tasks. Finally, individuals have to be provided the opportunity to work on the task for which they are qualified and motivated. This may seem like a simple equation, but as we see regularly across organisations of all types around the world, meeting these three conditions is rather difficult for many organisations. First, because they do a poor job of hiring whereby rather than ensuring that individuals have the right skills they are most often focused on the person's qualifications or pedigree. Next, in cases where the job has changed organisations are reluctant to provide training as it is seen as an unnecessary expense. Finally, the notion of providing the right environment so that individuals are motivated is rather complex because it requires addressing things at the macro, meso and micro levels.

The good news is that this can be done, as many successful organisations have demonstrated. The bad (tough) news is that it requires a lot of effort on the part of HR departments and line managers. This is where this book can come in handy. The findings of this book are quite provocative and can go a long way in helping individuals across all types of industry and nations rethink their Performance Management Systems and use the AMO model to drive high performance in their organisations.

Happy reading!
Arup Varma, PhD
Distinguished University Research Professor
Quinlan School of Business
Loyola University Chicago

Foreword II

I have worked in financial services for over a decade and half of that time closely with one of the authors of this book. I recall when the study and analysis that underpin this book was being completed, the passion for the topic coupled with the thought patterns, data and conclusions drove my own thinking and approaches forward in a way that I didn't expect.

The thinking has pushed and continues to push me to improve my own practices and approaches for enabling high-performing teams for productivity and process improvement. It provides a logical and insightful analysis and conclusions to drive your own improvement for enabling high-performing teams.

Jason Rensen
Head of Productivity and Process Improvement
Commonwealth Bank of Australia

Preface

> By developing individual strengths, guarding against weaknesses and appreciating the strengths of other types, life will be more amusing, more interesting and more of a daily adventure than it could possibly be if everyone were alike.
>
> Isabel Briggs Myers

> Your workforce is your most valuable asset. The knowledge and skills they have present the fuel that drives the engine of the business, and you can leverage that knowledge.
>
> Harvey Mackay

The above quote from Isabel Briggs Myers highlights the importance of understanding an individual's true strengths to lead a meaningful and fulfilling life. The quote from Harvey Mackay enforces the value knowledge has as the engine of all businesses and its everchanging employee assets. Knowledge is frequently defined to be the acquisition of information coupled with skills through experience, education and exposure. Whereas personality profiling is extensively known as a process to understand human attributes, values and skills, it also allows employers to set organisational goals to maximise job performance and individual contribution to the organisation. Personality profiling helps identify traits within individuals for unlocking their potential and aid the employer to comprehend the productive capacity of their employees better.

Further, the importance of research on high-performance work systems, which are known as a set of workplace practices that collectively have a positive impact in influencing employees' performance, has been established. Such an approach directs the focus of an organisation to achieve its efficiency, effectiveness and financial goals. Employing such an approach allows individuals to appreciate their abilities in a tangible and systematic manner to add the highest level of value to their organisations.

This book will posit on each of these areas to explore and understand the Australian banking and financial ecosystem. This book also evaluates the intricacies and extraordinary landscape of banking and finance to produce a view for organisations converging their strengths and providing an idiosyncratic competitive advantage. This, we believe, will advance scholarship in this exciting new area, by blending micro-level individual foundations with meso-level organisational systems for delivering high performance.

The research presented in this book captures concepts such as knowledge work, personality profiling, productivity outcomes and high-performance work systems in an organisational context. We hope this book inspires further research into the emic dimensions of people and performance surrounding a range of organisation and business outcomes.

Dr Ami-Lee Kelly
Associate Professor Ashish Malik, PhD
Dr Philip Rosenberger III

Acknowledgements

This book is the product of an abundance of hard work and an ongoing dedication to understanding a new emerging area of research. I am extremely grateful and appreciative of my incredible mentors Dr Ashish Malik and Dr Philip J. Rosenberger III, who have spent countless hours providing me guidance and feedback on our book. Their personal dedication to my academic career is beyond any expectations I might have had. My inspiration comes directly from both of them. Not only have we created an incredible working team, but we have become close friends. I thank them both from the bottom of my heart for everything they do for me.

This book is dedicated to my loving husband Shaun; Shaun has supported me endlessly, breathing and living this book as an ever-present supporter. Shaun's ongoing love, encouragement and constant motivation have been the strongest driving force in my life, encouraging me immensely when writer's block hit or when I thought writing this book wasn't achievable. Shaun supports and inspires me to be the very best version of myself.

Shaun – you always know the right thing to say, you always support me, and, above all else, you always make me feel so loved; this book is for you.

Ami-Lee Kelly

A book that focuses on performance management, I must confess that I have reflected a lot about performance and performance management, especially during the COVID pandemic, and when I was on a sabbatical during the second half of 2020. Performance has many meanings, measures and purposes. Oftentimes, we perform to achieve or contribute to a goal. Interestingly, this goal is seldom our own; yet we feel an immense sense of pride and accomplishment once it is achieved. I take some solace in the learnings from the ancient principles of *Ayurveda*, which focuses on achieving the goal of holistic well-being – a concept that encompasses physical, mental, emotional, social, environmental and spiritual aspects of human wellness. Getting to this level of understanding has been a journey, which would not have been possible without several *gurus* in my life. I therefore dedicate this book to my mentors, teachers and gurus who have come in different forms and at different points in my life, always inspiring me to seek these different forms of well-being. Interestingly, well-being is temporal and requires continuous balancing. The good news is that it is possible to achieve this, as there is plenty of wisdom that can be accessed, and this is a journey that is exciting to embark on.

Ashish Malik

Glossary of Key Terms

Affective organisational commitment: It is represented by the statement, 'I am willing to work harder to help the company succeed?'

Coachee: an individual who receives coaching from a qualified coach.

Hard tasks: tasks that follow a set standard application; these tasks are clearly defined and structured; individuals follow the same methods to complete these tasks, with little to no user variation.

High-performance work systems (HPWS): HPWS are known to involve improvements to work practices to increase employee decision-making and investments in employee skills and changes to performance incentives to ensure that employees can undertake these bigger or greater responsibilities and that they actually want to do so (Boxall & Purcell, 2008).

Knowledge-based environment: the environment where individuals are employed to work on knowledge-based tasks or activities; typically speaking, work in this environment is complex and based on the high-level skill an individual possesses (Organisation X, 2017).

Mentee: an individual who receives mentoring from a qualified mentor.

Myers-Briggs Type Indicator (MBTI): The MBTI is an introspective self-report questionnaire with the purpose of indicating differing psychological preferences in how people perceive the world around them and make decisions (Quenk, 2009). This is usually reported as an individual having a 'personality type', with the MBTI featuring four dichotomous base pairs that result in an individual having one of 16 combined MBTI types such as INTJ or ESFJ.

Non-productivity roles: individuals employed in roles outside of the productivity-related roles, but are individuals who champion productivity skills through their productivity qualifications.

Non-routine tasks: tasks completed outside of the 'normal' day-to-day activities.

Organisation X: This is the pseudonym used to disguise the case organisation's identity, where data collection took place.

Organisational citizenship behaviour: employee behaviour that encourages others to try new and effective ways of doing their job and willingly share their expertise with co-workers.

Organisational commitment: employees' favourable attitude towards their organisation wherein they strive to work harder to see the organisation succeed.

Productivity: the effectiveness of productive effort, as measured in terms of the rate of output per unit of input. The intersection between cost, effort and quality (Oxford Dictionary.com, 2017).

Productivity experts: individuals who are trained in Lean Six Sigma such as Green Belt, Black Belt and Master Black Belt certified. These individuals have attended and completed training in a formal educational environment, and they have led project(s) using these newly acquired skills and have sit for a formal examination to display their understanding and application of these skills (Organisation X, 2017).

Productivity practitioners: individuals employed in productivity-related roles across Organisation X. These individuals are trained in the appropriate belt (Green, Black and Master Black Belts) to complete their daily responsibilities (Organisation X, 2017).

Productivity roles: individuals who are employed in productivity-based roles.

Productivity tasks: tasks that productivity experts complete daily, weekly, monthly or as required. These tasks are detailed in Appendix B. The tasks can broadly be placed into two categories, with the first being operational-based work, which is more straightforward and at times repetitive or task-focused, and the second category of tasks being more complex and requiring thinking, investigating and knowledge, thus requiring higher levels of skills to complete (Organisation X, 2017).

Routine tasks: tasks that are part of the everyday requirements.

Soft tasks: tasks that do not follow a set standard application; these tasks differ based on the task itself and the individual completing the task, and individuals follow different methods to complete these tasks, with user variation.

1 High performance in the Australian banking and financial services industry

Introduction

This chapter introduces the research topic and outlines the methodology echoing a structured approach to presenting the research. The "Background" section provides a summary on the background of the project, including the impact personality profiling or types, and specifically Myers-Briggs, have on productivity levels of workers in a knowledge-based environment. The "Purpose and motivation for the study" section then outlines the research purpose and motivation for undertaking the study, whilst the "Research method" section briefly summarises the research methods used. Next, the "Research scope" section discusses the scope of the research. The "Research problem and research questions" section discusses the research problem and research questions extensively, and the next section, "Research questions," defines the key terms. The "Structure of the research" section details the overall structure of the study, and, lastly, the "Conclusion" section concludes the chapter.

Background

A key problem facing organisations is not only how to remain locally or regionally competitive but also to become globally competitive (Argote & Ingram, 2000; Chowhan, 2016; Malik, Pereira & Tarba, 2019; Smith, Tucker & Pitt, 2011) and manage performance and growth both during normal business times as well as during the 'new normal' or in times of a crisis (Malik, 2013, 2018b; Malik & Sanders, 2021). Human-resource management (HRM), when used correctly, can play an important role in dealing with that challenge (Chowhan, 2016; Malik, 2018a; Malik, Pereira & Budhwar, 2018; Smith, Tucker & Pitt, 2011; Toivanen, 2011). Through the blueprint and enactment of high-performance work systems (HPWS) incorporating recruitment of appropriate employees with appropriate skills and personal attributes, such as their personality type (Athota, Budhwar & Malik, 2020; Athota & Malik, 2019) for a particular job, HRM can play a key role in shaping the fundamentals that underpin performance in an organisation, along with maintaining an organisational focus of creating and delivering value (Boxall, 2012; Malik, Boyle & Mitchell, 2017; Smith & Pitt, 2011; Stewart, Danford, Richardson & Pulignano, 2010).

Employee productivity, personality testing and high-performance work systems have been extensively studied (Boxall, 2012; Boxall & Macky, 2009; Bradley & Herbert, 1997; Drucker, 1999; Genco, 2006; Jabbour, 2013). However, there is limited research that integrates these three related and vital concepts together, especially in the context of employees tasked with enhancing productivity in a competitive and knowledge-based environment. It is important to study these topics together to enable firms and companies to create and monitor their competitive advantage in a tangible manner in an ever-changing and highly competitive business market. This advantage can be the difference between success and failure especially in an industry like the one being analysed, the banking and financial services industry, where the product offerings are commodities. As a consumer, the products offered by all of the financial institutions are all the same, and there is little that really differentiates them in this market; however, a well-built and monitored personnel framework and talent pipeline can be the change an organisation needs to be better than its competitors, thus necessitating companies and firms to focus on competitive advantage (Argote & Ingram, 2000; Fahy, Farrelly & Quester, 2002). Also, it is necessary for an individual looking for the best-fit career for them. As an individual seeking employment, they have to make a decision regarding the types of work or employment they intend to take up; having more information at their disposal enables the individual to choose the most appropriate role for them that suits their skills, thus making the decision-making process easier and more aligned with their interests and ambitions. Hence, there is a need to improve the understanding of these three related concepts, which this research does through its detailed analysis.

There are several strong themes that are pertinent to this research. The first theme looks into the idea of competitive advantage concerning organisations, and the following themes consider the effective use of productivity in knowledge-based environments, personality profiling using inventories, such as the Myers-Briggs Type Indicator (MBTI) and high-performance work systems (HPWS), noting that there are inherent problems in measuring and defining productivity for different organisational tasks. Stalk (1988) and Jabbour (2013) detail competitive advantage as a dynamic target that companies need to keep track of, which can be done effectively through the use of productivity in the workplace (Stalk, 1988). Stalk continues to explain that leading companies are looking for innovative ways to remain competitive, and recently the focus has been on productivity (Stalk, 1988). In short, productivity is the idea of achieving production quality at the lowest cost and in the timeliest manner. It can be used well within an organisation, and productivity, when used correctly, is an attribute that can provide a real competitive advantage for companies and firms in today's aggressive landscape (Drucker, 1999; Genco, 2006; Jabbour, 2013; Stalk, 1988).

A second theme in the 21st century is to increase the productivity of knowledge work and knowledge workers (Drucker, 1999; Genco, 2006; Jabbour, 2013; Mladkova, 2011). Recent research has highlighted the critical role of certain high-performance human resource management and work practices in improving the ability of firms to share and integrate knowledge and thus also improve their performance (Malik, Froese & Sharma, 2020; Malik & Nilakant, 2016; Lee, Malik, Rosenberger & Sharma, 2020).

Many firms endeavour to use productivity in a more agile, effective and efficient manner in their operations, reinforcing the thought that productivity, when used appropriately, can drive competitive advantage (Curtain, 1998; Grant, 2001; Van Der Voordt, 2004).

Research into employee productivity shows that many executives and managers have a hazy and uncertain understanding of what it takes to increase productivity in knowledge-based businesses and firms today, thus suggesting that parts of or their entire businesses operate in a complex and uncertain environment (Matson & Prusak, 2010). Further, workplaces suffer from procrastination, which is typically seen as a sub-optimal behaviour that undermines productivity (Gupta, Hershey & Gaur, 2012). There is some evidence of an increase in motivation- and ability-enhancing practices to promote firm performance and increase knowledge sharing (Lee, Malik, Rosenberger & Sharma, 2020). Further, a meta-analysis of the impact of motivational approaches has found support for enhancing employees' knowledge-sharing behaviours (Nguyen, Tuan, Froese & Malik, 2019), including the importance of certain cognitive processes such as provisions of learning to motivate employees to share knowledge (Nguyen & Malik, 2020).

The above said findings would suggest that the work itself is more diverse and amorphous, with some activities and tasks in the workplace not clearly defined or easily predictable, which, in turn, affects how performance metrics are defined and created, thereby making it a challenging exercise managing people and their desired levels of productivity (Matson & Prusak, 2010).

However, there are added complexities when analysing companies that exist in a knowledge-based environment, and these complexities are important to apprehend, as knowledge workers hired to complete complex tasks differ frequently, for example in project-based settings. Knowledge work is more complex than what we have traditionally known of in manufacturing or operational-based environments (Matson & Prusak, 2010; Mladkova, 2011). It is therefore challenging to manage these complexities and hire individuals that fit in a work organisation and remain 'productive' by delivering high-quality outcomes. Along with capturing the right performance metrics to understand current performance and look for improvement opportunities, a focus on employee satisfaction, organisational commitment and job behaviours is also relevant (Matson & Prusak, 2010; Mladkova, 2011).

Additionally, Van Der Voordt (2003) states that many firms are looking to increase their effectiveness through productivity, as organisations are looking to achieve a better performance at lower costs. Van Der Voordt continues that a common opinion exists that open structure within the work environment encourages more communication and an easier exchange of knowledge and skills, whereas the use of cockpits or concentration cells creates good conditions for concentrated work, but these structures are yet to be tested. In some areas, productivity is simple to measure, for example in the manufacturing industry, but the challenge arises when productivity is measured in knowledge-producing organisations. This perspective strengthens the need for this research to enable a deeper understanding of productivity but also to understand whether knowledge-based roles can successfully be measured and whether productivity workers perform in the most productive manner (Van Der Voordt, 2003).

Alongside productivity, there is a vast body of literature that focuses on the theme of personality profiling, an idea that enables organisations to achieve competitive advantage through its people, focusing on psychological bases of their talent profiles to ensure both business continuity and that an ongoing competitive advantage is sustained and maintained (Fahy, Farrelly & Quester, 2002; Stahl et al., 2012). The idea of using personality profiling is not new and aligns with earlier ideas of achieving a person-organisation fit in line with the best-fit approach (e.g. Boxall & Purcell, 2011; Huselid, Jackson & Schuler, 1997). Therefore, through this research an individual's type is also examined as an important variable in obtaining and maintaining competitive advantage for companies in today's challenging times (Argote & Ingram, 2000; Chowhan, 2016; Smith, Tucker & Pitt, 2011).

Conventionally firms assess the competence of a candidate during the recruitment process based on whether the individual presents culturally as a 'decent enough' fit for the organisation. There exists a limited understanding of personality-role fit as a basis for sustained levels of performance especially in productivity-based roles. But as far as research shows, there are no formal tools or frameworks that support this kind of assessment; instead, a subjective opinion is formed in a time-boxed interview–based environment where the employer and potential employee meet for a short time (Collins, 2006; Mook, 1996; Organisation X, 2017).

This research will assist by making recommendations that will enable developing a formal tool or framework that can be used to formally and tangibly assess a personality-based profile, similar to the best-fit of the individual for a given role (Organisation X, 2017).

It is clear from the available literature that the area of personality profiling has been explored extensively, and the topics vary greatly ranging from demographic related content such as preferences relating to gender differences (Herk, 2011) through skills such as management skills (Schullery, Knudstrup, Schullery & Pfaff, 2009) to diseases and illnesses such as hearing loss (Hutchinson & Alessio, 1996) and Asperger's Syndrome (Chester, 2006). There are several journals that have published extensive research using measures such as MBTI (e.g. *Journal of Psychological Type*, published by the Center for Applications of Psychological Type, and *Personalities and Individual Differences*). These journals have been reviewed extensively and in great detail; however, the topic of personality profiling in knowledge-based environments where HPWS are employed has not been studied or discussed, therefore leaving a gap in the literature relating to this important and relevant topic which needs to be addressed.

Finally, we need to consider how the theme of HPWS affects performance and plays into this research (Macky & Boxall, 2007; Boxall & Macky, 2009, 2014). HPWS have been receiving increased attention in the last 10–15 years both academically and professionally (Macky & Boxall, 2007; Boxall & Macky, 2009, 2014; Boxall & Purcell, 2008; Malik, 2018). HPWS constitute a claim that there exists a system of work practices for core workers in an organisation that leads in some way to exceptional performance (Patel, Messersmith & Lepak, 2013). It is argued that a focus on the high-involvement stream usefully grounds HPWS studies in an important area of workplace change in the current context and takes organisations away from eclectic and contentious selections of 'best practices' (Macky & Boxall, 2007; Boxall & Macky, 2009, 2014). Along with the idea that HPWS are commonly comprehended to involve work practices to increase employee involvement in decision making, which in turn invests in employee skills and changes to performance incentives to ensure that employees do more work and are motivated to do so (Boxall & Purcell, 2008). Boxall and Macky (2009) further contend that the path to better research lies in inspecting the underpinning processes experienced by workers when management seeks to pursue high-involvement systems and charting their links to employee and operational outcomes (Macky & Boxall, 2007; Boxall & Macky, 2009, 2014).

Furthermore, if firms are able to build effective HR systems that help to produce a more adaptive workforce, then this, in turn, may help to produce greater levels of innovation and consequently improved performance, both of which are key to a company achieving and maintaining competitive advantage (Patel, Messersmith & Lepak, 2013).

In the literature, there are different conceptualisations of HPWS. HR systems encompass the management of a work domain and the management of the people who do the work practices and employment practices. Work practices are concerned with how the work is organised and structured. In contrast, employment practices include all the practices that are used to recruit, deploy, motivate, consult, negotiate with, develop and retain employees and to terminate the employment relationship. Boxall and Macky argue that employment practices influence the abilities, motivations and opportunities of individual employees (Macky & Boxall, 2007; Boxall & Macky, 2009, 2014).

As HPWS are a logical focus for building and maintaining competitive advantage through business model, process or product innovations (Malik, Boyle & Mitchell, 2017; Malik, Pereira, & Budhwar, 2018; Malik et al., 2019a), it is underpinned by the Ability, Motivation and Opportunity (AMO) model (Bos-Nehles, Van Riemsdijk & Looise, 2013; Boxall & Purcell, 2011; Lee, Malik, Rosenberger & Sharma, 2020). In the AMO model, Ability is the idea that employees will perform because they possess the necessary knowledge and skills to do so. Similarly, Motivation is based on the fact that employers need to build the right environment, as this will enable employees to perform because they are motivated in the workplace to do so. Lastly, creating an environment that affords Opportunity for employees is built on the prospect that if the work structure and environment provides the necessary support for employees, they will use it (Bos-Nehles, Van Riemsdijk & Looise, 2013; Boxall & Purcell, 2009).

Changes to opportunity-enhancing practices such as involvement and participation has implication for ability and motivation enhancing practices (Macky & Boxall, 2007; Boxall & Macky, 2009, 2014). Therefore, the literature supports the idea that HPWS are strongly linked to competitive advantage for companies and firms in today's challenging times. Each of the concepts mentioned will be expanded on in greater detail in later chapters.

Purpose and motivation for the study

The purpose of this study is to focus on the impact of personality type and the wider contextual environment for managing people on a range of individual and organisational outcomes. More specifically, the theoretical aspects of HPWS, individual personality type and its impact on a range of individual and organisational outcomes will be examined in this research.

To remain successful, competitive and open for business for the foreseeable future, organisations need to understand their industry landscape, along with their internal operations, and achieve a best-fit – in terms of person, organisation and job – for their employees to remain effective and efficient in their day-to-day operations and with their future strategy (Chowhan, 2016). Therefore, it is important to undertake this research to ensure that organisations understand how to operate in the most effective and efficient manner, and ensure that the above gaps are addressed (Chowhan, 2016).

The first theoretical area relates to how the wider organisational context created through the use of HPWS would have an impact on performance (e.g. Macky & Boxall, 2007; Boxall & Macky, 2009, 2014). Writers in this line of thinking postulate the need to address the key tenets of the AMO framework, wherein **A** refers to Ability of employees, **M** refers to the need to Motivate employees through a range of approaches and finally **O** refers to allowing for employees the Opportunity to put their Ability and motivational attitude to productive use. The second theoretical aspect concerns an individual's personality type and their self-awareness of it at a workplace in influencing their performance. Further, contingency theorists have long argued for the need to align and fit individual personality types to certain roles for gaining the most effective productivity outcomes and to avoid having square pegs in round holes (Bos-Nehles, Van Riemsdijk & Looise, 2013; Curtain, 1998; Stewart, Danford, Richardson & Pulignano, 2010; Van Der Voordt, 2003).

Such an approach is increasingly finding its application in the financial services sector. For example, at the case organisation where this study is conducted, Organisation X,[1] the hiring managers come up with a set of questions they feel are appropriate to assess the individual's skills, capabilities, prior roles and education. They will interview the individual who has applied for the role and look into prior performance based on key performance indicators considering their last 12 months of performance (Organisation X, 2017). Further, the current recruitment framework used in the case organisation is the 3E model: experience, exposure and education. The first is experience, which receives a 70% allocation; it is believed that in terms of professional development, individuals gain their knowledge base from real on-the-job experience (Organisation X, 2017). Note that this also corresponds to the abilities of an individual. The second is exposure, which receives a 20% allocation, with the idea being that individuals learn based on what they are physically exposed to, the environment which presents the Opportunity. The third is education, which receives a 10% allocation, as individuals learn based on formal education programmes (Organisation X, 2017; Wranx, 2017). Note that this aspect also corresponds to Ability and Opportunity to apply their knowledge. This model is taken into consideration as part of the recruitment process by some hiring managers and is promoted as the preferred model at Organisation X. However, this model is not always employed by all hiring managers – it really comes down to their personal beliefs and what they deem as important (Collins, 2006; Organisation X, 2017; Wranx, 2017). We have conducted some analyses into interviewing at the case organisation and found that if an individual (being interviewed) can present well and convince the hiring manager they are the best-fit for the role, the individual will be hired. However, based on the research experience, a lot of the times the individual might not be the best-fit for the role which would become evident after several months of the individual being in the role (Organisation X, 2017).

As part of the recruitment process, the hiring managers will complete an ad hoc assessment of whether they think the individual will culturally fit with the new team; however, this activity is subjective and informal, as there is currently no objective way to measure best-fit in terms of the job, organisation and culture (Organisation X, 2017). This research will offer hiring managers with a more tangible and formal mechanism, a model or framework for completing their assessment of the best-fit for a role; thus, a further motivation for completing this research is that it will benefit organisations and hiring managers in determining the best-fit for open and available roles across their teams and related businesses (Organisation X, 2017).

If organisations are able to recruit and align their employees with the best roles for building and maintaining a talent pipeline, then it will help ensure that organisations have the most effective and efficient workforce (Stahl et al., 2012). Therefore, developing a formal approach for achieving the best-fit outcomes will allow organisations to formally and tangibly assess the best-fit for individuals operating in certain productivity-based roles. This means an organisation can gain further competitive advantage in a marketplace, where such an attribute can mean the difference between success and failure of the organisation. Current employment practices at Organisation X differ based on who is undertaking the recruitment, as this organisation does not currently consider the best-fit formally during the recruitment process (Collins, 2006; Wranx, 2017).

Furthermore, individuals can use parts of this research to enable a sense of self-awareness and actualisation; such an approach may enable individuals to critically analyse the best possible workplace roles that are suitable for them and their satisfaction (Quenk, 2013). An individual can use the results of their personality profiling to understand their preferences and desires relating to different situations and circumstances. They can also use the results to determine their self-awareness regarding the best-fit role for them in their career (Boult, Thompson & Schaubhut, 2017).

Another motivation for this research came from access at Organisation X. As practitioners and researchers focusing on productivity, the research team had a vast expertise, but this research noted differences in productivity across Organisation X taking into account project-related work, productivity training and facilitation and creation and implementation of the four productivity habits (these topics are detailed in Chapter 2). The variation amongst the different productivity roles in Organisation X was extensive, clearly displaying that differences were evident based on which part of the organisation an individual was employed by and, largely, the key performance indicators that were relevant to the team and role. Some preliminary investigations in Organisation X suggested differences existed in performance and key performance indicators across productivity roles. This sparked an interest in understanding whether there were certain types of productivity-based roles.

It was highly evident that the results resonated with team members in similar occupations across the organisation. These individuals were also surprised with the accuracy and with the Opportunity to learn more about themselves and their preferences. Therefore, the question was whether there existed a certain type of individual who was best suited for productivity-based work based on the MBTI assessment. The motivation for this study stems from that mindset.

A related inquiry was whether the presence of other factors such as high-performance work systems influenced the best-fit roles. Do Ability, Motivation and Opportunity play into the view of the organisation that individuals work for? Collectively, this led to the overarching research question: *What influence does employee personality type have on employee and organisational outcomes in the presence of HPWS?*

This study's objective was to address several gaps in the extant literature. Specifically, this study focused on productivity drivers in knowledge-based environments such as that evident in the Australian Banking and Finance industry by focusing on personality profiling using MBTI in an HPWS workplace context. The review points to the existing gaps in personality profiling, using the MBTI in relation to productivity-based environments for knowledge-based workers. In addition to this, there was a lack of pipeline management for talent and talent development at Organisation X, which this research focused on. There existed no analysis of the impact of personality type as measured through MBTI on productivity in the Australian Banking and Finance industry. Further, there were gaps in relation to HPWS, specifically the AMO model, and its application in the Australian Banking and Finance industry. To this end, this research addressed the above said gaps.

The Australian Banking and Finance services sector employs 432,500 employees across Australia (ausbanking.org.au, 2018). Financial institutions make a large contribution to the Australian economy on a par with the mining industry, accounting for 9% of the gross domestic product (ausbanking.org.au, 2018). The choice of Australia's Banking and Finance sector for this research was timely in view of the challenges confronted by the industry as well as the need to better understand whether certain HPWS practices, employee roles and personality types were critical in achieving sustained levels of productivity.

Research method

This study employed a quantitative case research design to obtain relevant information and specific answers to relevant questions. The data was obtained using a cross-sectional survey within a large case organisation (Cavana et al., 2001). The case organisation is a large, Australian financial services organisation that operates internationally and features in excess of 50,000 employees worldwide. The banking and financial services industry has an annual revenue turnover of $205 billion, along with the employment of 221,303 employees internationally; please note these numbers only include the big four financial services organisations within Australia (Reserve Bank of Australia Annual Report, 2017; Wu, 2020). The population of employees at Organisation X was then narrowed down to all productivity workers, including those with Lean Six Sigma qualifications. This refinement process resulted in a sample frame of 803 potential sample respondents, who were then invited and encouraged to participate in this research. Sample respondents completed a self-administered, online survey that featured measures adapted from the literature. Data collection took place over a two-week period in August 2017. After the data-screening procedure, 263 responses were deemed usable for further analyses.

Data analysis was completed in Microsoft Excel v15 and SPSS v24. The collected data was first analysed using descriptive statistics to profile the sample and data set. Next, additional analyses were conducted pertaining to assessing the conceptual model using one-way, two-way and three-way ANOVAs along with hierarchical multiple regressions.

Research scope

The focus of this research is on the productivity environment, specifically that in a knowledge-based setting at one of Australia's largest financial services organisations. Other fields outside of productivity and outside of knowledge-based milieus are not covered in this research. Accordingly, the banking and finance industry especially is the scope of this research. Whilst the formal definition for the banking and finance industry includes investment funds, insurance companies and real estate firms, this research, when referring to the banking and finance industry, refers only to banks and other financial institutions (such as credit unions), with investment funds, insurance companies and real estate firms falling outside of the scope of this research (Australian Bureau of Statistics, 2017).

Next, in this context, the key constructs investigated were personality type (e.g. MBTI), aspects of HPWS, including Ability, Motivation and Opportunity

(AMO), along with organisational citizenship behaviour. MBTI is used for assessing the personality profiling 'tests'. Aspects of high-performance work systems were considered within this research using the key elements of AMO model (e.g. rewards relating to pay and performance, affective commitment, organisational citizenship behaviour and high-performance human resource practice perceptions). Lastly, the methodological scope of the research is restricted to the sample collected in the online, cross-sectional survey of productivity employees of one large Australian financial services organisation.

Research problem and research questions

The main objective of this research was to investigate the influence of personality type on employee and organisational HPWS. Therefore, the following overarching research problem was developed to set out the domain of the study:

What influence does employee personality type have on employee and organisational outcomes in the presence of HPWS?

Research questions

In order to address this problem and understand the relationships between personality preferences (specifically the MBTI), productivity and HPWS, the following three related and overarching research questions (RQs) were developed to guide the study.

RQ1: What influence does employee personality type have on employee HPWS, namely, Ability, Motivation and Opportunity?
RQ2: What influence does employee personality type have on organisational outcomes, namely, organisational citizenship behaviours and affective organisational commitment?
RQ3: What influence does employee personality type have on productivity?

In order to address the research problem and research questions, a critical review of the literature was undertaken (Chapter 2), leading to the development of a conceptual framework (Figure 2.4) that guided the ensuing research design (Chapter 3).

Structure of the research

This book follows a five-chapter structure, which supports the documentation and contribution of knowledge for original review, analysis and examination of the ideas undertaken in the research area. A brief description of the focus of each chapter follows.

Chapter 1 (High performance in the Australian banking and financial services industry) presents an overview of the research; specifically, it details the topic of interest along with the research problem and its related research questions. Chapter 1 also explains the purpose, justification, importance and research method in detail, along with details surrounding limitations and the overall structure of the research. Chapter 2 (Micro and meso-level understanding of high performance: a review) provides a comprehensive review of the literature, where each topic is detailed and the available research is discussed. The literature review draws from prior research and academic studies in the related domains. Lastly, Chapter 2 discusses the gaps in the available literature and the research questions related to this research along with the theoretical framework. Chapter 3 (Research context and data collection at a large Australian financial institution) addresses the context and methodology used to empirically explore the model developed in Chapter 2. The research strategy and design used in the research are detailed, along with a discussion related to the data-collection methods, data-analysis techniques and ethical considerations in relation to the research. Chapter 4 (High performance in a large Australian financial institution – key findings) discusses the data and analyses related to the statistical results of the study. Chapter 4 goes into greater detail discussing the sample profile, preliminary data analysis and the assumption checking undertaken prior to the primary analysis, and addressing essentiality of the research questions and further analyses. Finally, Chapter 5 (Key learning for practice and future directions) summarises the findings related to this study, along with comprehensive conclusions linking the findings to theory and practice. The limitations of the research and areas for future study are detailed. We also provide technical appendices to the interested reader for a substantive treatment of the analysis of the data.

Conclusion

This chapter has introduces the focal topic of the research, as well as briefly outlines the literature related to the conceptual areas of interest. These areas include productivity in a knowledge-based environment, personality profiling (specifically Myers-Brigg's Type Indicator, MBTI) and the linkages to high-performance work systems (HPWS). This chapter then discusses the justification and purpose of the study along with the scope of the research. Following this, the research questions have been outlined which will be explored in more detail in subsequent chapters. This chapter then concludes with an overview of the structure of the research.

Note

1 'Organisation X' is the pseudonym used to disguise the identity of the case organisation where the data collection for this research took place.

References

Argote, L., & Ingram, P., (2000). Knowledge Transfer: A Basis for Competitive Advantage in Firms. *Organisation Behavior and Human Decisions Processes*, 82(1), 150–169.

Athota, V.S., Budhwar, P., & Malik, A., (2020). Influence of Personality Traits and Moral Values on Employee Well-Being, Resilience and Performance: A Cross-national Study. *Applied Psychology*, 69(3), 653–685.

Athota, V.S., & Malik, A., (2019). *Managing Employee Well-Being and Resilience for Innovation: Evidence from Knowledge-Intensive Service Industries.* Springer.

Bos-Nehles, A.C., Van Riemsdijk, J.V., & Looise, J.K., (2013). Employee Perceptions of Line Management Performance: Applying the AMO Theory to Explain the Effectiveness of Line Managers HRM Implementation. *Human Resource Management,* Wiley Online Library, Wiley Periodicals Inc., 52(6), 861–877.

Boult, M.J.L., Thompson, R.C., & Schaubhut, N.A., (2017). Well-Being and MBTI Personality Type in the Workplace. An International Comparison. CPP White Paper, Asia Pacific, 1–33.

Boxall, P., (2012). High Performance Work Systems: What, Why How and for Whom? *Asia Pacific Journal of Human Resources,* Australia, 50(2), 169–186. Retrieved on 19 November 2017 from http://onlinelibrary.wiley.com/doi/10.1111/j.1744-7941.2011.00012.x/full

Boxall, P., & Macky, K., (2009). Research and Theory on High Performance Work Systems: Progressing the High Involvement Stream. *Human Resource Management Journal,* Blackwell Publishing Ltd., 2(6), 177–185. Retrieved on 19 November 2017 from http://www.sciepub.com/reference/83569

Boxall, P., & Macky, K., (2014). High Involvement Work Processes, Work Intensification and Employee Well-Being. *Sage Publications,* 28(6), 3–23. Retrieved on 19 November 2017 from http://journals.sagepub.com/doi/abs/10.1177/0950017013512714

Boxall, P., & Purcell, J., (2008). *Strategy and Human Resource Management.* Second Edition. Palgrave Macmillan.

Bradley, J.H., & Hebert, F.J., (1997). The Effect of Personality Type on Team Performance. *Journal of Management Development,* 16(5), 337–353. Retrieved on 19 November 2017 from http://www.emeraldinsight.com/doi/abs/10.1108/02621719710174525

Cavana, R., Delahaye, B., & Sekeran, U., (2001). *Applied Business Research: Qualitative and Quantitative Methods.* John Wiley & Sons.

Chester, R.G., (2006). Asperger's Syndrome and Psychological Type. *Journal of Psychological Type,* 66(12), 114–137.

Chowhan, J., (2016). Unpacking the Black Box: Understanding the Relationship Between Strategy, HRM Practices, Innovation and Organisational Performance. *Human Resource Management Journal,* 26(2) 112–133.

Collins, C.J., (2006). The Interactive Effects of Recruitment Practices and Product Awareness on Job Seekers Employer Knowledge and Application Behaviors. *Journal of Applied Psychology,* 92(1), 180–190.

Curtain, R., (1998). The Workplace of the Future: Insights from Futures Scenarios and Today's High Performance Workplaces. *Australian Bulletin of Labour,* ABI/INFORM Collection, 24(4), 279–294.

Drucker, P., (1999). Knowledge-Worker Productivity: The Biggest Challenge. *California Management Review,* 41(2), 76–156.

Fahy, J., Farrelly, F., & Quester, P., (2002). Competitive Advantage Through Sponsorship: A Conceptual Model and Research Propositions. *European Journal of Marketing,* 38(8), 1013–1030.

Genco, J.T., (2006). Relationships Between MBTI Personality Types and Coping Styles: A Pilot Study. *Journal of Psychological Type,* Center for Applications of Psychological Type, 66(6). Retrieved on 19 November 2017 from https://www.capt.org/research/psychological-type-journal.htm

Grant, R.M., (2001). The Resource Based Theory of Competitive Advantage: Implications for Strategy Formulation. *California Management Review,* Spring 1991, 33(3), 3–23.

Gupta, A., & Sahu, G., (2013). Factors Influencing Adoption of Relationship Marketing Practices for Overall Growth of Firm an ISM-Based Model Validation. *International Journal of Electronic Customer Relationship Management*, 7(1), 21–44.

Herk, N.A., (2011). Ethnic and Gender Differences in Best-Fit Type. *Journal of Psychological Type*, Center for Applications of Psychological Type, 71(4). Retrieved on 19 November 2017 from https://www.capt.org/research/article/JPT_Vol71_01_1211.pdf

Huselid, M.A., Jackson, S.E., & Schuler, R.S., (1997). Technical and Strategic Human Resource Management Effectiveness as Determinants of Firm Performance. *Academy of Management Journal*, 40(1), 171–188.

Hutchinson, K.M., & Alessio, H.M., (1996). Influence of Personality Type on Susceptibility to the Effects of Noise Exposure. *Journal of Psychological Type*, 39, 30–36.

Jabbour, L., (2013). Market Thickness, Sunk Costs, Productivity and the Outsourcing Decision: An Empirical Analysis of Manufacturing Firms in France. *Canadian Journal of Economics*, Canada, 46(1) 103–134. Retrieved on 19 November 2017 from http://onlinelibrary.wiley.com/doi/10.1111/caje.12007/abstract

Lee, Y.K., Malik, A., Rosenberger, P.J., & Sharma, P., (2020). Demystifying the Differences in the Impact of Training and Incentives on Employee Performance: Mediating Roles of Trust and Knowledge Sharing. *Journal of Knowledge Management*, 24(8), 1990–2000.

Macky, K., & Boxall, P. (2007). The relationship between 'high-performance work practices' and employee attitudes: an investigation of additive and interaction effects. *The International Journal of Human Resource Management*, 18(4), 537–567, DOI: 10.1080/09585190601178745

Malik, A., (2013). Post-GFC People Management Challenges: A Study of India's Information Technology Sector. *Asia Pacific Business Review*, 19(2), 230–246. doi:10.1080/13602381.2013.767638

Malik, A., (2018a). *Strategic Human Resource Management and Employment Relations*. Springer.

Malik, A., (2018b). *Human Resource Management and the Global Financial Crisis: Evidence from India's IT/BPO Industry*. Routledge.Malik, A., Boyle, B., & Mitchell, R., (2017). Contextual Ambidexterity and Innovation in Health Care: The Role of HRM. *Personnel Review*, 46(7): 1358–1380

Malik, A., Froese, F.J., & Sharma, P., (2020). Role of HRM in Knowledge Integration: Towards a Conceptual Framework. *Journal of Business Research*, 109, 524–535.

Malik, A., & Nilakant, V., (2016). Knowledge Integration Mechanisms in High-Technology Business-to-Business Services Vendors. *Knowledge Management Research & Practice*, 14(4), 565–574. doi:10.1057/kmrp.2015.9

Malik, A., Pereira, V., & Budhwar, P., (2018). Value Creation and Capture Through Human Resource Management Practices: Gazing Through the Business Model Lens. *Organizational Dynamics*, 47(3), 180–188.

Malik, A., Pereira, V., & Tarba, S., (2019a). The role of HRM Practices in Product Development: Contextual Ambidexterity in a US MNC's Subsidiary in India. *The International Journal of Human Resource Management*, 30(4), 536–564.

Malik, A., & Sanders, K., (2021). Managing Human Resources in Organisations during a Global Crisis. *British Journal of Management*, 1–19. doi:10.1111/1467-8551.12484

Malik, A., Sinha, P., Pereira, V., & Rowley, C., (2019b). Implementing Global-Local Strategies in a Post-GFC Era: Creating an Ambidextrous Context Through Strategic Choice and HRM. *Journal of Business Research*, 103, 557–569.

Matson, E., & Prusak, L., (2010). Boosting the Productivity of Knowledge Workers. *EBSCOhost*, 41(2), 79–94. Retrieved on 19 November 2017 from http://www.

mckinsey.com/business-functions/organisation/our-insights/boosting-the-productivity-of-knowledge-workers

Mladkova, L., (2011). Knowledge Management for Knowledge Workers. *Electronic Journal of Knowledge Management*, 9(3) 260–267. Retrieved on 19 November 2017 from http://connection.ebscohost.com/c/articles/78296183/knowledge-management-knowledge-workers

Mook, J.R., (1996). Personality Testing in Today's Workplace: Avoiding the Legal Pitfalls. *Employee Relations Law Journal*, Winter, 22(3), 65.

Nguyen, M., & Malik, A., (2020). Cognitive Processes, Rewards and Online Knowledge Sharing Behaviour: The Moderating Effect of Organisational Innovation. *Journal of Knowledge Management*, 24(6), 1241–1261.

Nguyen, T.M., Tuan, N., Froese, F., & Malik, A., (2019). Motivation and Knowledge Sharing: A Meta-Analysis of Main and Moderating Effects. *Journal of Knowledge Management*, 23(5), 998–1016.

Patel, P., Messersmith, J.G., & Lepak, D.P., (2013). Walking the Tightrope: An Assessment of the Relationship between High Performance Work Systems and Organisational Ambidexterity. *Academy of Management Journal*, 56(5), 1420–1442. Retrieved on 19 November 2017 from http://amj.aom.org/content/56/5/1420.abstract

Quenk, N.L., (2009). *Essentials of Myers-Brigg's Type Indicator Assessment*. Second Edition. John Wiley & Sons.

Reserve Bank of Australia Annual Report 2017, *Mathematica*, 47–54.<www.rba.gov.au/publications/annual-reports/rba/index.html>

Schullery, N., Knudstrup, P., Schullery, S.E., & Pfaff, L.A., (2009). The Relationship between Personality Type and 360 Degree Evaluation of Management Skills. *Journal of Psychological Type*, Center for Applications of Psychological Type, 69(11), 141–155.

Smith, A., & Pitt, M., (2011). Sustainable Workplaces and Building User Comfort and Satisfaction. *Journal of Corporate Real Estate*, Emerald Group Publishing, 13(3), 144–156.

Smith, A., Tucker, M., & Pitt, M., (2011). Healthy, Productive Workplaces: Towards a Case for Interior Plantscaping. *Facilities*, 29(5/6), 209–223.

Stahl, G., Björkman, I., Farndale, E., Morris, S.S., Paauwe, J., Stiles, P., Trevor, J., & Wright, P., (2012). Six Principles of Effective Global Talent Management. *Sloan Management Review*, 53(2), 25–42.

Stalk, G., (1988). Time – The Next Source of Competitive Advantage. *Harvard Business Review*. July Issue, 41–51.

Stewart, P., Danford, A., Richardson, M., & Pulgnano, V., (2010). Workers Experiences of Skill, Training and Participation in Lean and High Performance Workplaces in Britain and Italy. *Employee Relations*, Emerald Group Publishing, 32(6), 606–624.

Toivanen, S., (2011). Workplaces of the Future – How are the Studied? A Literature Study of Foresight and Delphi Methods. *Nordic Journal of Working Life Studies*, 1(1), 161–167.

Van Der Voordt, T.J.M., (2004). Productivity and Employee Satisfaction in Flexible Workplaces. *Journal of Real Estate*, ABI/INFORM Collection, 6(2), 133–148.

Wranx, (2017). 70 Experience, 20 Exposure and 10 Education Recruitment Model. Retrieved on 19 November 2017 from http://blog.wranx.com/70-20-10-model-experience-exposure-and-education

Wu, T., (2020). Finance in Australia. Break the bank: Cash rate cuts and the COVID-19 pandemic have caused revenue to fall, *IBISWorld*, 10–16.

2 Micro- and meso-level drivers of high performance

Introduction

This chapter examines the relevant theoretical literature to analyse the impact of personality type on employee outcomes, such as productivity, in productivity-based roles in a knowledge-intensive firm, paying special attention to the influence of high-performance work systems HPWS in the chosen case organisation. There is a significant body of literature on the topic of personality profiling, productivity and HPWS. This literature review will extensively examine each of these important and related topics individually and the importance of each topic is followed by the gaps in the literature for each theme. This will lead to the development of a theoretical conceptual model, which will guide this research.

Following this, the research seeks to address the gaps in the literature by examining the influence of an individual's personality type on the established relationship between HPWS and employee performance. This research also considers the impact of personality on satisfaction, organisational commitment, job behaviours and intentions of employees (Athota, Budhwar & Malik, 2019; Athota & Malik, 2019; Jensen, Patel & Messersmith, 2013; Kehoe & Wright, 2013; Patel, Messersmith & Lepak, 2013). Based on our review of research related to these topics embedded in a knowledge-based environment, we contend further research is needed how these aspects interact with personality traits (Athota, Budhwar & Malik, 2019; Athota & Malik, 2019; Boxall & Purcell, 2008; Robbins & Barnwell, 2002; Robbins, Judge, Millett & Waters-Marsh, 2008). The research examining the relationship between the role of personality type in examining an organisation's people management practices and its impact on employee attitudes, behaviours and performance is far from conclusive, often leading to equivocal findings, thereby warranting further research on the topic (Barnuto, Phipps & Xu, 2009; Barrick & Mount, 1991; Bathurst, 2000; Chang et al., 2016; Da Cunha & Greathead, 2007; Engstrom et al., 2010; Jarlstrom & Valkealahti, 2010; Zhang et al., 2019). On this basis, the central research question that is the focus of this research is, ***What influence does employee personality type have on employee and organisational outcomes?***

- The rest of this chapter is organised in the following manner. The "Personality profiling" section will discuss personality profiling, and the "Myers-Briggs personality profiling" section will detail Myers-Briggs Type

Indicator (MBTI). The "Productivity" section will discuss productivity the "High-performance work systems" section will deal with HPWS in detail, each section outlining the topic at hand. The "Gaps in the literature" section will delve into gaps within the literature pertaining to each topic that has been discussed, and then the "Theoretical framework and hypotheses" section will outline the theoretical framework and associated hypotheses. The final section, "Summary and conclusion", will provide a summary and closing of the chapter.

Personality profiling

A personality profile or test is a tool often used by organisations, management or individuals to evaluate and understand personal characteristics relating to preferences, values and skills in work and life. Personality profiling makes an effort to understand and capitalise on an individual's performance and contribution to an organisation or provide a level of self-awareness, along with details on how individuals act in the workplace or in romantic situations, or how they interact with friends (16personalities.com, 2017; Oxford Dictionary, 2017).

More recently, the much publicised Oxford Analytica's profiling of personalities and its link to behaviours and performance discusses the idea of dimensionality reduction technologies in the field to distil masses of information into a few essential strands, which is said to feature in more research efforts to organise the world around us (Oxford Analytica, 2018). The five essential personality dimensions have found a variety of real-world applications. Social media has given researchers a new pathway to assess an individual's personality traits using their social media trail. Dimensionality reduction technology has allowed researchers to identify five essential components of human personality that can be used to identify essential qualities worth measuring. This study claims the techniques used are powerful because they present a way of listening to the data instead of organising it along ex ante theories or beliefs. A potential area for profiling is companies, where comparisons could be made compared with firm performance. This research found that big data has increased the possibilities to obtain important insights into people, firms and the world. Dimensionality reduction technology will increasingly be used to understand essential components otherwise lost in large datasets.

Personality tests are created to provide information about an individual's temperament; character traits; decision-making methods; communication styles and techniques; and their behaviours and attitudes towards their life, work, education, recreation and people. Personality profiling helps individuals understand why they think, feel and behave the way they do and why other people may behave differently when they are faced with the same or similar situations (Eagle, 2017; Penney, David & Witt, 2011; Quenk, 2009).

There is a plethora of personality profiling 'tests' available that provide individuals with information on the different types and their determined type. Individuals can search on the internet to obtain as much information as they desire on the topic or they can see professional assessments. The interest in profiling an individual's personality and its impact on a range of attitudes and behaviours has been around since the early 1920s, when they were created and used in assessment centres to assist in the process of personnel selection (Penney, David & Witt, 2011; Quenk, 2009).

It is argued that when individuals align their behaviour(s) with their personality profiling everything becomes simpler and easier. Individuals have more energy, greater health; they are more resourceful; they make more money; and they find interpersonal relationships more fulfilling (Eagle, 2017; Quenk, 2009).

There are many different types of personality related profiling available. Some of the tests include I-Ching, Keirsey Bates Temperament Sorter, iPersonic Personality Type, Enneagram, DISC, INSIGHT, Holland's theory of career choice, Wealth Dynamics, Talent Dynamics Profile, Wealth Spectrum Test, the Minnesota Multiphasic Personality Inventory, the 5-factor model, Revised NEO Personality Inventory, the Big 5 and lastly Myers-Briggs Personality Profiling (Eagle, 2017). (Appendices A3, B6 and 7 provides additional information available on personality inventories.)

Previous research into personality types in an organisational context has explored the relationship between psychological type and the motivation of workers (Barbuto, Fritz, Lim & Xu, 2008), employee flexibility (Beltran-Martin & Roca-Puig, 2013), knowledge worker productivity (Erne, 2011), maximising knowledge worker productivity levels (Maruta, 2012) and boosting productivity of knowledge workers (Matson & Prusak, 2010; Mladkova, 2011). Such studies ignore the importance of other contextual factors through the use of HPWS. For example, early research found that personality types are an important factor governing successful team performance (Bradley & Hebert, 1997; Kasman, Kasman, Ayhan & Torun, 2013; Ones & Dilchert, 2009). More recently, however, research has identified that there are linkages between personality preferences and learning environments (Chesborough, 2005), happiness (Francis & Jones, 2000), coping styles (Genco & Mitchell, 2006) sunk costs and outsourcing (Jabbour, 2013), as well as the fit between type and roles (Herk et al., 2009) which strengthens the concept that personality profiling, specifically MBTI, has relevance in understanding an individual's preferences or behaviours; more than relevancy MBTI has a presence and place in understanding why an individual behaves as they do, which adds importance and linkage to the research (Boxall & Purcell, 2008; Robbins & Barwell, 2002; Robbins, Judge, Millett & Waters-Marsh, 2008).

Myers-Briggs personality profiling

The MBTI is an introspective, self-report questionnaire that is designed to indicate psychological preferences in how individuals view the environment around themselves and engage in decision-making (Quenk, 2009). The MBTI works on the approach that there are four principal psychological functions by which humans experience the world, namely, Sensing, Intuition, Feeling, and Thinking, as these are commonly noted functions that individuals engage in from time to time, though its distribution and combination vary in the population (Boult, Thompson & Schaubhut, 2017; Quenk, 2009).

The MBTI instrument came about in 1917 when Katharine Cook Briggs met her future son-in-law and she observed some noticeable differences in his personality compared to her family members (Boult, Thompson & Schaubhut, 2017; Quenk, 2009). Katharine began research into these differences, which eventually emerged as what is known today as MBTI. The available literature discusses some key strengths and facets of MBTI that are important in understanding how the instrument works; these are based on the structure of MBTI, creation of the tool and understanding and interpretation of the results, see the categories detailed in Table 2.1 (Boult, Thompson & Schaubhut, 2017; Quenk, 2009).

Table 2.1 Myers-Briggs Category Descriptions

Type	*Category*	*Description*
E	Extrovert	People who prefer extroversion draw their energy from action. Extroverts act, then reflect, then act further. If they are inactive, their motivation tends to decline. To rebuild their energy.
I	Introvert	Introverts "expend" energy through action: they prefer to reflect, then act, then reflect again. To rebuild their energy, introverts need quiet time alone, away from activity.
S	Sensing	People who prefer Sensing are more likely to trust information that is in the present, tangible, and concrete: that is, information that can be understood by the five senses. They prefer to look for details and facts. For them, the meaning is in the data.
N	Intuition	Those who prefer Intuition tend to trust information that is less dependent on the senses, that can be associated with other information (either remembered or discovered by seeking a wider context or pattern). They may be more interested in future possibilities. For them, the meaning is in the underlying theory and principles which are manifested in the data.
T	Thinking	Those who prefer Thinking tend to decide things from a more detached standpoint, measuring the decision by what seems reasonable, logical, causal, consistent, and matching a given set of rules.
F	Feeling	Those who prefer Feeling tend to come to decisions by associating or empathising with the situation, looking at it 'from the inside' and weighing the situation to achieve, on balance, the greatest harmony, consensus and fit, considering the needs of the people involved. Thinkers usually have trouble interacting with people who are inconsistent or illogical, and tend to give very direct feedback to others.
J	Judging	Types with a preference for Judging show the world their preferred Judging function (Thinking or Feeling). TJ types tend to appear to the world as logical and FJ types as empathetic. Judging types like to "have matters settled".
P	Perceiving	Those types who prefer perception show the world their preferred Perceiving function (Sensing or Intuition). SP types tend to appear to the world as concrete and NP types as abstract.

The table above outlines each of the individual Myers-Briggs type and some basic information on each main type.

Table 2.2 outlines 16 personality types that exist across 4 different categories collectively representing the entire population and distribution of individuals. Each type is different from others. It is worth providing some concise information on each type to demonstrate how they are similar to those in their categories but completely different at the same time (Boult, Thompson & Schaubhut, 2017). Appendix G provides further details about each MBTI personality type. Another way to look at the MBTI types is to break them down into opposing categories. It is stated that extroversion and introversion relate to an individual's attitude and how they operate in the external world, and it is argued that there is a preference for one or the other depending on the situation or environment (Boult, Thompson & Schaubhut, 2017; Quenk, 2009).

Sensing and Intuition and Thinking and Feeling relate to the psychological aspects of an individual's predisposition. As such, according to the typology, relative to others, a person may use each of these four elements to varying degrees of dominance; however, all of the functions are used by individuals based on circumstances or situations. Judging and Perceiving relates to an individual's preferences towards their lifestyle as compared to the outside world (Boult, Thompson & Schaubhut, 2017; Quenk, 2009). See Appendix G for further details.

The available literature discusses strengths and weaknesses pertaining to MBTI, which are important in understanding the instrument and its importance to the individual and the organisation. One of the key strengths regarding MBTI is that it follows a structured approach to personality profiling, whereby

Table 2.2 Myers-Briggs Major Categories

Category	*Type*	*Detail*
Analysts	INTJ INTP ENTJ ENTP	Analysts are defined as being rational and impartial, independent, open-minded, strong-willed, imaginative and strategic thinkers. Analysts are known to execute intellectual debates and enjoy scientific or technological fields.
Diplomats	INFJ INFP ENFJ ENFP	Diplomats are known to focus on empathy and cooperation, shining in diplomacy and counselling; they are harmonisers and warm, empathic and influential individuals; they rely exclusively on cold rationality or difficult decisions.
Sentinels	ISTJ ISFJ ESTJ ESFJ	Sentinels are cooperative, practical, secure and stable; they are known as meticulous and traditional hard-working people; they rely on logistical, administrative fields that have clear hierarchies and rules. Sentinels stick to their plans and they do not shy away from difficult tasks.
Explorers	ISTP ISFP ESTP ESFP	Explorers are able to connect with their surroundings in a way that no other type can; they are utilitarian and practical; they are best suited to situations that require quick reaction and the ability to think on their feet. Additionally, they are the masters of tools and techniques, and unsurprisingly these individuals are irreplaceable in crises.

Source: 16.personalities.com (2017), Boult, Thompson and Schaubhut (2017) and Mook (1996).

the questions asked and answers provided are considered closed, that is, responses provided are definitive and can easily be compared. The MBTI itself is deemed consistent and allows for comparison across individuals completing MBTI profiling, feeding into the mindset that the MBTI produces quality outcomes (Quenk, 2009; Varvel, Adams, Pridie & Ulloa, 2004).

Over time MBTI profiling has become more and more tailored and specific to a modern audience of individuals who are seeking information pertaining to their preferences (Boult, Thompson & Schaubhut, 2017). Available literature on the MBTI discusses the extent the methodology has become more accurate and concise as more individuals have completed the instrument over time (Boult, Thompson & Schaubhut, 2017; Quenk, 2009). Further, the literature states that the MBTI is relevant and accurate enough to represent the entire population, allowing for exploring similarities and differences. The profiling tool is popular for its ease of use and available interpretations of each type for individuals to get a sense of their type without much expert help (Quenk, 2009; Varvel, Adams, Pridie & Ulloa, 2004).

However, in contrast to this, the literature offers a critique of the use of MBTI. Although the MBTI is a comprehensive theory that provides a context for understanding individual complexity, an adequate understanding of the theory is needed to correctly administer and interpret the instrument (Quenk, 2009). Some argue that to accurately understand the results an individual would need to be appropriately trained to understand and correctly interpret the results (Moreno & Bartlett, 2016; Quenk; 2009).

The literature also points out that the MBTI is often viewed as too simplistic when it comes to the questions being asked, and that the typology itself is simple and static rather than complex and dynamic (Quenk, 2009). This leads to interpretation issues by the individual completing the MBTI, as the tool itself has an added layer of complexity, which needs to be recognised and understood for it to be correctly utilised (Moreno & Bartlett, 2016; Quenk, 2009).

The MBTI is a self-report instrument, which means individuals can potentially choose to respond as they feel; if they determine certain results are required individuals can answer accordingly to produce those results. This means an individual can respond as they 'think they should' as opposed to how they really feel, therefore enabling the results to be faked, which results in an outcome that's not precise for the individual and shouldn't be relied on (Quenk, 2009). An individual needs to ensure they are being truthful and transparent with their responses to ensure there is a level of honest consistency pertaining to their results; it is often advised that an individual should respond with 'their first preference' (often stated as 'their gut response') to ensure the responses provided and produced are both accurate and concise (Quenk, 2009; Varvel, Adams, Pridie & Ulloa, 2004).

Other critiques of MBTI have argued that the MBTI terminology is vague and too general and ultimately confuses the respondent. Therefore, results evidently become interpreted as the individual understands them based on their skills or knowledge (Quenk, 2009). A further criticism discussed in the literature regarding the MBTI is if an individual retests themselves within five weeks of their initial 'test' it is argued that there will be a 50% chance that the individual might return a different result (Boult, Thompson & Schaubhut, 2017; Quenk, 2009). An individual needs to be aware that their responses need to be as accurate as possible to avoid this anomaly and to ensure they respond accurately and with their preferences in mind; this will ensure their results are an accurate reflection of themselves and their preferences (Boult, Thompson & Schaubhut, 2017; Quenk, 2009).

Further, studies have explained the concept of misuse with regard to the MBTI instrument. One of the largest concerns with personality testing comes from the thought process of misusing the results to incorrectly label other individuals or themselves. Individuals completing profiling or testing need to be aware that they don't incorrectly label themselves or other individuals; labelling incorrectly can be damaging to the individual(s) and can result in outcomes being misinterpreted or misunderstood (16personalities.com, 2017; Ones & Dilchert, 2009; Quenk, 2009). Therefore, results should only be used for individual consumption such as self-awareness, self-development and personal use or in the instance of professional use with a qualified and trained MBTI expert who exercises extreme care and is aware of the seriousness of labelling of results (Boult, Thompson & Schaubhut, 2017; Quenk, 2009).

Next is the idea that the instrument from a normative standpoint has positive type descriptions that may be glossed over too easily, meaning real psychological problems might not be seen clearly and can be labelled as part of one's type rather than a real health related issue that needs medical care and attention (Boult, Thompson & Schaubhut, 2017; Quenk, 2009; Van Asselt, Dirksen, Arntz & Severens, 2008). Therefore, the individual needs the right level of understanding and interpretation to ensure results are accurately understood, and anything that doesn't appear within normal guidelines should be taken to a medical provider for further assessment and deliberation (Mook, 1996; Quenk, 2009; Van Asselt, Dirksen, Arntz & Severens, 2008).

Lastly looking into the MBTI itself, there are two criticisms that relate to demographics. First, within the MBTI there are no items that show and discuss gender differences pertaining to the instrument, and second, only a few items are discussed that relate to the sample respondent's age (Quenk, 2009). Critics argue that to be accurate and concise, demographics should be taken into account to ensure the results are detailed and relatable to the general population. It is clear from day-to-day interactions that males and females have different preferences related to how they perceive and act similarly, along with the thought that age also determines one's preferences, for which MBTI is often criticised and questioned in relation to accuracy – How accurate can MBTI be if it doesn't take gender or age into consideration?

In summary, personality profiling provides some important insights relating to an individual's behaviours and preferences. Understanding these factors is of high importance to organisations who want to get the best out of their workforce. It is clear from the reviewed literature that there is a robust and extensive story relating to personality profiling and the use of MBTI. However, some further investigations and research are required to determine whether there is any linkages between personality profiling, productivity and HPWS relating to an individual's workplace, for this research and future research recommendations.

While significant literature exists surrounding personality profiling and the variety of tools and instruments available, the MBTI instrument is one of the primary tools an individual can use to understand their behavioural preferences. Although a plethora of different profiling tools available to the individual seeking more information about their inner workings, the MBTI was chosen for this research due to the depth and abundance of information and documentation that exist for the tool. The MBTI as a tool has been discussed at great length throughout this chapter, displaying various studies on the topic. The MBTI was chosen as the primary tool for these reasons and the fact that the tool has been in use since 1917, showing not only the depth of the instrument but also its widespread appeal and application.

Productivity

The literature on the topic of productivity states that the central challenge is to make knowledge workers more productive (Drucker, 1999). It is argued that for making knowledge workers productive, changes are needed not only in their attitudes but also on a range of other organisational support systems (Drucker, 1999; Matson & Prusak, 2010; Mladkova, 2011; Smith, Smith & Offodile, 2011). As the supply of young people available for manual work shrinks rapidly, organisations, to make this transition successful, need to prepare themselves by having their supply of young people prepared, educated and trained for knowledge work (Drucker, 1999; Jabbour, 2013). To summarise what the literature states, survival for an organisation in current times can be directly linked to how the organisation uses its resources and productivity to differentiate itself (Drucker, 1999). As the demand for employees with an academic education has increased by 190% between 1975 and 2004, there has been a concurrent decline in the demand for employees with a lower educational background (Erne, 2011).

Productivity defined

Workplace productivity is defined by the Department of Labour as a productive workplace that is built on teamwork and a shared vision. Shared vision depicts a common understanding of where the business is heading and a commitment towards investing in employee skills. In a productive workplace, everyone's role is valued and all staff are encouraged to contribute ideas to improve the operations of the organisation (Erne, 2011; George, Rowlands, Price & Maxey, 2005). Put simply, the term productivity is defined as the ratio of output to inputs used in a production process (Erne, 2011; George, Rowlands, Price & Maxey, 2005; Sye, 2004). Available literature states that there are four major types of productivity dissipations, which are represented in Table 2.3.

Table 2.3 Productivity Definitions

Type	*Definition*
Labour productivity	Output per person
Capital material productivity	Ratio of outputs to the input of physical capital
Material productivity	Ratio of output to the input of materials
Total factor productivity	All factors as a ratio of output to the input

Source: George, Rowlands, Price and Maxey (2005), Sye (2004), and Erne (2011).

When researching the topic of productivity, it is clear that productivity is not a new term. Productivity measures have been shifted from the manufacturing factory and have been applied to all companies or firms across every industry (George, Rowlands, Price & Maxey, 2005; Sye, 2004). The literature argues that in an environment where a company is turning over items the translation is simple, and that the real challenge comes when productivity is applied in knowledge-based environments where individuals whose skills were concentrated in academic or more intellectual roles, wherein productivity measures aren't as clear (Sye, 2004).

The difficulty comes with trying to relate productivity to a knowledge-based environment when those individuals are working on projects or activities that relate to the individuals' mindset or behaviour or improvement initiatives over time, especially as some of these attributes aren't tangible (George, Rowlands, Price & Maxey, 2005; Sye, 2004). At Organisation X, productivity is defined at the intersection between low cost, appropriate time and appropriate levels of quality and service delivered (Organisation X, 2017).

Productivity in knowledge-based environments

Productivity in knowledge-based environments is a term that was popularised by Drucker (1999). There are six major factors that determine knowledge-worker productivity. It demands that we ask the question, 'What is the task?' It demands that we impose the responsibility for their productivity on the individual knowledge workers themselves because knowledge workers have to self-manage, and should have autonomy in their jobs (Drucker, 1999; LePine, Buckman, Crawford & Methot, 2011; Mladkova, 2011). Motivating workers to share their knowledge through formal and informal mechanisms, or through use of online platforms, requires a range of behaviours and mediating and moderating mechanisms, such as the presence of organisational innovation culture, tangible and intangible incentives, and investment in training and development (Lee, Malik, Rosenberger & Sharma, 2020; Nguyen & Malik, 2020; Nguyen, Tuan, Froese & Malik, 2019). The importance of research examining the impact of several human resource management (HRM) practices on a range of innovation and performative outcomes in knowledge-based environments (Malik, 2018a; Malik, Froese & Sharma, 2019; Malik & Nilakant, 2016), such as business model innovation (Malik, Pereira & Budhwar, 2018), product and process innovations (Malik, Boyle & Mitchell, 2017; Malik, Pereira & Tarba, 2019; Sanz-Valle & Jiménez-Jiménez, 2018) and firm performance (Malik & Rowley, 2015; Malik, Sinha, Pereira & Rowley, 2019), both during munificent times as well as during a crisis (Malik, 2013, 2018b; Malik & Sanders, 2021), is emphasised.

Continuing innovation is a requirement of the work; there needs to be a linkage between the work, the task and innovation. Knowledge work requires ongoing learning for the knowledge worker and a layer of ongoing teaching by the knowledge worker. Further productivity of the knowledge worker is not a matter of quantity of output; there is a necessary lens of quality associated with the work. Lastly, knowledge-based work must consider knowledge workers as assets, rather than costs (Drucker, 1999; Erne, 2011; Mladkova, 2011). Therefore, productivity of knowledge work has to aim first at obtaining quality and not the minimum quality, but optimum, if not maximum, quality (Drucker, 1999; Erne, 2011; Mladkova, 2011).

Methodology used to execute productivity

The following sections will outline the different methodologies that have been utilised at Organisation X at different times to execute productivity successfully. These methodologies include Lean, Six Sigma and Lean Six Sigma (Sye, 2004).

Lean management principles

Lean management is a pragmatic method for removing or reducing waste. Lean methodology comes from the manufacturing environment, where the focus is to remove tasks, as these tasks do not add value and cause wastage across processes (George, Rowlands, Price & Maxey, 2005; Sye, 2004). It is argued that lean methodology as a management philosophy came from the Toyota Production System in the 1990s. Typically, a trained professional in lean methodology would assess a given process and remove the elements of waste. These elements of waste form the seven-letter acronym TIMWOOD (Sye, 2004). T refers to *transport* wherein products that don't actually need moving to perform the process are moved, I refers to *inventory*, which is the unfinished product not being processed. M relates to *motion*, where people or equipment are moving more than what is required to perform the process, and W refers to *waiting*, which represents interruptions in the process where there is waiting on a person or product. The first O relates to *overproduction*, where there is more product than demand, and the second O refers to *overprocessing*, where there is production of product outside of what is required. D refers to *defects*, where there is an *error* (George, Rowlands, Price & Maxey, 2005; Sye, 2004).

Six Sigma

The Six-Sigma approach was created in by Bill Smith and Mikel J. Harry while they were working for Motorola. Six Sigma was also central to General Electric's business strategy starting in 1995 (Sye, 2004). Six Sigma is focused on the idea that to improve the quality of outputs of a defined process, it is essential to evaluate the capability of processes using a set of quality management tools, largely through statistical methodologies (Sye, 2004).

Processes that have successfully been evaluated under the Six Sigma approach tend to produce long-term results. Typically, the process is measured in defects per million Opportunity (DPMO) below 3.4. However, companies should determine the most appropriate sigma level relative to their business processes and the industry. Six Sigma's credibility can clearly be noted when Motorola in 2005 stated that Six Sigma had attributed to over US$17 billion dollars in savings for the company between 1995 and 2005 (George, Rowlands, Price & Maxey, 2005; Sye, 2004).

Lean Six Sigma

Lean Six Sigma refers to a managerial approach that combines Six Sigma methods and tools employing a lean manufacturing philosophy. The Lean Six Sigma approach strives to eliminate waste in a system to which it is applied, thus assuring its quality in the production and organisational processes, whilst also controlling variation, errors and waste in a system or process (George, Rowlands, Price & Maxey, 2005; Sye, 2004).

In recent years, there has been the combination of Lean Methodology and Six Sigma, thus referred to as Lean Six Sigma. Companies all around the world, in various industries, have now taken Lean Six Sigma methodology on board and implemented programmes involving business-trained and qualified subject matter experts to improve quality, to reduce costs and to improve the customer experience (Smith, Smith, & Offodile, 2011; Smith, Tucker & Pitt, 2011). The application of Six Sigma and Lean Six Sigma to emerging knowledge-based industries such as information technology and business process management services has seen a surge in investment for the above certification programmes and other quality management systems in a bid to boost the performance of the process and a business unit (Malik & Blumenfeld, 2012; Malik, Sinha & Blumenfeld, 2012).

The methodology used to execute Lean Six Sigma is called "DMAIC" methodology. There are five phases to this framework: the first phase is "Define", which articulates the problem and scope, and analyses how the customer, process and business see the problem at hand. The "Measure" phase involves data collection taking a look into the as-is and to-be process capabilities, while "Analyse" phase delves into the data to determine the root causes of the problem. The "Improve" phase starts to think through the possible solutions and how to best prioritise these for maximum impact, and lastly comes the "Control" phase, which hands the solved problem back to the business for ongoing management and monitoring (George, Rowlands, Price & Maxey, 2005; Stewart, Danford, Richardson & Pulgnano, 2010). Productivity experts at Organisation X utilise a toolkit based on Lean Six Sigma which is focused on the aforementioned DMAIC framework when solving a business problem (Smith, Smith, & Offodile, 2011; Smith, Tucker & Pitt, 2011; Sye, 2004).

Productivity habits in practice at Organisation X

Productivity habits in practice at Organisation X will depict how the case organisation views productivity and how it is structured across the organisation with necessary linkages to literature to support the way the role is positioned.

Owing to the diverse and expansive nature of Organisation X, those in productivity-based roles have to complete an array of tasks defined by their key performance indicators (KPIs). They lead targeted projects that follow Lean Six Sigma methodology, facilitate the training and coaching of productivity-based knowledge syllabus and create and implement the four productivity habits, namely, visual management board (VMB) creation and management, huddles, continuous improvement initiatives and standard operating procedure creation and management.

The productivity expert is responsible for the end-to-end management of their projects or initiatives; these projects follow the 'DMAIC' methodology outlined above. Projects will follow different timelines and utilise different funding and resource requirements; however, the outcomes will be similar as productivity experts are expected to improve the different parts of the business, making them more effective and efficient in their day-to-day functioning (Organisation X, 2017).

Another role and responsibility of productivity experts is to train and coach individuals across the organisation in productivity-based knowledge. There is a demand at Organisation X from individuals who want to learn and develop their productivity-based skills. This demand has led to a formal team being constructed for imparting training. The entire population of staff at Organisation X is said to be around 50,000 personnel worldwide. Training is available to the entire population. Not only has productivity become a topic area that is sought after, but all senior managers or individuals who want to become part of senior management are required to be productivity certified to ensure they are aware of the different ways they can manage and prioritise their teams or divisions.

A further area of focus is the development and implementation of the four productivity habits (Dossegger, 2017). These four habits have been used by Organisation X for almost seven years now. The four habits have been included in all employees' key performance indicators (KPIs), meaning all staff need to know and understand the four habits, and learn how to use them, and they are expected to be in production on a daily, weekly or monthly basis (Dossegger, 2017).

VMBs hold information that pertains to a project and business as usual functions; this information is based around project status updates and general progress, team allocation and prioritisation, general team information and related project metrics. VMBs are an important tool in managing and monitoring team work and engagement as it shows what is completed and what is left on the roadmap (Dossegger, 2017).

Typically speaking huddles occur each week or several times a week around VMBs, and information is shared around projects, business as usual endeavours and ways to improve what employees currently do (Dossegger, 2017). Continuous improvement initiatives are often captured on VMBs to ensure progress is being made. The value of continuous improvement initiatives is that they can be small, for example making a little change to an email that is going to a customer, or medium in size, for example eliminating a step in a process through big technologic changes like the implementation of a new technology system (Dossegger, 2017). The ideas are usually managed through the PDCA framework, which is *plan*, *do*, *check* and *act*, and ideas are progressed through this framework to ensure progress (Dossegger, 2017; Maruta, 2012; Sokovic, Pavletic & Pipan, 2010). The nature of continuous improvement follows this usual cycle of control, plan is where identifying and analysing of the problem or opportunity occurs (Dossegger, 2017; Sokovic, Pavletic & Pipan, 2010).

Lastly are the standard operating procedures (SOPs), which are the backbone of any well-planned and documented organisation; they are undertaken to keep the business functioning smoothly. Capturing of business intelligence has quickly become a critical matter for businesses, as failure to capture this information can lead to substantial consequences from being unable to capture precious business information for continuity management to not being able to implement new processes. A lack of transparency around organisational structures leads to failure in using technology systems (Bandara, Gable & Rosemann, 2005; Dossegger, 2017). If an individual moves onto a new role, or worse still to a new organisation, the information they retain can be lost and at times prevent the organisation from being able to deliver their products and services to their customers. Therefore, documentation of SOPs should not be downplayed or overlooked, as organisations need to accurately capture business information to ensure successful business continuity (Bandara, Gable & Rosemann, 2005). This research adopts a view that there is a specific productivity 'type' that is best suited to productivity-based roles. Specifically, therefore, the question is, *What influence does employee personality type have on employee and organisational outcomes?'*

A further point for deliberation should be discussed. The case organisation has been on a productivity-related journey for the last seven years. The introduction of a new CEO saw a new business strategy implemented that was partly focused on using productivity-related tools and methods in an effort to make the business more effective and efficient at delivering the best possible customer experience. An important part of this journey was the introduction and implementation of productivity to drive competitive advantage. The last seven years have been focused on being as effective and efficient to offer the best products and services to the customer, which is highly important when the products within this industry are commodities. This journey means that the organisation has been developing and evolving and learning from challenges, and is growing. Therefore, when considering the case organisation against its competitors one would expect to see considerable differences with how the organisation views and uses productivity in their operations. The case organisation projects a level of maturity regarding its productivity practices (Organisation X, 2017).

Productivity practices, such as the ones mentioned here, if executed well, can be the difference for an organisation seeking competitive advantage, especially when dealing with products and services that are commodified in the banking and financial services industry.

High-performance work systems

First, it is worth defining high-performance work systems, which can be described as a set of workplace systems that are designed to make workers as effective as it can (Boxall, 2012; Heffernan & Dundon, 2016; Macky & Boxall, 2007). A high-performance workplace is a delicate balancing act of managing investment in people, business processes, the physical space (environment) and technology to enhance the talents of workers to learn, ascertain, revolutionise and lead, and to achieve efficiency and financial benefit (Boxall & Macky, 2009; Macky & Boxall, 2008; Robbins & Barnwell, 2002).

In conjunction with HPWS, high-performance teams should also be defined, as a group of people with specific roles and responsibilities along with their talents and skills, that are aligned to a common purpose. High-performance teams have reported high levels of collaboration and innovation, which consequently results in superior results (Boxall & Macky, 2009; Macky & Boxall, 2008; Markos & Sridevi, 2010). In a similar vein, Pak and Kim (2018) have argued for the role of an effective team for achieving high performance. Pak and Kim examined whether HPWS is positively related to performance outcomes, examining team-level factors contributing to an effective implementation. This study expands on HPWS in two ways, the first through conceptualising team level HPWS intensity and identifying antecedents of variance across teams. Specifically, attention is given to the visible role of team members in the process of HPWS implementation as a primary interpretive filter that makes team members perceive differences in the HPWS intensity which is said to, in turn, affect team performance.

Second, it is posited that if human resource policies are viewed as an exchange agreement between the organisation and its employees, then a team manager would more actively enforce espoused HR practices. These practices may positively influence the sense of human resource management–induced psychological contract fulfilment of team members, which, in turn, may influence individual in-role performance and organisational citizenship behaviour.

The analysis from the research demonstrated that HPWS is meaningful at the team level since aggregation is justified. This result supported the social interaction perspective, which suggests that shared HR experiences are created as team members share similar work contexts and interact frequently within their work groups. Furthermore, the study also confirmed that HPWS intensity is significantly influenced by team managers' enforcement of intended HR practices, the strength of the HRM system and the situational factors. To create a strong work environment, HR messages should be delivered to individuals in a distinctive, consistent, and consensual manner. In addition, HR experiences are influenced by adjacent filters, that is, the team manager's actions.

The major contribution of this study is in identifying the factors influencing the HPWS and performance relationship. HPWS research has focused on unlocking the black box that leads to expected performance outcomes, while studies examining the role of line managers have created a separate research stream. The examination of team managers' implementation of espoused HR practices recognises team managers as agents of the organisation with the responsibility of enforcing HR policies in their work groups, proposing ways in which team members implement HR policies as primary interpretative mechanisms through which employees make sense of actual HR experiences. The study concludes that the degree to which a team manager acts as a deliverer and an advocate of the espoused HR policies in the work group is significantly related to HPWS intensity at the team level and to subsequent work group and individual outcomes.

HPWS have been commonly referred to as the framework that reforms work practices to increase employee involvement, specifically in decision-making, and companion investments in employee skills and changes to performance incentives to ensure they can and want to undertake these highly important responsibilities (Boxall & Purcell, 2008). Underpinning the HPWS framework is a secondary model that is aimed at building individual and organisation performance, and this managerial approach is known as the AMO framework (Chowhan, 2016). Broadly the AMO model is concerned with the individual's performance when Ability, Motivation and Opportunity are present. It is argued that if managers want to enhance their staff performance they need to influence the three parts of the AMO model positively. Both HPWS and the AMO model frameworks will be discussed in greater detail within this section (Hughes, 2007; Robbins & Barnwell, 2002).

Ali, Lei, Freeman and Khan's (2019) research on perceived high-performance work system and its effect on branch performance examines the influence of high-performance work systems on unit performance relative to the mediating roles of collective human capital at the unit level and perceived HPWS at the employee level. This study outlined the important role high-performance work systems have in organisational performance. Limited research exists on how HPWS affect employees' perceptions of themselves and their impact on unit performance. Little evidence exists that differentiates the experiences of managers and employees in organisational HR practices. The relationship between HPWS and performance is quite robust, but there remain significant challenges in regard to the specific benefits of HPWS in relation to organisational performance. First, most prior research on HPWS show a direct and positive relationship with performance. Second, existing research almost exclusively takes a managerial perspective on the relationship between HR and performance, implicitly assuming that managers' opinions are consistent with employees' perceptions. Researchers have argued that employees' perceptions of the relationship between HPWS and performance should be addressed, because as the actual recipients of such practices, employees are in an ideal position to say how far and how well HPWS are executed within the organisation. Third, such studies generally confine themselves to organisational-level data, ignoring individual-level responses.

This study takes into account the concerns raised surrounding HPWS and contributes to the new stream of research building on existing literature by addressing calls for studies that better account for the relationship between HPWS and performance from both the managerial and employee perspectives. Eight hundred employees and 400 managers from different branches of the four banks were invited to participate in a survey. From this group, 181 branch managers and 504 employees responded to the questionnaire. The results show that the predictor and criterion variables of this study are positively associated with each other. On average, branch managers do actively implement HPWS. Employees' responses showed that they perceive a fairly high level of HPWS. In addition, manager-implemented HPWS and employee-perceived HPWS were correlated with each other. The average scores indicated that branch managers, in general, play an important role in creating unit performance. HPWS are also positive and highly correlated with collective human capital, perceived unit performance and perceived market performance, respectively.

Similarly, Andersén and Andersén (2019) found the influence of management position and gender on the relationship between HPWS and employees' affective commitment. The study found that employees become more affectively committed to organisations through an HPWS. The authors argue that management position and gender likely influence how individuals respond to HPWS. The purpose of the research was to examine how HPWS affects affective commitment among managers and subordinates. The study examined a hierarchical linear model of 356 employees in 26 Swedish small- and medium-sized manufacturing companies. The findings showed that managers and women showed high affective commitment in organisations using HPWS. For men with non-managerial positions the results indicated a reversed relationship, with HPWS reducing affective commitment. The findings show that there is a need to consider individual differences when examining the effect of HPWS and the usefulness of relational-oriented theories when studying the employee outcomes of HRM systems. The study showed the importance of not considering employees as a homogenous entity in response to HPWS in a similar manner based on the idea of reciprocal exchange. Further, when examining consequences for employees of HPWS, the study outlined it is important to consider that individuals belong to different social groups and this affects their identification with, and response to, HPWS. Also in respect of the influence of HPWS on attitudinal and performance outcomes, Kloutsiniotis and Mihail (2018) examined the Greek banking sector and the indirect effects of high-performance work systems on service quality, specifically the effects of employees' perception of HPWS in relation to their trust towards their managers, service quality and the mediating role of employee outcomes. Trust is also examined as a potential moderator in the relationship between HPWS and employee outcomes. Analysing a sample of 350 front-line employees working in the Greek banking sector, the study found employee outcomes to mediate the relationship between HPWS and service quality. While trust mediated the relationship between HPWS and employee outcomes, support was lacking for a moderating effect. Finally, trust was found to play a mediating and moderating role in the relationship between HPWS and service quality. In a similar vein Lee, Malik, Rosenberger and Sharma (2020) found the mediating role of trust in their study examining the relationship between ability and motivation-enhancing practices and formal and informal knowledge sharing, which, in turn, has an impact on employee and business level outcomes.

The presence of a trusting environment and social relations at work has attracted researchers to explore the importance of allowing flexible working arrangements and how this can have an impact on performance. Stirpe, Trullen and Bonache (2018) studied the effects of HPWS and flexible work programmes (FWPs) on retention of ageing workforces, employing data from the Workplace Employment Relations Study 2011, a government-funded survey designed to provide representative data on a wide range of employment practices across all sectors of the UK economy, with workplace as its unit of analysis. The Workplace Employment Relations Cross-Section Management Questionnaire is completed through face-to-face interviews with HR managers. The survey provided the information required for testing the hypotheses. The study sample comprised 736 workplaces. This study showed that workforce age composition matters in the relationship between HPWS and retention. Although the analysis confirmed that HPWS are valuable tools for retaining employees, their expected retention payoff changes as a function of workforce ageing. While HPWS may increase the retention of younger workforces, this does not appear to be the case for older workforces, where retention may even be impaired. Hence, the conventional view that HPWS generate more appealing work environments, thereby reinforcing employee attachment to the firm, does not seem to hold for older talent. This study argues that older employees will perceive HPWS-related resources less positively and HPWS-related demands more negatively than younger ones, thereby reducing the appeal of HPWS for ageing workforces, and hence their retention potential. Related to the stream examining social relations, employee participation and organisational innovation outcomes in the presence of HPWS, Zhou, Fan and Son (2019) explored the interaction effects between HPWS, employee participation, and human capital on organisational innovation. This study examines the contingency view of HRM in the context of China-specific research and investigates how human capital and employee participation jointly moderates the relationship between HPWS and organisational innovation.

The authors investigate a three-way interaction effect of HPWS, direct voice mechanisms, corporate governance participation, and human capital on organisational innovation. It was found that HPWS resulted in different innovation outcomes when employees who possessed distinct degrees of human capital were involved in employee participation (i.e. direct voice mechanism and corporate governance participation). Specifically, for firms with lower levels of employee human capital (i.e. lower education levels), HPWS combined with high direct voice mechanism or low corporate governance participation were positively related to organisational innovation. In contrast, for firms with higher levels of employee human capital (i.e. higher education levels), HPWS together with high direct voice mechanism or low corporate governance participation were negatively related to organisational innovation.

Investigating the moderating roles of organisational orientations aims to integrate strategic human resource management and transformational leadership literature to address gaps in each of the two literature. This study proposes that an organisational HPWS affects team managers' transformational leadership and the emergence of transformational leadership and the effectiveness of transformational leadership on team performance and the contingent organisational and efficiency orientations. The study reported a positive relationship between HPWS and transformational leadership which was positively and negatively moderated by adaptation and efficiency orientations, respectively. Transformational leadership was seen to positively relate to team performance and negatively moderate efficiency orientation. The results support a multilevel, moderated-mediation effect, with the indirect effect of HPWS on team performance through a transformational leadership varying significantly as a function of adaptation and efficiency orientations.

Shahzad et al. (2019) attempted to study the relationship between high-performance work systems and innovation performance in small- and medium-sized companies. Using the Ability, Motivation and Opportunity paradigm, this study examined the mediating roles of innovation-specific ability, motivation and voice behaviours between HPWS and SME innovation performance. The research found that human capital, motivation and employee voice mediate the relationship between HPWS and innovation performance in Pakistani SMEs.

The adoption of HPWS and its variants, high-involvement and commitment practices, has been linked to creating an ambidextrous context, which is critical for a firm to stay innovative and agile, and to sustain its competitive position through a range of innovative activities (Malik, Boyle, & Mitchell, 2017; Malik, Froese & Sharma, 2019; Patel, Messersmith & Lepak, 2013). Caniëls and Veld (2019) examined whether and how innovative work behaviour is related to explorative and exploitative activities. Polynomial regression analyses were employed to examine the relationship between organisational ambidexterity and employees' innovative work behaviours. The authors found that balance at a high level, as well as specialisation, is conducive to innovative work behaviour. The aim was to distinguish three situations: first whether there is a balancing of explorative and exploitative activities; second, whether there is an unbalanced scenario where exploitative activities dominate explorative activities and third, whether exploration outweighs exploitation. The study revealed that HRM practices have a positive impact on the innovative behaviour of individual employees who undertake a combination of explorative and exploitative activities.

Conceptual model of high involvement

According to the literature, for HPWS to work well, there needs to be a focus on two different frameworks; the first is the conceptual model of high-involvement work processes, and the second is the parallel framework of Ability,

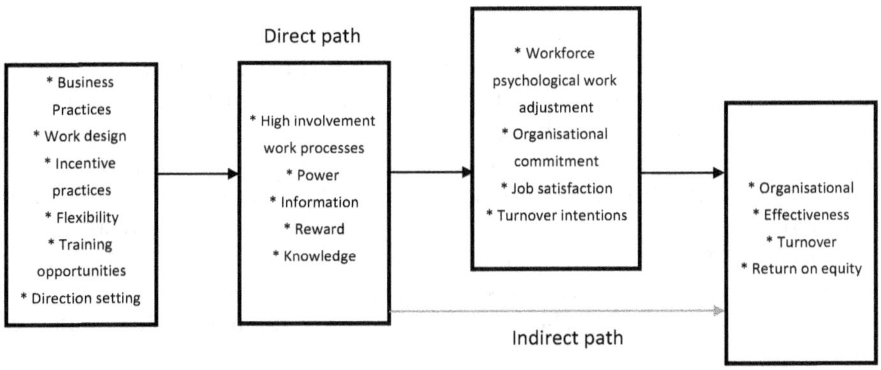

Figure 2.1 Conceptual Model of High-Involvement Work Processes.
Source: Boxall and Purcell (2008).

Motivation and Opportunity, which is otherwise known as the AMO framework (Bos-Nehles, Van Riemsdijk & Looise, 2013; Boxall & Macky, 2009; Hughes, 2007; Robbins, Judge, Millett & Waters-Marsh, 2008). The first, the conceptual model of high-involvement work processes, is best represented in Figure 2.1 (Boxall & Purcell, 2008; Robbins, Judge, Millett & Waters-Marsh, 2008).

There are two distinctive paths that can be followed through the above Conceptual Model. The first is a cognitive path, known also as the direct path, whereby the greater skills of employees are taken (Boxall & Purcell, 2008). The second path known as the indirect path, which is more of a motivational path where the processes involved aim to increase worker's satisfactions and other affective reactions are explored (Boxall & Purcell, 2008; Markos & Sridevi, 2010; Robbins, Judge, Millett & Waters-Marsh, 2008). The direct path enhances employee skill levels and firm-related knowledge, and is important for enabling personnel to solve work-related problems in a more effective and efficient manner (Boxall & Purcell, 2008; Robbins & Barnwell, 2002; Robbins, Judge, Millett & Waters-Marsh, 2008). The indirect path focuses on employee motivation and satisfaction, with an effort to lower turnover rates; this path is also important in ensuring that staff want to solve work-related problems and their continued responsibility for doing so remains at the forefront of their mind (Boxall & Purcell, 2008; Robbins & Barnwell, 2002).

The AMO framework stands hand in hand with this conceptual model; the AMO framework is described as an individual's will to perform when they have the Ability, which is essentially having the knowledge and skills to perform, the Motivation to do the job because they are interested and rewarded to do so and lastly the Opportunity to perform as the structure and environment supports them to perform (Boxall & Purcell, 2008; Robbins, Judge, Millett & Waters-Marsh, 2008).

Ability, Motivation and Opportunity

The AMO framework in practice is best depicted in Figure 2.2.

Previous research argues that not only does HRM practices impact employees but employees are also motivated through other ways such as through work processes, but also through the environment they are working in, and that it is easier to perform when a company is successful (Boxall & Macky, 2009; Boxall & Purcell, 2008; Dropulic-Ruzic, 2014; Macky & Boxall, 2007). For this research, one way to conceptualise HPWS is that when systems have an impact on the AMO factors. In this approach, we will analyse the HPWS of a large organisation and the impact it has on an individual's productivity levels along with their personality type (Boxall & Purcell, 2008; Robbins, Judge, Millett & Waters-Marsh, 2008).

The AMO framework is suitable for the HPWS context, as studies have found for the AMO framework to work it must positively affect employee abilities, motivations and opportunities in order for them to contribute to the organisation. Improvements in knowledge enhance Ability, whilst empowerment and information enhance the Opportunity to contribute (Boxall & Purcell, 2008; Robbins, Judge, Millett & Waters-Marsh, 2008).

Rewards are a direct attempt to enhance Motivation, which may also be improved through empowerment of information and knowledge (Boxall & Macky, 2009; Robbins & Barnwell, 2002).

High-performance work systems including performance-related pay, various employee communication means, training and team-based work mutually reinforce each other to generate superior organisational performance (Boxall &

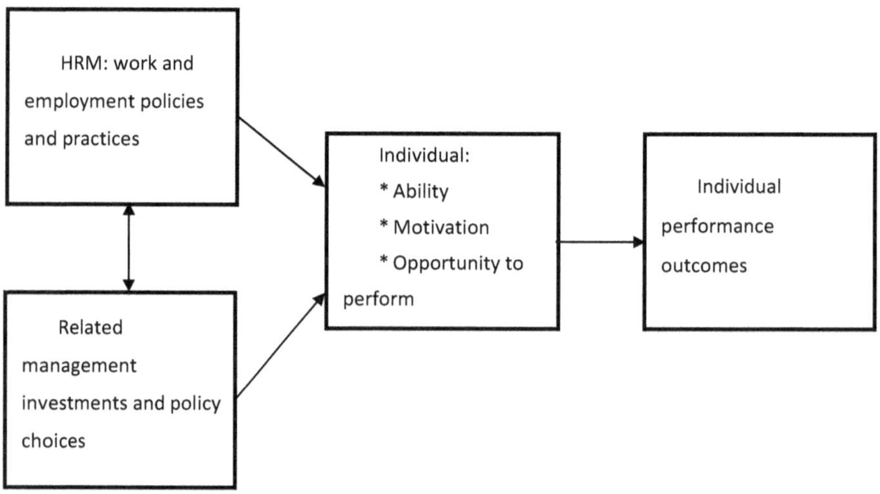

Figure 2.2 The AMO Framework.
Source: Boxall and Purcell (2008).

Purcell, 2008; Robbins, Judge, Millett & Waters-Marsh, 2008). Advocates of the HPWS school argue that improvements in organisational performance is generated because these practices enhance employee discretion which, in turn, can flow into an improved attitude towards the work undertaken by employees (Boxall & Purcell, 2008; Robbins, Judge, Millett & Waters-Marsh, 2008). Conversely, critics suggest that high-performance work practices lead to work intensification, with any gains in discretion being small to none (Boxall & Purcell, 2008; Robbins, Judge, Millett & Waters-Marsh, 2008).

There is a large volume of literature in this area. However, there are very few studies that have examined the impact of HPWS on an organisation's employees; therefore, this area of topic needs further research. In addition, the main feature of high-performance work systems is understood as a change from being a 'Tayloristic' work organisation to being a more holistic work organisation, which is characterised by flat, horizontal hierarchical structures, enhanced skills through job rotation of employees, along with teams that are self-responsible, individuals that are capable of multi-tasking, non-managerial employees in decision-making, horizontal (rather than vertical) communication channels throughout the organisation and a greater sense of autonomy for employees over the way they execute their tasks related to their roles and responsibilities (Boxall & Purcell, 2008; Robbins, Judge, Millett & Waters-Marsh, 2008). It is said that innovative workplace practices are often accompanied by complementary human resource practices and performance (Andreeva & Sergeeva, 2016; Beltran-Martin & Roca-Puig, 2013; Smith, Tucker & Pitt, 2011).

Looking more closely at the AMO model, abilities are the level of physical, financial, cognitive, emotional or social resources a person can apply to perform a specific task (Boxall & Purcell, 2008; Robbins, Judge, Millett & Waters-Marsh, 2008).

Motivation is the needs and wants of an individual and how these may influence them to behave in a certain way. Motivation encourages employees to act in a particular way (Boxall & Purcell, 2008; Robbins & Barnwell, 2002; Robbins, Judge, Millett & Waters-Marsh, 2008). Opportunity is the relevant restrictions, such as the availability of time and resources that also enable behaviours; generally speaking, employees seek opportunities to complete a task that will result in a benefit for them or for others (Boxall & Purcell, 2008; Robbins, Judge, Millett & Waters-Marsh, 2008). For employees, Motivation is provided by incentives and rewards for the type of expected behaviour and outcomes that benefit the organisation. Opportunities, for example, engage employees in activities that make them feel like they are helping the organisation be successful. This may lead to new capabilities or skills through training and increasing knowledge and talents used on the job (Boxall & Purcell, 2008; Robbins & Barnwell, 2002; Robbins, Judge, Millett & Waters-Marsh, 2008).

Research suggests organisations that are able to focus on these three elements can achieve increased organisational performance in the form of increased and improved profitability, productivity, customer satisfaction, quality of deliverables and lastly growth of market share (Patel, Messersmith & Lepak, 2013).

Motivation is said to have a direct influence on behaviour, which is then moderated by both Ability and Opportunity (Boxall & Purcell, 2008; Robbins, Judge, Millett & Waters-Marsh, 2008).

Exploring the Ability-Motivation-Opportunity paradigm for enhancing firm performance, Kundu and Gahlawat (2018) present evidence from India and discuss key challenges such as rapid enhancement in productivity levels, reduction in various costs and management of de-skilling and multi-skilling issues. The authors note that managers of Indian firms are compelled to think of the human factors in organisations and rely on human resource systems to facilitate organisational learning, promotion of empowerment and enhancing the employee adaptability at workplaces through the use of high-performance work systems. The research examined the question around whether Western methods of human resource management can be effective in India. To unlock the 'black box,' the study introduced affective commitment as a mediating variable between HPWS and firm performance. This study claims to be distinct from other studies as it is aimed at examining the relationship between HPWS and performance effects through the AMO paradigm. This theoretical understanding focuses on empirical evidence of how the HPWS components are linked to firm performance via the affective commitment of the employees.

The study reinforced the significant role of HPWS in Indian organisations. The results demonstrated that through the adoption of the three AMO components, the HR practices enhanced employees' affective commitment as well as the firm's performance. Overall, the study provides an understanding of whether contemporary HRM systems can work within the context of emerging economies in general, and for organisations in India, in particular.

In this study, high-performance work systems have been reviewed and discussed; simply put the findings showcase that if the organisation's systems are designed in the right way, with the right elements to support individuals, the organisation can maximise the way its workforce performs. Specifically, if you hire people with the Ability and give them the right Motivation and Opportunity they will perform 'better', which, in turn, enables the organisation to perform 'better' (Gahan et al., 2004; Jensen, Patel & Messersmith, 2013). The interactions between key factors and the AMO are detailed below in Figure 2.3.

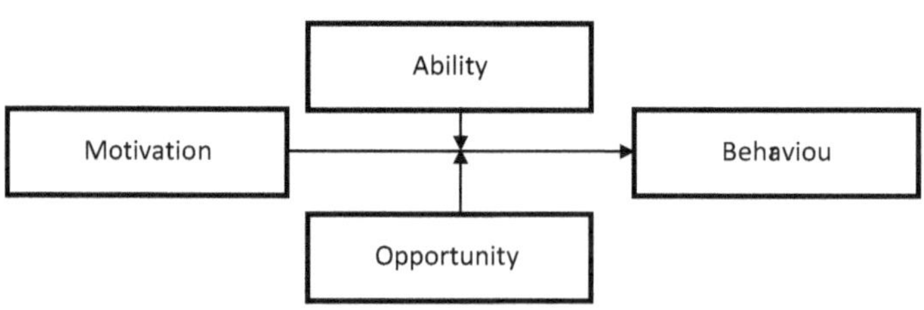

Figure 2.3 The AMO Framework Interacting.

Out of each of the topics explored, namely, personality profiling, productivity and HPWS, HPWS is the most researched and explored. HPWS are an important element in understanding linkages between the organisation an individual works for and what motivates the individual to do the best possible job. Gaps regarding the relationship between personality profiling and productivity are therefore explored.

Gaps in the literature

So far, this literature review chapter has defined, detailed and discussed each of the theoretical areas accordingly. As evident from what we have discussed above, of all the topics, the interactions between personality profiling using MBTI, productivity and HPWS are areas that have not been extensively researched and discussed at great length. The following will outline the identified gaps in the literature, showing linkages as to why this research is so imperative for advancing theory and practice.

MBTI

It is worth discussing the available literature with consideration to personality profiling, specifically the MBTI, as the application of MBTI to productivity-based roles or productivity-based environments is non-existent; currently there is no research that considers these factors together, therefore highlighting the importance of this research. But more than just a gap in available literature, there is an importance that comes with the personality profiling, as MBTI allows an organisation to understand the best-fit individuals for the roles within their organisation and to subsequently manage their talent pipeline for business continuity (Stahl et al., 2012). There are key gaps in the literature surrounding HRM and pipeline management for organisations; therefore, this research seeks to provide tangible insights into the best ways to manage the talent pipeline (Stahl et al., 2012). Personality profiling being important to an individual's self-awareness allows for an individual the Opportunity to understand their preferences, which, in turn, enables individuals to pick the best possible career options that complement their preferences and personal requirements. A context that allows for employees such decisions is more likely to create opportunities for them to be motivated to apply their skills effectively.

While MBTI is a topic that has been explored in great depth, there is a lack of research that considers MBTI within the Australian banking context. Significant research exists that considers a vast variety of other topics, such as their impact on mental illnesses, education selection and sporting preferences, but there is no research available that considers MBTI and preferences as regards banking and finance within the Australian market (Barbuto, Fritz, Lim & Xu, 2008; Genco & Mitchell, 2006; Herk, 2008; Loffredo & Opt, 2006). Therefore, this type of research would be able to provide individuals and organisations with important information that determines how MBTI is seen to act in the banking and finance industry within the Australian market, filling an obvious gap.

Research exists when considering MBTI and the impact on productivity in manufacturing and production-based environments; as previously mentioned this is potentially due to the simplicity of the translation of productivity in manufacturing compared to that in knowledge-based work (Bong-Chang & Gurbaxani, 2012; Kasman, Kasman, Ayhan & Torun, 2013). However, there are limitations when MBTI is reviewed for knowledge-based productivity; critics argue this is due to the complexity of knowledge-based environments and the current shift from production into knowledge-based domains (Drucker, 1999; Jabbour, 2013).

Lastly, there is no research that considers MBTI preferences with HPWS, specifically how an individual acts within the workplace if they have the right abilities, motivations and opportunities, therefore warranting further research to understand whether there are any positive or negative linkages between the two concepts. These linkages would provide greater insights into the preferences that drive an individual's view of Ability, Motivation and Opportunity (Rastogi & Dave, 2004). Further, linked closely to the idea of HPWS is the concept of employee outcomes; employee outcomes have been described for this study as the way an individual feels and therefore views the case organisation. As there is no research that considers MBTI and HPWS there is also no research that considers the flow of impact onto employee outcomes. This research would provide individuals and organisations with information they can use to better understand the complexities in the relationship an employee has with the case organisation. This study will also provide insights into how an individual views the case organisation.

In addition, some of the weaknesses of MBTI need to be further researched to understand the impact of these weaknesses on the outcome of the profiling, as literature has failed to investigate some of these topics. Also, the previously mentioned issue surrounding individual interpretation of results deserves attention; an individual can misinterpret the results of the MBTI if they do not understand the questions or outcomes of the MBTI. No research has explored this in greater detail to determine whether there are real issues associated with this and how to mitigate misinterpretation of the MBTI (Quenk, 2009). Moreover, there are gaps in the literature on the MBTI in Australia; as most studies deal with the dominant American style preferences, the Australian context warrants further research to explore any differences due to national, industry and cultural variations in MBTI profiles (Hautala, 2007; Reeder & McPeek, 2011; Smolka, 2005).

Productivity

Productivity has been discussed taking into consideration the available literature and considering how one of Australia's largest financial services organisations deals with the topic, and from the discussion it is evident that there are some gaps in the literature. The first gap is based on the limited research that is available when an individual transitions from productivity in a manufacturing environment into productivity in a knowledge-based environment; in this regard ample research pertaining to physical labour, manufacturing and operational environments exists, as the translation of productivity in those spaces is regarded as simple (Drucker, 1999; Sye, 2004). However, complexity comes into play when productivity is attempted to be translated in a knowledge-based environment, thus resulting in limited available research on the topic; therefore, there is a requirement to review this topic further to understand any potential linkages. Secondary to this is the limited available research in the banking and finance industry in the Australian market, due to the complexity of the topic when transitioning into knowledge-based spaces. In addition, productivity in knowledge-based environments, specifically the banking and finance industry, has not been explored as a topic; the same in Australian context has not been explored either. That said, this research is a compelling and significant requirement to developing and discussing an unknown topic in a field/industry in a geographical location for which data doesn't exist currently, providing future researchers the Opportunity to further deliberate and enhance this topic to glean more intellectual and detailed findings. In this research, productivity has been discussed as it relates to one of Australia's largest financial services organisations and is therefore unique to that company; there are gaps in relation to how productivity is viewed and utilised for different roles in different industries and companies in the Australian market, with this research being a starting point for those insights. It is highly likely that different productivity roles in different companies and industries are performed completely differently based on the company's needs and where they are in their productivity journey. The productivity journey for Organisation X has been underway for the last seven years, meaning Organisation X is more likely to be further advanced when compared to other financial services organisations in terms of productivity (Organisation X, 2017).

High-performance work systems (HPWS)

The topic of HPWS is also an area that has a large robust inventory of research relating to it, but from the available literature it is clear there are gaps relating to the view of HPWS within Australia and banking and finance as an industry. As this is a significant industry contributing over $200 billion annually to the GDP and employs in excess of 221,303 employees internationally, a study on HPWS in Australian Banking and Finance industry is both significant and compelling.

The literature discusses the AMO model at length, specifically the thought process underpinning the AMO model, that is, if you focus on employee Ability, Motivation and Opportunity, individuals can achieve increased performance. By implementing a set of HPWS, organisations can achieve a range of employee and business productivity outcomes, such as increases in profitability, productivity, customer satisfaction, quality of deliverables and growth of market share, which leads to achieving competitive advantage (Patel, Messersmith & Lepak, 2013). However, the model needs further exploration to understand whether there are any factors that might impact this relationship (Ferrari, O'Callaghan & Newbegin, 2005; Steel, 2007). It is argued that procrastination is dangerous in the workforce and a concept that HPWS should critically consider, as teams in the workforce are said to consistently delay the bulk of their work until the deadlines approach (Steel, 2007). There are gaps in the available literature regarding the level of impact that procrastination has on the AMO model, if any; however, it should be explored to understand whether workforce procrastination is a real risk and concern organisations are faced with. Through the study of personality type an organisation can gain an understanding of employee personality preferences, thus highlighting those who have a preference for procrastination in the workplace and potentially being aware of those individuals; with this knowledge organisations can then build the most appropriate methods and tools to mitigate this behaviour where possible.

There are some further gaps in the research regarding HPWS when reviewed against banking and finance as an industry. That said, the topic should be explored further to determine if there are any differences in the research and its findings. Moreover, as there is limited research conducted in Australia in this regard, this geographic location should be explored to determine if there are any tangible differences between the research already conducted, which appears to be mostly in the United States and New Zealand, and that conducted within Australia (Boxall, Hutchinson & Wassenaar, 2015; Boxall & Macky, 2009; Jensen, Patel & Messersmith, 2013; Patel, Messersmith & Lepak, 2013).

HPWS have also been explored with regard to productivity and the impact HPWS has on employee productivity levels within organisations; however, there is limited research that has reviewed HPWS with regard to MBTI and productivity, thus necessitating further research in this area (Boxall, 2012; Boxall & Macky, 2009; Kasman, Kasman, Ayhan & Torun, 2013; Macky & Boxall, 2007; Messersmith, Lepak, Patel & Gould-Williams, 2011).

Research questions

A good research question needs to be grounded in current theoretical and empirical knowledge; it needs to set context; must be doable as well as worthwhile undertaking; should address a specific, clear, well-defined and to-the-point topic; and needs to lead to new information (Malhotra, 2010; Sekaran & Bougie, 2013). Further to this, a good research question should demand a lot more than looking something up. It needs to be ethical, should be dichotomous and needs to be relevant (Malhotra, 2010; Sekaran & Bougie, 2013). In review of the above, the main objective of this research was to investigate the influence of personality type on employee and organisational outcomes. With that objective, the following overarching research problem was developed to set out the domain of the study: *What influence does employee personality type have on employee and organisational outcomes?* In order to address this problem and understand the relationships between personality preferences (profiled specifically with the aid of the MBTI), productivity and HPWS, the following three overarching research questions (RQs) were also developed to guide this research.

RQ1: What influence does employee personality type have on employee HPWS, namely, Ability, Motivation and Opportunity?
RQ2: What influence does employee personality type have on organisational outcomes, namely organisational citizenship behaviours and affective organisational commitment?
RQ3: What influence does employee personality type have on productivity?

In order to address the research problem and research questions, a critical review of the literature was undertaken (Chapter 2), leading to the development of a conceptual framework (Figure 2.4) that guided the ensuing research design (Chapter 3).

Theoretical framework and hypotheses

The theoretical framework is designed to answer the research problem, related research questions and linked hypotheses which have been outlined and will be discussed in greater detail.

Theoretical framework

The guiding theoretical framework represents beliefs on how certain phenomena are related to each other and an explanation of why these variables are associated with each other (Sekaran & Bougie, 2013). The theoretical framework consists of the conceptions and their delineations and reference to pertinent scholarly literature and existing theory that is used for this study (Abend, 2013). The variables in the study's guiding theoretical framework are defined as follows.

1 **HPWS:** HPWS involve improvements to work practices to increase employee decision-making and investments in employee skills and changes to performance incentives to ensure that employees can undertake bigger or greater responsibilities and that they actually intend to fulfil these responsibilities (Boxall & Purcell, 2008; Gahan et al., 2004). The HPWS focus in this study is on the AMO model, that is, Ability, Motivation and Opportunity, which, when used effectively, is said to drive increased organisational performance in the form of improved and enhanced profitability, productivity, customer satisfaction, quality of deliverables and, lastly, growth of market share (Patel, Messersmith & Lepak, 2013).
2 **Personality**: A personality profile test using a questionnaire or other standardised instrument is designed to reveal aspects of an individual's character or psychological make-up. Specifically, this study will use and reference the MBTI, which is based on 16 personality types that depict the population.

3 **Productivity**: the effectiveness of an employee's productive effort, as measured in terms of the rate of output per unit of input, and the intersection between cost, effort and quality (Sye, 2004). For the purposes of this study, it is made up of Task Enjoyment and Task Duration.
4 **OCB**: Organisational citizenship behaviour is an individual's voluntary commitment to activities that are not part of their contractual tasks. Typically, employees who are committed to their organisation feel a connection; they feel they 'fit in', and they understand the goals of the organisation (Boxall & Purcell, 2008).
5 **AOC**: Affective organisational commitment depicts how committed an individual is to their place of employment or how they emotionally feel about their organisation (Buitendach & De Witte, 2005).
6 **Behaviours and intentions**: Behaviours and intentions are the way in which one acts or conducts oneself, especially towards others (Oxford Dictionary, 2017). In relation to this study behaviours and intentions are related to how an individual engages with the organisation they work for.

Figure 2.4 shows the relationships between the variables. The focus of this study is based on the MBTI and the related relationships between HPWS (specifically AMO) and individual and organisational behaviours, and lastly its relationship with productivity outcomes. The conceptual model is outlined in Figure 2.5 below; this model shows the relationships between independent variables (IVs) and dependent variables (DVs). The relationships have been detailed which show that the MBTI is one of the main variables being tested with how it interacts with HPWS (AMO), OCB, AOC and productivity.

This study attempts to bridge the theoretical gap by analysing the impact of personality type and high-performance work systems on productivity in the context of the Australian Banking and Finance services sector. Moreover, the

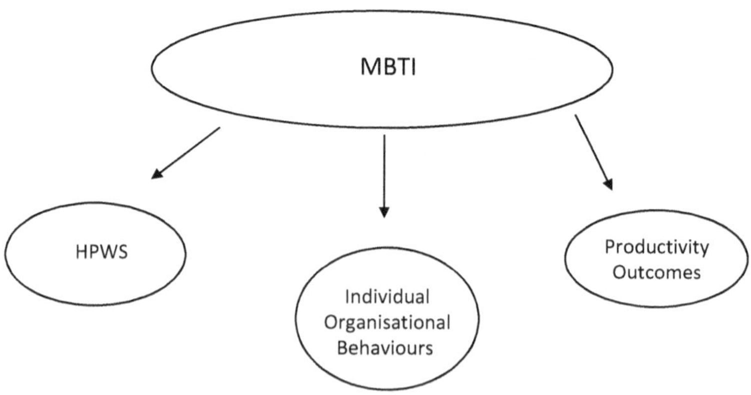

Figure 2.4 Moderation Effects.

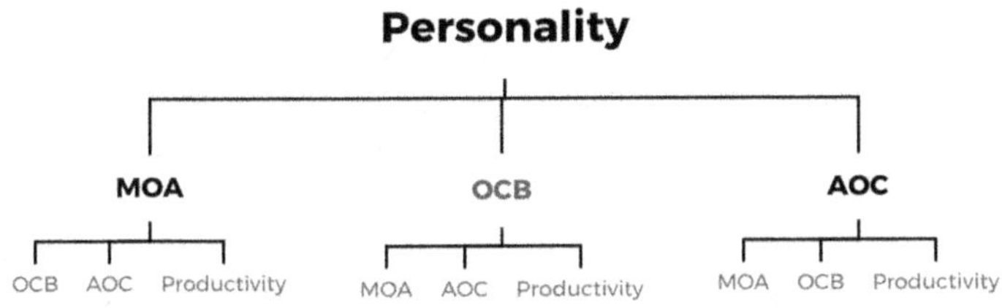

Figure 2.5 The Conceptual Model.
Note: *Arrows represent relationships between variables. For clarity of presentation, the personality profile's direct influences on the constructs of the model are not shown.*

research is expected to yield insights related to the most suited personality type for high productivity work in a knowledge-based environment. The findings of this research would allow firms to more effectively allocate resources and achieve a better employee-job fit and help them maintain their competitive advantage.

Hypotheses

A hypothesis is defined as a tentative, testable statement expected to be found in an empirical data set (Malhotra, 2010; Sekaran & Bougie, 2013). Hypotheses are unproven statements or propositions about a factor or phenomenon that is of interest (Malhotra, 2010). Good hypotheses have certain characteristics to be successful. The first is the power of prediction; hypotheses need to predict for the future, and they also need to have a close contact with observable things, should be simple, clear and testable empirically, and relevant to a particular research problem (Bryman & Bell, 2011).

A relationship is expected to occur between the personality type of an individual and their commitment to an organisation, reinforcing the idea that the tasks and preferences an individual enjoys will drive satisfaction because they are enjoyable activities which will lead to commitment, happiness and high performance (Boxall & Purcell, 2008; Robbins & Barnwell, 2002; Robbins, Judge, Millett & Waters-Marsh, 2008).

It is expected that a relationship between productivity and personality as MBTI preferences would drive productivity, meaning people will work harder because they enjoy completing the assigned tasks. Also a relationship between HPWS and productivity is expected to be observed in this research because if the right environment is built employees will want to work harder to produce quality key performance indicators. And, lastly, a relationship is expected to be observed between personality and HPWS, as employees' preferences will make them want to work harder to contribute to a performing environment or workplace (Patel, Messersmith & Lepak, 2013). To address the information needs of the research problem and questions, the following hypotheses have been examined as part of this research.

Research Question One: *What influence does employee personality type have on employee HPWS (AMO)?*

This group of hypotheses is linked to research question one and are designed to analyse whether there is a relationship between an HPWS element (i.e. AMO) and MBTI type, including both the overall MBTI – 16 type and the constituent base pairs (i.e. the MBTI – 4). A significant relationship is expected to be present in this regard based on prior research (e.g. Drucker, 1999; LePine, Buckman, Crawford & Methot, 2011; Mladkova, 2011), which is detailed in the "Productivity" section. Previous literature detailed that HPWS and AMO have an impact on employees and their motivation, through work processes and the environment they are working in (Boxall & Macky, 2009; Boxall & Purcell, 2008; Macky & Boxall, 2007). The available research on the topic of personality type and HPWS (AMO) has found that personality types in an organisational context have explored many different relationships, including, but not limited to, the relationship between psychological type and the motivation of workers (Barbuto, Fritz, Lim & Xu, 2008), which maximises knowledge worker productivity levels (Maruta, 2012) and boosts productivity of knowledge workers (Matson & Prusak, 2010; Mladkova, 2011). Therefore, based on the literature, a relationship between MBTI and AMO is expected.

H1a: Personality type, as represented by the MBTI – 16, has an effect on Motivation.
H1b: Personality type, as represented by the MBTI – 16, has an effect on Opportunity.
H1c: Personality type, as represented by the MBTI – 16, has an effect on Ability.

This leads to a further examination of the following sub-hypotheses related to the AMO model.

Motivation

H2a–d: The MBTI – 4 dimensions of (a) Introvert/Extrovert, (b) Intuition/ Sensing, (c) Thinking/Feeling and (d) Perceiving/Judging will have an influence on Motivation.

Opportunity

H3a–d: The MBTI – 4 dimensions of (a) Introvert/Extrovert, (b) Intuition/ Sensing, (c) Thinking/Feeling and (d) Perceiving/Judging will have an influence on Opportunity.

Ability

H4a–d: The MBTI – 4 dimensions of (a) Introvert/Extrovert, (b) Intuition/ Sensing, (c) Thinking/Feeling and (d) Perceiving/Judging will have an influence on Ability

Research Question Two: *What influence does employee personality type have on organisational HPWS (AMO), namely, organisational citizenship behaviours and organisational commitment?*

The second group of hypotheses looks into whether there is a relationship between an individual's personality type and the level of organisational citizenship. The above factors form part of the concepts surrounding organisational commitment, and it can be argued organisational commitment is seen through the level of incentive an individual possesses and the knowledge they hold, along with their productivity levels, which all feed into the commitment they maintain to the organisation they work for. Studies have found that personality types are an important factor in successful team performance, which again is linked to the level of commitment one displays (Bradley & Hebert, 1997; Kasman, Kasman, Ayhan & Torun, 2013; Ones & Dilchert, 2009). Therefore, a relationship is expected between the individual's personality type and the level of commitment behaviours they display in the workplace.

H1d: Personality type, as represented by the MBTI – 16, has an effect on OCB.
H5a–d: The MBTI – 4 dimensions of (a) Introvert/Extrovert, (b) Intuition/Sensing, (c) Thinking/Feeling and (d) Perceiving/Judging will have an influence on OCB.

In order to understand the AOC an individual possesses the AMO model should be reviewed. Studies have found for the AMO framework to work it must positively affect employee abilities, motivations and opportunities in order for them to contribute to the organisation. Improvements in knowledge enhance Ability, whilst empowerment and information enhance the Opportunity to contribute (Boxall & Purcell, 2008; Robbins, Judge, Millett & Waters-Marsh, 2008).

Advocates of the HPWS school argue that improvements in organisational performance enhance employee discretion, which, in turn, can flow into an improved attitude towards the work undertaken by employees (Boxall & Purcell, 2008; Robbins, Judge, Millett & Waters-Marsh, 2008). That said, a relationship is expected between MBTI and affective organisational commitment displayed by employees.

H1e: Personality type, as represented by the MBTI – 16 has an effect on AOC
H6a: The MBTI – 4 dimensions of (a) Introvert/Extrovert, (b) Intuition/Sensing, (c) Thinking/Feeling and (d) Perceiving/Judging will have an influence on AOC

Research Question Three: *What influence does employee personality type have on productivity?*

The third group of hypotheses covers productivity outcomes, which, for the purpose of this study, include Task Enjoyment linked to satisfaction and Task Duration.

In the first instance employee personality type and enjoyment were reviewed to understand whether there is a relationship between the factors. In order to understand personality type and enjoyment, individuals at the case organisation provided insights into the activities employees enjoy or not, as part of their jobs.

Underpinning these hypotheses is the HPWS concept, which is aimed at building individual and organisation performance (Chowhan, 2016). Considering the HPWS concept is the AMO model, which is concerned with an individual's performance when Ability, Motivation and Opportunity are present. The literature argues that if managers want to enhance their staff performance they need to influence the three parts of the AMO model positively (Hughes, 2007; Robbins & Barnwell, 2002).

To this end, if the AMO model is followed closely and successfully executed, a relationship would be found between an individual's MBTI and their enjoyment within the workplace. Linked to the idea of enjoyment is satisfaction, as studies have found that personality types may have a role to play in explaining employee performance in the organisational context. For example, early research found that personality types are an important factor in successful team performance (Bradley & Hebert, 1997; Kasman, Kasman, Ayhan & Torun, 2013; Ones & Dilchert, 2009). The conceptual model of high-involvement work processes is examined as part of this literature review specifically, and the indirect path as part of that model is referenced. The indirect path is said to focus on employee motivation and satisfaction, with an effort to lower turnover rates; the indirect path is important to ensure that staff want to solve work-related problems and their continued responsibility to do so remains at the forefront of their mind (Boxall & Purcell, 2008; Robbins & Barnwell, 2002).

H1f: Personality type, as represented by the MBTI – 16 has an effect on Task Enjoyment.

H7a–d: The MBTI – 4 dimensions of (a) Introvert/Extrovert, (b) Intuition/Sensing, (c) Thinking/Feeling and (d) Perceiving/Judging will have an influence on Task Enjoyment.

The final group of hypotheses is created to understand whether personality type has an effect on the duration of tasks completed (by productivity experts). These hypotheses are loosely linked to the prior group of hypotheses in that behaviours and intentions are investigated, which is achieved by applying the AMO model. Abilities are the level of physical, financial, cognitive, emotional or social resources a person can afford to perform a specific behaviour (Boxall & Purcell, 2008; Robbins, Judge, Millett & Waters-Marsh, 2008).

Motivation are the needs and wants of an individual and the encouragement for behaviour (Boxall & Purcell, 2008; Robbins & Barnwell, 2002; Robbins, Judge, Millett & Waters-Marsh, 2008). Opportunity is the relevant restrictions, such as the availability of time and resources, that also enable employee behaviours (Boxall & Purcell, 2008; Robbins, Judge, Millett & Waters-Marsh, 2008). Research suggests organisations that are able to focus on these three elements can achieve increased organisational performance in the form of increased and improved profitability, productivity, customer satisfaction, quality of deliverables and, lastly, growth of market share (Patel, Messersmith & Lepak, 2013). If an organisation can effectively tap into the parts of the AMO model they can increase organisational performance through greater productivity; therefore, one can assume that an individual would complete more tasks in a shorter timeframe with greater quality attached to those deliverables. That said, it is expected that a positive relationship should be ascertained between MBTI and Task Duration.

H1g: Personality type, as represented by the MBTI – 16 has an effect on Task Duration.

H8a: The MBTI – 4 dimensions of (a) Introvert/Extrovert, (b) Intuition/Sensing, (c) Thinking/Feeling and (d) Perceiving/Judging will have an influence on Task Duration.

Therefore, it was expected that a relationship would be found between MBTI and productivity, specifically Task Enjoyment linked to satisfaction and Task Duration.

Summary and conclusion

This chapter has critically reviewed the literature and identified key research findings in the area of personality profiling, productivity and HPWS with regard to the case organisation. Each of these terms has been discussed individually, then collectively for further analysing the gaps in the available literature, thereby highlighting why this research has such an importance and needs to be undertaken. Next, the relevant research questions have been conferred at a greater level of detail. Following this, the concepts have been evaluated; finally, a guiding theoretical framework has been developed in detail along with the relevant hypotheses relating to this research.

References

16personalities.com, (2017). *Personality Types.* Retrieved on 19th November 2017 from https://www.16personalities.com/personality-types

Abend, G., (2008). The Meaning of Theory. *Sociological Theory* 26, 173–199.

Ali, M., Lei, S., Freeman, S., & Khan, M.M., (2019). Implemented and Perceived High-Performance Work System and Its Effect on Branch Performance. *Employee Relations: The International Journal,* 41(4), 793–810.

Andersén, J., & Andersén, A., (2019). Are High-Performance Work Systems (HPWS) Appreciated by Everyone? The Role of Management Position and Gender on the Relationship between HPWS and Affective Commitment. *Employee Relations: The International Journal,* 41(5), 1046–1064.

Andreeva, T., & Sergeeva, A., (2016). The More the Better….or Is It? The Contradictory Effects of HR Practices on Knowledge Sharing Motivation and Behaviour. *Human Resource Management Journal,* 26(2), 151–171.

Athota, V.S., Budhwar, P., & Malik, A., (2019). Personality Influencing Wellbeing and Resilience Via Values and Moral Foundations: A Cross-National Study. *Applied Psychology: An International Review,* 69(3), 653–685.

Athota, V.S., & Malik, A., (2019). *Managing Employee Well-being and Resilience for Innovation: Evidence from Knowledge-Intensive Service Industries.* Springer.

Bandara, W., Gable, G. G., & Rosemann, M., (2005). Factors and Measures of Business Process Modelling: Model Building through a Multiple Case Study. *European Journal of Information Systems,* 14(4), 347–360.

Barbuto, J.E., Fritz, S.M., Lim, J.C.S., & Xu, Y., (2008). Using the MBTI Instrument and the Motivation Sources Inventory to Test the Relationships between Jung's Psychological Types and Sources of Motivation. *Journal of Psychological Type,* Center for Applications of Psychological Type, 105, 1155–1158.

Barrick, M., & Mount, M.K., (1991). The Big Five Personality Dimensions and Job Performance: A Meta-Analysis. *Personnel Psychology,* 44(1), 1–26.Barnuto, Jr., J.E., Phipps, K.A., & Xu, Y., (2009). Testing Relationships between Personality, Conflict Styles and Effectiveness. *International Journal of Conflict Management,* 21(4), 434–447.

Bathurst, J., (2000). The Relationship between Reported Type and Best-Fit Type: Evidence for Administrator Bias? *Journal of Psychological Type,* Center for Applications of Psychological Type, 54, 5–11.

Beltran-Martin, I., & Roca-Puig, V., (2013). Promoting Employee Flexibility Through HR Practices. Human Resource Management. *Wiley Periodicals,* 52(5), 645–674. Retrieved on 19 November 2017 from http://onlinelibrary.wiley.com/doi/10.1002/hrm.21556/abstract

Bong-Chang, Y., & Gurbaxani, V., (2012). Information Technology Outsourcing, Knowledge Transfer and Firm Productivity: An Empirical Analysis. *MIS Quarterly,* 36(4), 1043–1063.

Bos-Nehles, A.C., Van Riemsdijk, J.V., & Looise, J.K., (2013). Employee Perceptions of Line Management Performance: Applying the AMO Theory to Explain the Effectiveness of Line Managers HRM Implementation. *Human Resource Management,* 52(6), 861–877.

Boult, M.J.L., Thompson, R.C., & Schaubhut, N.A., (2017). Well-Being and MBTI Personality Type in the Workplace. An International Comparison. *CPP White Paper,* Asia Pacific, 1–33.

Boxall, P., (2012). High-Performance Work Systems: What, Why, How and for Whom? *Asia Pacific Journal of Human Resources,* 50(2), 169–186.

Boxall, P., & Macky, K., (2009). Research and Theory on High Performance Work Systems: Progressing the High Involvement Stream. *Human Resource Management Journal,* 2(6), 177–185.

Boxall, P., & Purcell, J., (2008). *Strategy and Human Resource Management.* Second Edition. Palgrave Macmillan.

Boxall, P., Hutchison, A., & Wassenaar, B., (2015). How Do High-Involvement Work Processes Influence Employee Outcomes? An Examination of the Mediating Roles of Skill Utilisation and Intrinsic Motivation. *The International Journal of Human Resource Management,* 26(13), 1737–1752.

Bradley, J.H., & Hebert, F.J., (1997). The Effect of Personality Type on Team Performance. *Journal of Management Development,* 16(5), 337–353.

Bryman, A., & Bell, E., (2011). *Business Research Methods.* Third Edition. Oxford University Press.

Buitendach, J.H., & De Witte, H., (2005). Job Insecurity, Extrinsic and Intrinsic Job Satisfaction and Affective Organisational Commitment of Maintenance Workers in a Parastatal. *Business Management,* 36(2), 27–38.

Caniëls, M.C., & Veld, M., (2019). Employee Ambidexterity, High Performance Work Systems and Innovative Work Behaviour: How Much Balance Do We Need? *The International Journal of Human Resource Management*, 30(4), 565–585.

Chang, E., Lee, A., Byeon, E., Seong, H., & Lee, S.M., (2016). The Mediating Effect of Motivational Types in the Relationship between Perfectionism and Academic Burnout. *Personality and Individual Differences*, Elsevier Ltd., 89, 202–210.

Chesborough, S., (2005). Do Athletes Learn Differently? Implications for Improving the Learning Environments for Athletes. *Journal of Psychological Type*, Center for Applications of Psychological Type, 64(4), 31–40.

Chowhan, J., (2016). Unpacking the Black Box: Understanding the Relationship between Strategy, HRM Practices, Innovation and Organisational Performance. *Human Resource Management Journal*, 26(2), 112–133.

Da Cunha, A.D., & Greathead, D., (2007). Does Personality Matter? An Analysis of Code-Review Ability. *Communications of the ACM*, 50(5), 109–112.

Dossegger, A., (2017). *Four Productivity Habits That Can Make You More Successful. CommSec Advisor Service*. Retrieved on 19 November 2017 from http://www.investing.commsecadviserservices.com.au/empowered/articles/four-productivity-habits-that-can-make-you-more-successful/

Dropulic-Ruzic, M., (2014). Direct and Indirect Contribution of HRM Practice to Hotel Company Performance. *International Journal of Hospitality Management*, Elsevier, 49, 56–65.

Drucker, P., (1999). Knowledge-Worker Productivity: The Biggest Challenge, *California Management Review*, 41(2), 76–156.Eagle, A., (2017). *What is the Best Personality Test? NLP Coaching Hypnotherapy*. Retrieved on 19 November 2017 from http://www.abbyeagle.com/nlp/what-is-my-personality-type.php

Engstrom, M.C., Boozer, R.W., Maddox, E.N., & Forte, M., (2010). Psychological Type, Emotional Intelligence and the Work Outcomes of Job Satisfaction and Organisational Commitment. *Journal of Psychological Type*, Center for Applications of Psychological Type, 11, 123–133.

Erne, R., (2011). Making Knowledge Workers Productive – A Cross Industrial View, International *Journal of Management Cases*, 13(3) 59–76.

Ferrari, J.R., O'Callaghan, J., & Newbegin, I., (2005). Prevalence of Procrastination in the United States, United Kingdom, and Australia: Arousal and Avoidance Delays among Adults. *North American Journal of Psychology*, 7(1), 1–6.

Francis, L.J., & Jones, S.H., (2000). Psychological Type and Happiness: A Study Among Adult Churchgoers. *Journal of Psychological Type*, Center for Applications of Psychological Type 54, 36–41.

Gahan, P., Robin, M., Butar, I., Evans, M., & Harley, B., (2004). *The Paradox of High Performance Work Practices (or if HPWS Are Good For Performance Why Don't We Use Them More?)* Managing for Peak Performance.

Genco, J.T., & Mitchell C.W., (2006). Relationships between MBTI Personality Types and Coping Styles: A Pilot Study. *Journal of Psychological Type*, Center for Applications of Psychological Type, 66(6), 49–57.

George, M.L., Maxey, J., Rowlands, D.T., & Upton, M., (2004). *Lean Six Sigma Pocket Toolbook*. McGraw-Hill Professional Publishing.

Hautala, T., (2007). Impact on Followers Type on Their Expectations of Leaders: An Individual Consideration of Transformational Leadership. *Journal of Psychological Type*, Center for Applications of Psychological Type, 67(4), 30–38.

Heffernan, M., & Dundon, T., (2016). Cross-Level Effects of High Performance Work Systems (HPWS) and Employee Well-Being: The Mediating Effect of Organisational Justice. *Human Resource Management Journal*, John Wiley & Sons, 26(2), 211–231.

Herk, N.A., & Thompson, R.C., (2009). Ethnic and Gender Differences in Best-Fit Type. In *Poster Presented at the APTi International Conference*, Dallas, TX.

Hughes, J., (2007, January). The Ability-Motivation-Opportunity Framework for Behavior Research in IS. In *2007 40th Annual Hawaii International Conference on System Sciences (HICSS'07)* (pp. 250a–250a). IEEE.

IBIS: Tommy Wu. IBISWorld (2020) Finance in Australia. Break the bank: Cash rate cuts and the COVID-19 pandemic have caused revenue to fall, pages 10–16.

Jabbour, L., (2013). Market Thickness, Sunk Costs, Productivity and the Outsourcing Decision: An Empirical Analysis of Manufacturing Firms in France. *Canadian Journal of Economics*, Canada, 46(1) 103–134.

Jarlstrom, M., & Valkealahti, K., (2010). Person Job Fit Related to Psychological Type of Finnish Business Students and Managers: Implications for Change in the Management Environment. *Journal of Psychological Type*, Center for Application of Psychological Type, 4, 41–52.

Jensen, J.M., Patel, P.C., & Messersmith, J.G., (2013). High-Performance Work Systems and Job Control: Consequences for Anxiety, Role Overload, and Turnover Intentions. *Journal of Management*, 39(6), 1699–1724.

Kasman, A., Kasman, S., Ayhan, D., & Torun, E., (2013). Total Factor Productivity and Convergence Evidence from Old and New EU Member Countries Banking Sectors. *Journal of Business Economics and Management*, 14(1), 13–35.

Kehoe, R.R., & Wright, P.M., (2013). The Impact of High-Performance Human Resource Practices on Employees' Attitudes and Behaviors. *Journal of Management*, 39(2), 366–391.

Keith Macky & Peter Boxall (2007) The relationship between 'high-performance work practices' and employee attitudes: an investigation of additive and interaction effects, The International *Journal of Human Resource Management*, 18:4, 537–567, DOI: 10.1080/09585190601178745

Kloutsiniotis, P.V., & Mihail, D.M., (2018). The Link between Perceived High-Performance Work Practices, Employee Attitudes and Service Quality. *Employee Relations*, 40(5), 801–821.

Kundu, S.C., & Gahlawat, N., (2018). Ability–Motivation–Opportunity Enhancing Human Resource Practices and Firm Performance: Evidence from India. *Journal of Management and Organization*, 24(5), 730–747.

Lee, Y.K., Malik, A., Rosenberger, P.J., & Sharma, P., (2020). Demystifying the Differences in the Impact of Training and Incentives on Employee Performance: Mediating Roles of Trust and Knowledge Sharing. *Journal of Knowledge Management*, 24(8), 1987–2006.

LePine, J.A., Buckman, B.R., Crawford, E.R., & Methot, J.R., (2011). A Review of Research on Personality in Teams: Accounting for Pathways Spanning Levels of Theory and Analysis. *Human Resource Management Review*, Elsevier Ltd., 21, 311–330.

Loffredo, D.A., & Opt, S.K., (2006). Argumentativeness and Myers-Briggs Type Indicator Preferences. *Journal of Psychological Type*, Center for Applications of Psychological Type, 66(7), 59–68.

Macky, K., & Boxall, P., (2007). The Relationship between 'High Performance Work Practices' and Employee Attitudes: An Investigation of Additive and Interaction Effects. *The International Journal of Human Resource Management*, Australia, 18(4), 537–567.

Malhotra (2010), *Marketing Research: An Applied Orientation*. Pearson United States of America, Prentice Hall, chapter 3 and 5.

Malik, A., (2013). Post-GFC People Management Challenges: A Study of India's Information Technology Sector. *Asia Pacific Business Review*, 19(2), 230–246. doi:10.1080/13602381.2013.767638

Malik, A., (2018a). *Strategic Human Resource Management and Employment Relations*. Springer.

Malik, A., (2018b). *Human Resource Management and the Global Financial Crisis: Evidence from India's IT/BPO Industry*. Routledge.

Malik, A., & Blumenfeld, S., (2012). Six Sigma, Quality Management Systems and the Development of Organisational Learning Capability: Evidence from Four Business Process Outsourcing Organisations in India. *International Journal of Quality & Reliability Management*, 29(1), 71–91.

Malik, A., Boyle, B., & Mitchell, R., (2017). Contextual Ambidexterity and Innovation in Health Care: The Role of HRM. *Personnel Review*, 46(7), 1358–1380.

Malik, A., Sinha, P., Pereira, V., & Rowley, C., (2019). Implementing global-local strategies in a post-GFC era: Creating an ambidextrous context through strategic choice and HRM. *Journal of Business Research*, 103, 557–569.

Malik, A., Froese, F.J., & Sharma, P., (2019). Role of HRM in Knowledge Integration: Towards a Conceptual Framework. *Journal of Business Research*, 109, 524–535.

Malik, A., & Nilakant, V., (2016). Knowledge Integration Mechanisms in High-Technology Business-to-Business Services Vendors, *Knowledge Management Research and Practice*, 14(4), 565–574.

Malik, A., Pereira, V., & Budhwar, P., (2018). Value Creation and Capture through Human Resource Management Practices: Gazing through the Business Model Lens. *Organizational Dynamics*, 47(3), 180–188.

Malik, A., Pereira, V., & Tarba, S., (2019). The Role of HRM Practices in Product Development: Contextual Ambidexterity in a US MNC's Subsidiary in India. *The International Journal of Human Resource Management*, 30(4), 536–564.

Malik, A., & Rowley, C. (Eds.)., (2015). *Business Models and People Management in the Indian IT Industry: From People to Profits*. Abingdon: Routledge.

Malik, A., & Sanders, K., (2021). Managing Human Resources in Organisations during a Global Crisis. *British Journal of Management*, (1), 1–19.

Malik, A., Sinha, A., & Blumenfeld, S., (2012). Role of Quality Management Capabilities in Developing Market-Based Organisational Learning Capabilities: Case Study Evidence from Four Indian Business Process Outsourcing Firms. *Industrial Marketing Management*, 41(4), 639–648.

Markos, S., & Sridevi, S.M., (2010). Employee Engagement: The Key to Improving Performance. *International Journal of Business and Management*, 5(12), 89–96.

Maruta, R., (2012). Maximising Knowledge Work Productivity: A Time Constrained and Activity Visualised PDCA Cycle. *Knowledge and Process Management*, 19(4), 203–214.

Matson, E., & Prusak, L., (2010). Boosting the Productivity of Knowledge Workers, *McKinsey Quarterly*, September, 1–4.

Messersmith, J.G., Lepak, D.P., Patel, P.C., & Gould-Williams, J.S., (2011). Unlocking the Black Box: Exploring the Link between High Performance Work Systems and Performance. *Journal of Applied Psychology*, USA, 96(6), 1105–1118.

Mladkova, L., (2011). Knowledge Management for Knowledge Workers. *Electronic Journal of Knowledge Management*, 9(3) 260–267.

Mook, D.G., (1996). *Motivation: The Organization of Action*. Norton.

Moreno, A., & Bartlett, K., (2016). Personality Profiles, Learning Styles, and the Japanese Student: An Exploratory Study. *Kwansei Gakuin University Humanities Review*, 21, 73–80.

Nguyen, M., & Malik, A., (2020). Cognitive Processes, Rewards and Online Knowledge Sharing Behaviour: The Moderating Effect of Organizational Innovation. *Journal of Knowledge Management*, 24(6), 1241–1261.

Nguyen, T.M., Tuan, N., Froese, F., & Malik, A., (2019). Motivation and Knowledge Sharing: A Meta-Analysis of Main and Moderating Effects. *Journal of Knowledge Management*, 23(5), 998–1016.

Ones, D., & Dilchert, S., (2009). Personality Tests in the Workplace. In the black. *ABI/INFORM Complete*, 60(4), 995–1027.

Oxford Analytica, (2018). Profiling Beyond Personality Will Rise, *Oxford Analytica Daily Brief Service* Retrieved from https://dailybrief.oxan.com/Analysis/DB235213/Profiling-use-will-expand-beyond-human-personalities on 01 September 2020.

Pak, J., & Kim, S., (2018). Team Manager's Implementation, High Performance Work Systems Intensity, and Performance: A Multilevel Investigation. *Journal of Management*, 44(7), 2690–2715.

Patel, P., Messersmith, J.G., & Lepak, D.P., (2013). Walking the Tightrope: An Assessment of the Relationship between High Performance Work Systems and Organisational Ambidexterity. *Academy of Management Journal*, 56(5), 1420–1442.

Penney, L.M., David, E., & Witt, L.A., (2011). A Review of Personality and Performance: Identifying Boundaries, Contingencies and Future Research Direction. *Human Resource Management Review*, Elsevier, 21, 297–310.

Quenk, N.L., (2009). *Essentials of Myers-Briggs Type Indicator Assessment*. Second Edition. John Wiley & Sons.

Rastogi, R., & Dave, V., (2004). Managerial Effectiveness: A Function of Personality Type and Organisational Components. *Singapore Management Review*, 26(2), 79–87.

Reeder, R.M., & McPeek, R.W., (2011). Using Psychological Type-Related Teaching Tools to Improve Reading Comprehension. *Journal of Psychological Type*, 71(3), 46–53.

Robbins, S.P., & Barnwell, N., (2002). *Organisational Theory*. Fourth Edition. Pearson Education Australia, Prentice Hall.

Robbins, S.P., Judge, T.A., Millett, B., & Waters-Marsh, T., (2008). *Organisational Behaviour*. Fifth Edition. Pearson Education.

Sanz-Valle, R., & Jiménez-Jiménez, D., (2018). HRM and Product Innovation: Does Innovative Work Behaviour Mediate That Relationship? *Management Decision*, 56(6), 1417–1429.

Sekaran, U., & Bougie, R., (2013). *Research Methods for Business: A Skill Building Approach*. Sixth Edition. Wiley & Sons Ltd.

Shahzad, K., Arenius, P., Muller, A., Rasheed, M.A., & Bajwa, S.U., (2019). Unpacking the Relationship between High-Performance Work Systems and Innovation Performance in SMEs. *Personnel Review*, 48(4), 977–1000.

Smith, A.A., Smith, A.D., & Offodile, O., (2011). March Madness and Perceived Influences on Workplace Productivity by Business Professionals: An Exploratory Study. *Sport, Business and Management: An International Journal*, Emerald Insight, 1(1), 43–60.

Smith, A.A., Tucker, M., & Pitt, M., (2011). Healthy, Productive Workplaces: Towards a Case for Interior Plantscaping. *Facilities*, 29(5/6), 209–223.

Smolka, C.M., (2005). Cognitive Orientations and Leader Member Alignment. *Journal of Psychological Type*, Center for Applications of Psychological Type, 65(3), 17–26.

Sokovic, M., Pavletic, D., & Kern Pipan, K., Quality Improvement Methodologies – PDCA Cycle, RADAR Matrix, DMAIC and DFSS, *Journal of Achievements in Materials and Manufacturing Engineering* 43(1), 476–483.

Stahl, G., Björkman, I., Farndale, E., Morris, S.S., Paauwe, J., Stiles, P., Trevor, J., & Wright, P., (2012). Six Principles of Effective Global Talent Management. *Sloan Management Review,* 53(2), 25–42.

Stirpe, L., Trullen, J., & Bonache, J., (2018). Retaining an Ageing Workforce: The Effects of High-Performance Work Systems and Flexible Work Programmes. *Human Resource Management Journal*, 28(4), 585–604.

Steel, P., (2007). The Nature of Procrastination: A Meta-Analytic and Theoretical Review of Quintessential Self-Regulatory Failure. *American Psychology Association,* 133(1), 65–94.

Stewart, P., Danford, A., Richardson, M., & Pulgnano, V., (2010). Workers Experiences of Skill, Training and Participation in Lean and High Performance Workplaces in Britain and Italy. *Employee Relations*, 32(6), 606–624.

Swanson, R.A., (2013). *Theory Building in Applied Disciplines.* Berrett-Koehler Publishers.

Sye, G.L., (2004). *Process Mastery with Lean Six Sigma.* Second Edition. Soarent Vision.

Van Asselt, A., Dirksen, C., Arntz, A., & Severens, J., (2008). Difficulties in Calculating Productivity Costs: Work Disability Associated with Borderline Personality Disorder, *International Society for Pharmacoeconomics and Outcomes Research*, 11(4), 637–644.

Varvel, T., Adams, S., Pridie, S., & Ulloa, B., (2004). Team Effectiveness and Individual Myers-Briggs Personality Dimensions. *Journal of Management in Engineering,* 20(4), 141–160.

Zhang, J., Bal, P.M., Akhtar, M.N., Long, L., Zhang, Y., & Ma, Z., (2019). High-Performance Work System and Employee Performance: The Mediating Roles of Social Exchange and Thriving and the Moderating Effect of Employee Proactive Personality. *Asia Pacific Journal of Human Resources*, 57(3), 369–395.

Zhou, Y., Fan, X., & Son, J., (2019). How and When Matter: Exploring the Interaction Effects of High-Performance Work Systems, Employee Participation, and Human Capital on Organizational Innovation. *Human Resource Management*, 58(3), 253–268.

3 Research context and data collection at a large Australian financial institution

Introduction

As identified earlier in Chapter 2, there is limited research undertaken on the impact of personality profiles in examining the relationship between High Performance Work Systems (HPWS), evidenced through Ability-, Motivation- and Opportunity-enhancing practices, on employee- and firm-level outcomes in an Australian context (Boxall, Hutchinson & Wassenaar, 2014; Boxall & Macky, 2009; Jensen, Patel & Messersmith, 2013; Patel, Messersmith & Lepak, 2013). Context has been identified as a critical factor affecting the nature and extent of relationships, as well as, sometimes, the directions of the relationships (Cooke, 2018; Johns, 2006; Malik, Boyle & Mitchell, 2017). This warrants an understanding of the research context to situate the findings in a way that aligns with the structure, context and performance expectations imposed by the context. The Australian financial services industry is a multi-billion dollar sector that necessarily requires certain ways of working and performance, especially as the sector is also heavily regulated. Such an approach puts constraints on operations, as well as lends the sector an opportunity to experiment and try out new ways of work and organisation to overcome any institutional isomorphic pressures (Boon et al., 2009). To this end, this chapter begins by providing an overview of the Australian financial services industry and then proceeds to explain the research methodology used in this research to explore the impact an individual's personality has on their productivity in a knowledge-based environment in the banking and finance industry. Following this, the chapter outlines the research strategy and the high-level design details that were chosen to address the information needs for addressing the research problem, research questions and hypotheses.

Following this is a discussion of the research design in further granular detail, focusing on the sample population, sample design and the sample framework, along with the time-dimension characteristics and the survey-instrument development and questions used. The chapter then details the data-collection methods employed, including how sample respondents were recruited and the mitigation plan that was developed to manage a low response rate, along with important details on ensuring the reliability and validity of the data. The chapter then outlines how the data was screened and cleaned for use and the techniques used to analyse the data. Lastly, Chapter 3 closes with a discussion of ethical considerations for the research and a brief conclusion of the research methodology.

The Australian financial services industry

The financial services industry in Australia is one that is highly competitive, along with financial products being complex yet critical to an individual's well-being. The Australian banking sector component of this industry is oligopolistic in its structure, with a handful of major providers (the 'Big Four') and a large number of smaller providers. It is clear the four major Australian banks as a group hold substantial market power, which is down to their size, their brands and their broad geographical reach. As a result of their power, the major banks have the choice to pass on cost increases and the ability to set prices that maintain their extremely high levels of profitability with minimal loss of their market share. The recent Productivity Commission inquiry states that adding costs to the larger banks without altering their market power does not lift competition, but it harms consumers and is seen as counter-productive. These key banks in Australia benefit from the view that 'we are too big to fail', and it is this mentality and status that reflects an expectation of government intervention should one or more of these banks fall into financial difficulty (Australian Government Productivity Commission, 2018) (Figure 3.1).

As with other advanced Western economies, the Australian financial services industry is highly regulated; however, competition is said to be poor

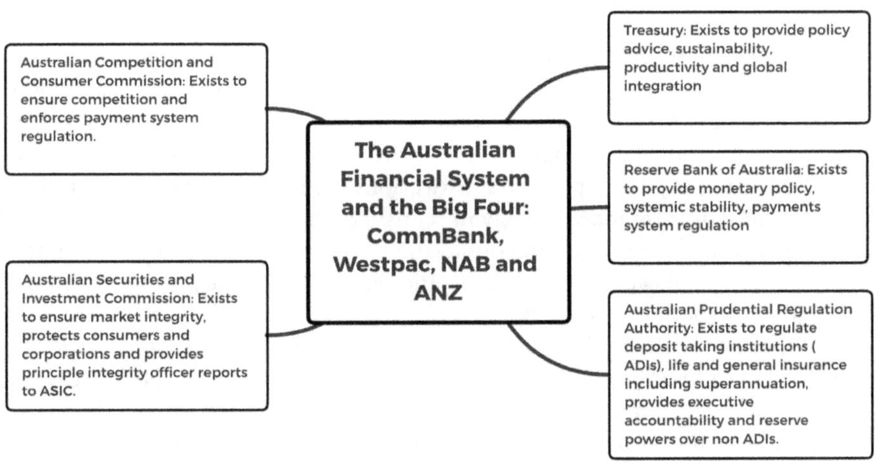

Figure 3.1 The Australian Financial Services Industry and Its Regulators.

Source: Authors' Compilation: Adapted from Figure 5: Embedding competition and consumer interests into financial system regulatory structures, Australian Productivity Commission (2018).

(Wu, 2020a). The four major banks hold over 80% of the market and the majority of Australian individual and organisational customers' money. In 2019, the Commonwealth Bank of Australia had 23% of the market, ANZ 21%, Westpac 20% and National Australia Bank 18%. The major banks argue that they do not exercise market power; however, there is a view that they have successfully protected themselves from competition and have been able to sustain massive returns despite the global financial crisis. The Productivity Commission inquiry claims that there is evidence that the major banks are sustaining prices above competitive pricing levels, that they are continuing to offer low-quality quality products to several groups of its customers and that they have subsumed much of the broker industry and taken action that could inhibit the expansion of smaller competitors in some markets. The major banks are said to hold market power that allows them to set interest rates to borrowers and depositors that allows them to remain highly profitable without significant loss of market share (Australian Government Productivity Commission, 2018).

Large Australian banks, in particular, have been able to maintain consistently high returns on equity (ROEs). It is said that many consumers find financial products and services less interesting than other consumer products and the differentiation point is minimal to non-existent between the major banks. This leaves little scope for consumers to collectively apply competitive pressure on the major banks' product and service offerings. Whilst there is the existence of a large number of marginally different products on offer, which can be perceived as allowing close tailoring to consumer needs, this is not often the case and can instead result in choice overload for consumers. This results in creating an illusion of choice and the perception of a greater degree of competition amongst providers than what actually exists (Australian Productivity Commission, 2018).

The Australian Securities and Investments Commission (ASIC) governs the Australian market and financial system and has the responsibility of ensuring competition is not put first. However, the role of juggling competition and financial stability falls to the Australian Prudential Regulatory Authority (APRA) (Reserve Bank of Australia, March 2018). The Productivity Commission inquiry report recommends that competition needs to be heard and that the current environment has a strong emphasis on institutions with macro-prudential interventions, likely to feature more notably in regulator activity for some years to come (Australian Productivity Commission, 2018). It is evident from the inquiry that finesse in the application of regulatory decisions that impact competition can and definitely should be improved.

The inquiry further deliberates that a competition champion would add immense value to the Australian financial system and this role would be best suited to the Australian Competition and Consumer Commission (ACCC), as they have long-standing expertise in competition issues and an emerging skill set in the financial ecosystem. The inquiry makes a list of recommendations that include improving scope for competition, looking to achieve favourable outcomes for customers in the home mortgage markets, shedding light on opaque practices that harm consumers, taking action on the payment system before incumbent positions become more entrenched and reducing the costs of stability. New entrants in the banking system are infrequent and challenging; the number of organisations with a banking licence has fallen by almost 40% since 2017 (Crowe, 2020). This is said to be largely due to mergers between institutions. Additionally, further tightening of regulations is likely as part of the ongoing response to the Banking Royal Commission. It is anticipated that tougher rules on insurance sales and a new oversight authority for ASIC and the Australian Prudential Regulation Authority will be introduced by the Government, along with a stronger focus on monitoring misconduct by ASIC being considered (Crowe, 2020).

Employment in the Australian finance and insurance industry

The financial services industry is one of largest employing industries in Australia, with the financial-and-insurance-services industry employing approximately 488,600 persons based on the Australian Bureau of Statistics trend data, which accounts for 3.9% of the total workforce. Over the past five years, employment in the industry has increased by 17%, with employment forecast, in 2020, to grow by 4.6% over the next five years to 2024. Employment is roughly split between men (53%) and women (47%). The median age for workers in this industry is 39 years and median weekly earnings are around $AUS 1500 per week, or $AUS 78,000 per year (Labour Market Information Portal, 2020).

Industry Growth

A decade after the global financial crisis of 2007–2008 sees the banking industry on firmer ground, as most banking sectors have gradually emerged better capitalised, better funded and more liquid. For example, the capital base of the largest banks about doubled over the past decade (S&P Global, 2020). In short, banks are now bigger, more profitable and more resilient, although the emergence of the Coronavirus in 2020 is providing testing times for the industry.

Pre-Coronavirus, according to The Banker's Top 1000 World Banks Ranking for 2018, total banking assets had reached $US 124 trillion, while return on assets (ROA) stood at 0.9%. US banks compared to European banks were ahead on multiple measures. Total assets in the United States reached a peak of $US 17.5 trillion. Return on equity (ROE) for the industry is at a post-crisis high of 11.8%. Efficiency ratios were said to be at their best in some time. Similarly, on other metrics, such as nonperforming loans and number of failed institutions, the US banking industry was strong. In contrast, the same could not be said of the banking industry in Europe. Structural deficiencies, overcapacity, low/negative interest rates and the absence of a pan-European banking regulatory agency had all likely contributed to European banks experiencing persistent profitability challenges. A large number of European banks have become smaller, total profits had dropped from $US 60 billion in 2007 to $US 17.5 billion in 2017. In the Asia Pacific region, there has been the growth of the Chinese banks, with the world's four largest banks in 2018 being Chinese whereas in 2007 none of the top ten banks in the world were Chinese (Deloitte, 2018). This trend in the growth of the Chinese banks has continued into 2020, with the big four Chinese banks significantly increasing their capital strength vis-à-vis the big four US banks, making them 72% larger in capital terms. Eleven of the top 25 banks are now Chinese, an increase of two over 2019 (The Banker, 2020).

The global banking industry shows some uncertainties, those being real GDP growth forecasts from the International Monetary Fund (IMF) point to a deceleration in all regions, including China and Emerging Asia (Deloitte, 2018). In the latest pre-Coronavirus forecast, Deloitte economists were predicting a 25% probability of a recession in the United States in 2018. In this scenario, tariffs and dilution of the stimulus effect could weaken US economic growth in late 2019 or early 2020. Deloitte advises technology remains a focus in the industry with the relationships between banks, fintechs and bigtechs evolving rapidly. Fintechs are increasingly no longer seen as scrappy adversaries; collaboration with incumbents is more the norm. With increasing industry convergence, the relationship between the banking industry and bigtech can be characterized as a bit guarded. Banks typically need bigtechs, and in some ways bigtechs also need banks, as the banking industry remains a big revenue source for many technology companies. Deloitte has urged banks and capital market institutions to accelerate their digital transformation. They encourage banks to discard visions of becoming technology companies and to focus on their customers.

According to recent IBISWorld reports on the Australian financial sector (Wu, 2020a) and National and Regional Commercial Banks (Wu, 2020b), declining private capital expenditure has led to lower demand for credit, while a downturn in the residential property market in 2018–2019 put further pressure on revenue. Falling interest rates have been the main factor causing subdivision revenue to fall over the past five years, as the COVID-19 outbreak prompted the Reserve Bank of Australia (RBA) to make two rate cuts in March 2020, with a third cut (to 0.10%) in November 2020. Due to the economic impact of the COVID-19 pandemic, subdivision revenue is anticipated to fall by 4.6% in the current year (Wu, 2020a). The decline has been primarily driven by cash rate cuts by the RBA since June 2019 and the COVID-19 outbreak. This is despite growth in lending volumes over the first half of the year. Industry profitability is projected to fall over the current year as the major players continue to face customer remediation costs, whilst some have allegedly breached anti-money laundering laws (Wu, 2020b) and been subject to large fines. Overall, Australian financial sector revenue is expected to decline at an annualised 1.4% over the five years through 2019–2020, to $195.7 billion. However, the outlook is forecast to be positive over the next five years, as revenue is forecast to grow at an annualised 4.3% over the five years through 2024–2025, to $AUS 241.1 billion (Wu, 2020a).

Changing industry focus

A recent report identified six powerful forces shaping the Australian banking industry today and driving change in the industry: changing demographics, technology, consumer behaviour, Asian governments and a subdued global economy (PWC, 2016). This report cautioned that for banks to create profit for shareholders, they need to focus their efforts on being simpler and more connected to their customers than ever before. The report also recommended five fundamental areas of focus for banks: (1) explicitly organise around the customer; (2) simplify the offer, face and voice; (3) optimise the footprint through the value chain; (4) proactively embrace regulation; and (5) put culture to work (PWC, 2016).

In addition to the reputational damage that was starting to become more apparent at the time due to poor practices and lack of accountability, the major blow to the industry came win the culmination of the *Final Report: Royal Commission into Misconduct in the Banking, Superannuation and Financial Services Industry* (Hayne, 2019).

By 2019, the Australian banking sector was said to be in a state of flux, with much debate around culture and reputation as well as uncertainty around the pace, scale and breadth of strategic disruption to the industry. This flux has continued into 2020 with the impact of the Coronavirus accelerating trends affecting aspects of the industry. In 2019, the Royal Commission conducted an inquiry into the misconduct in the banking, superannuation and financial services industry. This investigation commenced to determine if there had been misconduct in practices, behaviours or business activities by financial and insurance entities in Australia. Four main observations were made from this investigation, the first being that the conduct in issue was driven not only by the relevant entities pursuit of profit but also by individuals' pursuit of gain, this in the form of remuneration for the individual or profit for the individuals' business. Often providing service to customers was pushed to second place, with those who dealt with customers becoming sellers and the role of advisors being confused with those selling products.

The second observation was that entities and individuals in these industries acted in the ways they did because they could with little cause for justification. There was a clear imbalance of power between entities offering products and services and those acquiring it. The third observation was that consumers typically dealt with financial entities through an intermediary, this set up a false pretence that the person standing between the financial entity and the client would provide the right product or service in the client's interest. In many cases this was not the case. The fourth observation was that financial services entities that broke the law were not properly held to account. Misconduct often was not detected, denounced and justly punished; misconduct that yielded profit was not deterred. The Royal Commission report clearly outlines that the primary responsibility for the misconduct in the financial services industry lies with the entities concerned and those who acted in managerial roles, such as senior management team and board members. Close attention must be given to the culture of these entities, their governance and the remuneration practices in place.

The Royal Commission investigation forced a detailed examination of past, present and future practices for all entities involved. Seventy-six recommendations were made that would forever change the way these entities operate. These recommendations hinged on six fundamental principles, these being, first, obey the law; second, do not mislead or deceive; third, act fairly; fourth, provide services that are fit for purpose; fifth, deliver services with reasonable care and skill; and sixth, when acting for another act in the best interests of that other. The above investigations led to the establishment of a new Banking Code of Practice, sped up the transition away from a vertically integrated system and foreshadowed the likelihood of regulators becoming more interventionist as a result (Money Management, 2018), which is coming to fruition with the introduction of new legislation (Crowe, 2020).

New banking code of practice and Senate's inquiry into credit and hardship

One of the recommendations from the Royal Commission investigation into the misconduct in the Banking, Superannuation and Financial Services Industry was to update the Banking Code of Practice. The Banking Code of Practice was first introduced in 1993 and has undergone multiple improvements since responding to emerging issues and the changing needs of customers.

The 2019 update to the Banking Code of Practice sets out standards for practice and service in the Australian Banking Industry, offering safeguards and protections not set out in law (ABA, 2019).[1] The Banking Code of Practice works to complement the law and, in some circumstances, set even higher standards than the law. The Banking Code of Practice is underpinned by four guiding principles, which are trust and confidence, integrity, service and transparency and accountability. This translates to over 200 commitments Australian Banks have made to improve the rights of customers. The Banking Code of Practice protects the most vulnerable categories of customers, including customers experiencing death, disability, hardship, language barriers and domestic violence. The Banking Code offering services to protect those who need it the most. This development is reflected by the state of the banking and finance market, which shows it is estimated there are 950 financial counsellors in Australia and 2.5 million people who are living in households of high financial stress (ABA, 2019). These provisions for protecting the vulnerable will be particularly needed given the effects of the Coronavirus pandemic of 2020 – economic recession and job losses – will only further exacerbate the financial stress faced by many Australian households.

The Senate Economic Committee discussed a new trend in the banking and finance industry referred to as microfinance, which are services generally provided by community organisations. These funds for lending are provided by banks and some funding for administration is provided by the Department of Social Services and state governments. Essentially, microfinance services provide loans at a lower price than the market price, some with no or low interest. Loans are available for a limited range of purchases; these loans are provided to people who have a healthcare or pension or those with an income under $AUS 45,000.

There is no credit check and the borrower must have the willingness and capacity to repay the loan should the customer be unable to. Loans offered are generally from $AUS 800 to $AUS 3000, with 78% of the loans used for purchasing second-hand cars or for car repairs. Repayment periods range from three months to a year, and fees are half the cost of the major lenders and dishonour and default fees are far lower. Microfinance is delivered with what is described as financial literacy and education focused on building a trusted relationship between the consumer and the finance provider (Senate Economic Committee, 2019).

The sector was now well and truly reeling under regulatory, reputational and performance pressures. This was borne out in the 2019 *Financial Stability Review* by the Reserve Bank of Australia. The 2019 Financial Stability Review considered a global and domestic view of the financial market. The report shows that global economic growth had increased in 2019. Domestically, the Australian market reflected a declined cash rate that had been cut by 75 basis points along with banks' inflation and risk premiums showing low levels. Australia had seen rising prices of many assets, with house prices rising in Sydney and Melbourne (the two largest population centres in the country). The Australian domestic economic growth had slowed, which was linked to a downturn in the global economy. Interestingly, household debt in Australia was 190% of household combined income, which was typically higher than most other countries. The global financial environment impacts the Australian market through financial and economic mechanisms. Global financial vulnerabilities remained elevated, reflecting high asset prices, high debt levels and a range of country-specific factors. Banks in other jurisdictions reported varying results, with bank profitability being low in Europe and Japan with many banks facing declining margins and some European banks dealing with challenging low-performing loans (Reserve Bank of Australia, 2018).

The biggest challenges in the Australian banking and financial services market include the major banks facing challenges resulting from their many legacy IT systems and the ever present threat of cyber-attacks (Reserve Bank of Australia, 2018). These cyber-attacks are described as being able to disrupt the financial market with the ability to spread across the major banks targeting common systems or key financial market infrastructure. The review further explains that banks need to devote close attention to these risks while managing large changes to their operations. Changes to operations have come from several inquiries in the last few years, including the Royal Commission into the misconduct in the Banking, Superannuation and Financial Services Industry. Despite these risks, the Australian financial system is described as generally resilient with an overall improvement due to actions taken in response to the lessons learned from the financial crisis. And then, COVID-19 struck.

COVID-19 and its impact

The Australian Banking Association reports that the morning of the 11 March 2020 the CEOs of the Australian Banking Association met with Treasurer

Josh Frydenberg to discuss the strength of the economy and the impacts of COVID-19. The Australian banking industry discussed with the Government that they were prepared for the lasting impacts of the COVID-19 pandemic and were prepared to assist those Australians suffering from its effects. Matt Comyn, the CEO of the Commonwealth Bank of Australia, reinforced the view that "Australia has a very strong financial system with banks that are well-capitalised and have strong balance sheets". The banks have supported Australia throughout many difficult times in the past and would continue to do so as the country moves through these unprecedented times, with Matt Comyn stating, "We are very much open for business". Anna Bligh – CEO of the Australian Banking Association – said that banks stand ready to support those customers in need and those needing support should come forward. The banks were prepared to offer an array of support to those who needed it the most, reaffirming the strength of the Australian Banking industry (ABA, 2020a).

The COVID-19 pandemic of 2020 has seen Australian banks offer loan and mortgage deferrals and payment holidays to their customers at the start of the pandemic, with around 500,000 mortgages, and more than 200,000 small business loans, having paused repayments as of late June. However, improvements in the Australian economy due to the favourable situation of low levels of Coronavirus transmission had led to almost half (45%) of deferred mortgages getting back to making regular loan repayments by early October (ABA, 2020b). This recovery bodes well for the industry's revenue and profit outlook going into 2021, so long as the current level of economic impairment from the Coronavirus does not worsen.

Context summary

The above review and analysis highlights the importance of general and institutional contextual factors that are critical when investigating this industry. These affect business practices and the strategic choices firms make about the allocation of their resources (Kochan, McKersie, & Cappelli, 1984) as the macro-environmental forces change (Malik, 2013, 2018; Malik & Sanders, 2021; Malik, Sinha, Pereira & Rowley, 2019; Sharma et al., 2018). Context is also shaped by the wider cultural (Malik & Pereira, 2015, 2016; Pereira & Malik, 2015a, 2015b) and institutional make-up of any sector (Malik, Pereira & Budhwar, 2020; Pereira et al., 2020). Context can regulate and change the direction and causation of a number of factors that are in operation in any business or national setting, as has been highlighted in several studies (Cooke, 2018; Johns, 2006; Malik, Boyle & Mitchell, 2017).

Research strategy and design considerations

A study's research design provides a method or framework for the research study and it answers specific and targeted research questions. Adopting a positivism paradigm approach, where the belief is that the world is external and that there is a single objective reality to any research phenomenon or situation regardless of the perspective or belief (Bryman & Bell, 2011; Zikmund et al., 2017), the research strategy chosen for this research was deductive – i.e. theory driven – given the level of theoretical understanding in the literature on the topic. Accordingly, the research design featured a cross-sectional, self-administered, quantitative survey designed to test hypothesised theoretical relationships (Boxall & Purcell, 2008; Braunsberger, Wybenga & Gates, 2007; Malhotra, 2010; Sekaran & Bougie, 2013).

The design for this research

This section details the procedures that were employed to obtain the insights and information needed to address the research problem, research questions and hypotheses detailed in Chapters 1 and 2. It details the survey approach utilised, including the survey instrument as developed and the measures used, population sampling, design and sample framework and, lastly, the time dimensions and sample size.

Survey approach

This research used an anonymous, self-administered, web-based questionnaire. It took approximately eight to ten minutes to complete and used questions drawn and/or based on the HPWS literature, along with some context-specific measures (i.e. related to productivity).

As there were several topics that needed more candid or honest responses, the use of an self-administered survey meant that anonymity of participation could be exercised with regard to these more challenging topics and questions, which allowed sample respondents to be more open and honest with their responses (DeFranzo, 2012; Fowler, 2002; Sekaran & Bougie, 2013). The utilisation of a self-administered survey also allowed respondents flexibility when they completed the survey and without the researcher's involvement (Bryman & Bell, 2011; Malhotra, 2010; Zikmund et al., 2017).

An important consideration in this study was whether to use a paper-and-pencil postal survey or a web-based survey. The speed and lower cost of the web-based approach were crucial factors. Additionally, given the large geographical spread of Organisation X in having employees in a variety of operating units located around Australia, the web-based survey allowed geographic coverage at the lowest possible cost, whilst also ensuring respondent anonymity (Malhotra, 2010; Sekaran & Bougie, 2013; Zikmund et al., 2017).

Survey instrument development and measures used

As part of the design of this research there were some principles of wording that were taken into consideration as the survey was being designed and created. The first point relates to the content and purpose of the questions, where the purpose of each question was considered as part of the design to ensure that the variables were adequately measured and there were no supercilious questions asked (Sekaran & Bougie, 2013). Second, the language of each question was critically considered to ensure there were no misinterpretations in the language and questions being asked, questions included no abbreviations or idioms often used at Organisation X or in productivity work to ensure no misunderstandings or confusion were created (Fowler, 2002; Malhotra, 2010; Sekaran & Bougie, 2013; Zikmund et al., 2017).

Third, whilst a mixture of open-ended and closed-ended questions were included in the survey, where possible, open-ended questions were limited to ensure detailed data sorting and interpretation was not needed after the survey closed (Malhotra, 2010; Sekaran & Bougie, 2013). Closed-ended questions were used to ensure responses were consistent and able to be easily compared. The structured data collection meant questions were presented in a prearranged order that required sample respondents to choose from a set of determined answers (Fowler, 2002; Malhotra, 2010; Sekaran & Bougie, 2013). Fourth, positively worded questions were used (i.e. no reverse coded questions) to ensure there was consistency throughout the survey (Malhotra, 2010; Sekaran & Bougie, 2013). Fifth, double-barrelled, ambiguous recall, leading and loaded questions were avoided where possible to avoid any bias in the survey, question length was kept concise, clear and to the point, questions were sequenced in a logical pragmatic manner to enable the respondent to organically move through the topics and questions without too much difficulty (Malhotra, 2010; Sekaran & Bougie, 2013; Zikmund et al., 2017).

Sixth, several other design factors were taken into consideration. This included the general appearance/aesthetics of the survey, as a neat, appropriately designed survey shows quality and attention to detail, which adds to the legitimacy of the survey and allows responses to be easier to collect (Malhotra, 2010; Sekaran & Bougie, 2013). A clear introduction was written to provide sample respondents some background and basic information into the survey and research this assisted in building rapport with the audience, the questions were organised and clear instructions were provided to ensure sample respondents knew exactly what was required of them by when (Boxall & Purcell, 2008; Braunsberger, Wybenga & Gates, 2007; Fowler, 2002; Malhotra, 2010; Sekaran & Bougie, 2013).

Lastly, when it comes to optimal survey completion time, it is recommended completing a survey should take eight to ten minutes, as this reduces the potential of non-response error and improves the overall response rate (Bryman & Bell, 2011; Epstein & Kinkenberg, 2001; Malhotra, 2010; Sekaran & Bougie, 2013). The survey was designed to achieve this recommendation.

The survey structure can be seen in **Appendix A1**. Section A captured background information on the sample respondents to identify the different roles and responsibilities in the productivity community, with questions that focused on basic information, such as the position the individual was employed in, their business unit, tenure with the organisation, employment status, number of hours worked each week and their qualifications. Section B of the survey captured the respondent's Myers-Briggs personality 'type', whilst section C of the survey sought responses on a selection of productivity measures, such as the tasks they undertook, how often they undertook the tasks and how they felt about the tasks in terms of enjoyment. Section D of the survey focused on HPWS, with questions relating to how the respondent viewed the organisation and its performance. Lastly, section E of the survey featured demographics related to the individual, including age, gender and their highest qualification held. Section E was left optional, as sample respondents could potentially be identifiable by virtue of their role within the organisation and other demographic information provided in response to the survey.

However, there was an additional step required before completing this survey, as prior to the commencement of the online survey, potential sample respondents were asked to complete their MBTI and record the results. Potential sample respondents were asked to do their MBTI prior to commencing the survey in order to allow them to go straight through and complete the survey without distraction. Potential sample respondents were referred to the popular MBTI site, 16personalities.com, where the MBTI battery was estimated to take less than 12 minutes to complete (16personalities.com).

Significant prior research had been completed regarding the topic areas being discussed, including the HPWS field. Therefore, this research drew on prior measures in the development of the survey (Churchill, 1979). The measures for the key constructs in the survey, and the sources they were based on, are presented in Table 3.1. The new measures included in the survey were referred to in the remainder of the survey. These questions and metrics were built specially for this topic area and this research, such as the number of productivity projects completed or currently underway, along with the tasks that individuals complete and how they felt about those tasks.

Population, sampling design and sampling framework

Table 3.2 presents the sample population, sample frame, sample size and participation rate for this research. A population is the complete group that shares some common set of characteristics that the research decides to investigate (Zikmund et al., 2017), which in this case was all productivity-employed specialists in the financial services sector in Australia. This subgroup of employees was deemed suitable for the purposes of exploring the influence of employee personality type on individual and organisational outcomes, with the financial services sector being of interest from employment and perspectives (see "Research method" section).

The sample frame for this study comprised the list of productivity-based workers – otherwise known as 'productivity experts' – employed at Organisation X, where access was obtained. Organisation X is a large Australian financial services organisation, employing over 50,000 individuals and therefore represented a suitable organisation for recruiting potential sample respondents for the research.

Table 3.1 Survey Constructs, Items Used and Sources

Construct/Statement	*Source*
Motivation Pay raises are based on performance. Individuals in this job receive bonuses based on the profit of the organisation. Employees are paid accordingly based on their individual/group performance. Performance is more often measured with objective quantifiable results. Job security is almost guaranteed to employees.	Kehoe and Wright (2013) and Patel, Messersmith and Lepak (2013)
Opportunity Associates in this job area allowed to make important work-related decisions such as how the work is done or implement new ideas. Employees are provided the opportunity to suggest improvements in the way things are done.	Kehoe and Wright (2013) and Patel, Messersmith and Lepak (2013)
Ability The company hires only the very best people for the job. Great effort is taken to select the right person for the job. Long term employee potential is emphasised.	Kehoe and Wright (2013) and Patel, Messersmith and Lepak (2013)
Affective commitment I am willing to work harder to help this company succeed.	Kehoe and Wright (2013)
Organisation citizenship behaviour I encourage others to try new and effective ways of doing their job. I willingly share my expertise with my co-workers.	Kehoe and Wright (2013)

This resulted in approximately 803 potential sample respondents, which comprised the sample frame for this research. The sample frame included all individuals across all business units in Organisation X that were certified as either a Green Belt or a Black Belt or a Master Black Belt in Lean Six Sigma[2] along with individuals who were identified as either a 'productivity champion' or 'productivity practitioner'. A census sampling approach was used, whereby all potential sample respondents in the sample frame were selected to be contacted (Cavana, Delahaye & Sekaran, 2001; Malhotra, 2010; Zikmund et al., 2017). Table 3.2 presents the sampling characteristics for the study.

To ensure the sample frame initially identified was suitable for use, a series of steps were taken. First, a random selection of 30 potential sample respondents was selected and searched for on the internal corporate directory, whereby roles were checked and confirmed to ensure there was alignment between those qualified as productivity specialists and the role they hold being productivity related.

Table 3.2 Sampling Characteristics

Component	*Description*
Sample population	The population of interest was all productivity experts in the financial services industry within Australia.
Sample frame	The productivity experts at Organisation X.
Sample size	288 completed surveys were collected, with 263 deemed usable.
Participation rate	804 surveys were distributed, 515 did not respond, resulting in a participation rate of approximately 36%.

Second, these individual's online 'badges' were checked to ensure alignment. Every individual at Organisation X has a list of options they can flag as their 'badges', where these badges are appropriate to the individual and the role they hold. These badges range from Fire Wardens to Diversity Champions to First Aid Officers, for example, with there being roughly 30 different badges an individual could flag on their profile online, which is housed on the internal corporate directory. For example, there are several productivity-related badges that can apply, such as the Green Belt badge, Black Belt badge, Master Black Belt badge, Productivity Practitioner badge and the Productivity Champion badge. During this pre-check process, these individuals were also checked with reference to their qualifications and against their title, with the badges also reviewed to ensure the right people were being communicated with. This pre-check process resulted in no identified errors or defects in the pool of sample-frame sample respondents, and the sample frame was accordingly deemed suitable and ready for the commencement of data collection (Bryman & Bell, 2011; Organisation X, 2017).

Details of the time dimensions and sample size can be found in Appendix A2.

Data collection

The survey itself was created in and hosted on the Qualtrics online-research platform. Once ready for distribution, a link to the survey was pushed out via email to the sample frame as part of the invitation to participate in the research. At the end of data collection, the data was then exported from Qualtrics for analysis in SPSS.

Participant recruitment and measures to minimise low response

Sample respondents were recruited via an email with a link to the Qualtrics-hosted survey. An invitation to participate in the research was created that contained the link to the email. Data collection happened over a 15-day period. The concepts that informed participant-recruitment action are discussed first, followed by the recruitment timeline as implemented.

Steps were taken in the participant-recruitment process to encourage survey participation, including drawing on Dillman's (1991) Tailored (or Total)

Design Method for improving response rates, by such things as pre-notification, follow-up reminders and including interesting questions. Dillman et al.'s (2014) Tailored Design Method (TDM) draws on social-exchange theory with the aim of reducing costs, increasing benefits and engendering trust in potential sample respondents such that the expected benefits of responding would outweigh the costs of responding.

Pre-notification was used to notify sample respondents that the survey was coming, with the instructions on how to participate being included. In the email invitation that followed to launch the survey, sample respondents were provided some context into the topic, including background information on the research and some on the research team. Instructions were then provided, with a first step being that sample respondents who did not know their MBTI type were asked to complete their Myers-Briggs Personality Profiling by accessing a link on the 16Personalities.com webpage, which provides a free MBTI assessment and results,[3] and to note their four-letter identifier from the outcome of the MBTI test. In addition, two follow-up reminders were sent on a weekly basis and focused on reminding the individuals of the importance of the survey and how they could participate, which helped boost the number of responses received (Bryman & Bell, 2011; Converse, Wolfe, Huang & Oswald, 2008).

A mitigation plan was developed to deal with some common issues that surveys are faced with, these included perceived anonymity, social desirability, low response rates and respondent control. Perceived anonymity was mitigated through notifying sample respondents that their responses to the demographic questions might identify who they are and these questions were made optional to respondents. Social desirability bias was also mitigated through requesting sample respondents to provide the most candid and honest responses in an anonymous setting. Respondent control was provided through respondents being able to answer the survey at the times convenient to them (Bryman & Bell, 2010; Malhotra, 2010).

Reliability and validity issues

The quantitative data collected needed to be analysed for measurement reliability and construct validity to ensure that the data was of suitable quality to use in the intended analyses and that appropriate conclusions could be drawn from the findings. Reliability refers to the extent to which results are consistent over time and an accurate representation of the total population under a specific study, if the results can be reproduced it is said that the research instrument is reliable (Golafshani, 2003; Joppe, 2000; Sekaran & Bougie, 2013; Zikmund et al., 2017). The reliability tests undertaken were focused on the internal consistency of the multiple-item scales, including Cronbach's alpha and composite reliability. Next, internal consistency was analysed as a further measure of reliability within this study (Golafshani, 2003; Sekaran & Bougie, 2013).

Validity is whether the research truly measures that which it was intended to measure, being represented by content validity and construct validity in this study (Golafshani, 2003; Joppe, 2000; Sekaran & Bougie, 2013; Zikmund et al., 2017). Content (or face) validity refers to a scale appearing to accurately reflect what it purports to measure (Zikmund et al., 2017) – that is, that the items 'look right' (Churchill, 1979). Construct validity looks at how well the results from the use of the measure fit the theories around which the test is designed (Golafshani, 2003; Joppe, 2000; Sekaran & Bougie, 2013). The validity assessment utilised factor analysis and average variance extracted analysis (AVE).

Data analysis approach

This section describes the analysis tools that were utilised to test the hypotheses relating to this research. To begin with, descriptive statistics were used to understand and interpret the basic qualities of the dependent and independent variables relating to this research, along with assisting with the data screening and cleaning processes undertaken to prepare the data for more in-depth analysis. Next, group differences were explored using *t*-tests and ANOVAs. Lastly, multiple-regression analysis was utilised to understand and predict the value of the dependent variable based on the influence of multiple independent variables.

Data screening and cleaning

To screen the raw data (288 responses), incompletes were removed along with responses completed so quickly as to indicate inadequate time for considered reading of the survey questions, resulting in a usable sample of 263 responses. Open-ended-response questions, such as the individual's role/title, open-ended answers were reviewed and assigned to one of the existing categories as appropriate. Next, further recoding was undertaken to disaggregate the combined, four-character MBTI personality profile sample respondents reported (with 16 MBTI profiles possible, MBTI – 16 hereafter) into four new dichotomous variables representing the four MBTI – Four base pairs (i.e. Introverted vs Extroverted, Sensing vs Intuition, Feeling vs Thinking, Perceiving vs Judging). Finally, the data was reviewed to determine whether the dependent variables (e.g. affective commitment, organisation citizenship behaviours) were deemed to be normally distributed or not, as this is typically a requirement for the parametric techniques used (e.g. ANOVA). (A detailed description of the screening-and-cleaning process can be seen in Appendix A3.)

ANOVA (analysis of variance)

ANOVA requires one or more categorical independent variables (IV) and a metric dependent variable (DV) measured on an interval/ratio scale, seeking to determine if differences in the IV are matched by changes in the DV (Bryman & Bell, 2011; Malhotra, 2010; Sekaran & Bougie, 2013). One-way ANOVAs were used to examine the influence of MBTI – 16 profile as the IV and the individual A-M-O elements (HPWS dimensions) of as the DVs, as well as one-way

ANOVAs examining the relationship between the MBTI – 16 (IV) and DVs of OCB, AOC, Task Enjoyment and Task Duration. ANOVA has been used in previous studies investigating the influence of personality type on argumentativeness (Loffredo & Opt, 2006), well-being in the workplace (Boult, Thompson & Schaubhut, 2017) and in student performance and attitudes of psychological type (McPeek et al., 2011).

Multiple regression

Multiple regression was used in this research. Multiple regression is a multivariate analysis method used to develop predictions and explain the relative contribution of one or more IVs to predict an interval/ratio-scaled target DV (Kumar & Lawley, 2005; Malhotra, 2010; Sekaran & Bougie, 2013; Zikmund et al., 2017). Multiple regression allows examination of the relationship between one of the IVs while controlling the influence of the other variables in the model (Mendenhall & Sincich, 2012; Tabachnick & Fidell, 2013). Multiple regression also allows for the use of control variables (Tabachnick & Fidell, 2013), such as gender and age, which account for potential influences that are not the focus of interest, thus providing a clearer picture of the underlying relationship of interest.

In this study, a series of multiple regressions was used to evaluate the influence of the MBTI – Four pairs (IVs) on the DVs of the individual A-M-O elements, OCB, AOC, Task Enjoyment, Task Duration and whether there was a relationship with Routine, Non-routine, Hard and Soft Tasks. Multiple regression is a widely used technique, with several prior MBTI studies having used this technique (Bughi, Lie, Zia & Rosenthal, 2017; Loffredo & Opt, 2006; Mendenhall & Sincich, 2012).

Non-parametric analysis techniques

Non-parametric analysis techniques allow analysis of nominal (categorical) or ordinal data or non-normal interval/ratio data (Zikmund et al., 2017). Cross-tabulation is a non-parametric technique that describes two or more variables simultaneously and results in tables that depict the joint distribution of two or more variables that have a limited number of categories or distinct values (Malhotra, 2010; Zikmund et al., 2017). For this research, MBTI – 16 was cross-tabulated was examined with various other variables.

Ethical considerations

As this research involved engagement and participation of people who were asked to complete a self-administered online survey, approval was obtained from the Human Research Ethics Committee of the University of Newcastle Australia, ensuring safe and ethical research practices were to be followed. Data was voluntarily collected from individuals who were invited to respond to an online survey through an email invitation to complete an online survey. Prior to data collection starting, individuals were provided a Participant Information Sheet outlining that participation in this research was voluntary and anonymous, with consent implied with the completion and submission of the questionnaire. All data was aggregated for reporting purposes and subject to secure safekeeping. Furthermore, sample respondents were informed that completing any personal or organisational demographics was optional if they had concerns relating to privacy.

Conclusion

This chapter details the research context along with outlining the methodology utilised throughout this research, including the data-collection and data-analysis methods. A quantitative research method was used in the form of a self-administered, online survey hosted on the Qualtrics platform. Sample respondents comprised 288 productivity-related employees in a large, Australian, financial services organisation, which was reduced to 263 usable responses after data screening and cleaning. The constructs in the theoretical framework were measured using items drawn from the literature, along with performance and demographic information. The reliability and validity aspects of relevance for the data were identified and the analytical techniques used are detailed. Lastly, how the ethical concerns of the research were addressed is detailed.

Notes

1 The Banking Code of Practice has been temporarily amended to reflect the impact of COVID-19. It now incorporates a Special Note, which applies from 1 July 2020 until 1 March 2021. See here for more details: https://www.ausbanking.org.au/wp-content/uploads/2020/07/2020-Code-A4-COVID-19-Special-Note-WEB.pdf.

2 Lean Six Sigma is a method that uses fact-based, data-driven improvements to focus on defect detection and prevention. Lean Six Sigma focuses on driving customer satisfaction through improvements centred on reducing variation, waste and cycle time. Lean Six Sigma promotes a view of standardisation and when used effectively can create a competitive advantage for organisations. Lean Six Sigma brings together strategies of Lean methodology and Six Sigma in the pursuit of the reduction or elimination of process waste.

3 The 16 Personalities page offers not only a version of the MBTI, but it also includes details surrounding the results. The results include an overview of the results, strengths and weaknesses, an emotions section, romantic relationships, friendships, parenthood, career paths, workplace habits and a conclusion. Sample respondents completing the 16 Personalities page were then offered a copy of the premium profile for a cost, however, the available information provided free of charge was suitable for the purposes of this study, as well as being detailed and comprehensive enough for the individual to garner some real, tangible information on their personality profile.

References

ABA, (2019). *Banking Code of Practice: Setting the Standards of Practice for Banks, Their staff and Their Representatives.* Australian Banking Association.

ABA, (2020a). *Banks are Ready to Face Coronavirus Challenge.* Australian Banking Association. Retrieved on 13 November from https://www.ausbanking.org.au/banks-are-ready-to-face-coronavirus-challenge/

ABA, (2020b). *Repayments Have Resumed on Almost Half of Deferred Loans.* Australian Banking Association. Retrieved on 13 November 2020 from https://www.ausbanking.org.au/repayments-have-resumed-on-almost-half-of-deferred-loans/

Australian Government Productivity Commission, (2018). Competition in the Australian Financial System: Productivity Commission Inquiry Report: Overview and Recommendations. Report Number 89.

Boon, C., Paauwe, J., Boselie, P., & Den Hartog, D., (2009). Institutional Pressures and HRM: Developing Institutional Fit. *Personnel Review*, 38(5), 492–508.

Boult, M.J.L., Thompson, R.C., & Schaubhut, N.A., (2017). Well-Being and MBTI Personality Type in the Workplace. An International Comparison. CPP White Paper, Asia Pacific, 1–33.

Boxall, P., & Macky, K., (2009). Research and Theory on High Performance Work Systems: Progressing the High Involvement Stream. *Human Resource Management Journal*, 2(6), 177–185.

Boxall, P., & Purcell, J., (2008). *Strategy and Human Resource Management.* Second Edition. Palgrave Macmillan.

Braunsberger, K., Wybenga, H., & Gates, R., (2007). A Comparison of Reliability between Telephone and Web Based Surveys. *Journal of Business Research*, 60, 758–764.

Bryman, A., & Bell, E., (2011). *Business Research Methods.* Third Edition. Oxford University Press.

Bughi, S.A, Lie, D.A., Zia, S.K., & Rosenthal, J., (2017). Using a Personality Inventory to Identify Risk of Distress and Burnout among Early Stage Medical Student. *Education for Health*, Wolters Kluwer, 30(1), 26–30.Cavana, R.Y., Delahaye, B.L., & Sekaran, U., (2001). *Applied Business Research Qualitative and Quantitative Methods.* John Wiley & Sons.

Churchill, G., (1979). A Paradigm for Developing Better Measures of Marketing Constructs. *Journal of Marketing Research*, 16(1), 64–73.

Converse, P.D., Wolfe, D., Huang, X., & Oswald, F., (2008). Response Rates for Mixed-Mode Surveys Using Mail and E-mail/Web. *American Journal of Evaluation*, 29, 99–107.

Cooke, F.L., (2018). Concepts, Contexts, and Mindsets: Putting Human Resource Management Research in Perspectives. *Human Resource Management Journal*, 28(1), 1–13.

Creswell, J.W., (2009). *Research Design: Qualitative, Quantitative and Mixed Methods Approaches.* Sage Publications.

Crowe, D., (2020). *Draft Laws Put ASIC On Notice to Toughen Up.* The Sydney Morning Herald, p. 10.

Deloitte Centre for Financial Services, (2018). *2019 Banking And Capital Markets Outlook: Reimagining Transformation.* Deloitte Development LLC.

Dillman, D.A., (1991). The Design and Administration of Mail Surveys. *Annual review of sociology*, 17(1), 225–249.

Dillman, D.A., Smyth, J.D., & Christian, L.M., (2014). *Internet, Phone, Mail, and Mixed-Mode Surveys: The Tailored Design Method.* John Wiley & Sons.

Epstein, J., & Klinkenberg, W., (2001). From Eliza to Internet: A Brief History of Computerized Assessment. *Computers in Human Behavior*, 17(3), 295–314.

Fowler, F.J., (2002). *Survey Research Methods.* Third Edition. Sage Publications, Inc.

Golafshani, N., (2003). Understanding Reliability and Validity in Qualitative Research. *Qualitative Report*, 8(4), 597–606. Retrieved on 19 November 2017 from http://nsuworks.nova.edu/cgi/viewcontent.cgi?article = 1870&context = tqr

Hayne, K.M., (2019). *Final Report: Royal Commission into Misconduct in the Banking, Superannuation and Financial Services Industry.* Volume 1. Creative Commons Attribution 4.0 International Licence.

Jensen, J. M., Patel, P. C., & Messersmith, J. G. (2013). High-performance work systems and job control: Consequences for anxiety, role overload, and turnover intentions. *Journal of Management*, 39(6), 1699–1724.

Johns, G., (2006). The Essential Impact of Context on Organizational Behavior. *Academy of Management Review*, 31(2), 386–408.

Joppe, M., (2000). *The Research Process.* Retrieved on 19 November 2017 from http://www.ryerson.ca/~mjoppe/rp.htm

Kehoe, R.R., & Wright, P.M., (2013). The Impact of High Performance Human Resource Practices on Employees' Attitudes and Behaviors. *Journal of Management. Southern Management Association*, 39(2), 366–391.

Kochan, T., McKersie, R.B., & Cappelli, P., (1984). Strategic Choice and Industrial Relations Theory. *Industrial relations*, 23(1), 16–39.

Kumar, A., & Lawley, D., (2005). *Marketing Research. The Pacific Rim Edition.* John Wiley & Sons, Inc.Labour Market Information Portal, (2020). *Financial and Insurance Services.* Commonwealth of Australia. Retrieved on 13 November 2020 from https://lmip.gov.au/default.aspx?LMIP/GainInsights/IndustryInformation/FinancialandInsuranceServices

Loffredo, D.A., & Opt, S.K., (2006). Argumentativeness and Myers-Briggs Type Indicator Preferences. *Journal of Psychological Type*, Center for Applications of Psychological Type, 60–68.

Malik, A., (2013). Post-GFC People Management Challenges: A Study of India's Information Technology Sector. *Asia Pacific Business Review*, 19(2), 230–246.

Malik, A., (2018). *Human Resource Management and the Global Financial Crisis: Evidence from India's IT/BPO Industry.* Taylor & Francis.

Malik, A., Boyle, B., & Mitchell, R., (2017). Contextual Ambidexterity and Innovation in Healthcare in India: The Role of HRM. *Personnel Review*, 46(7), 1358–1380.

Malik, A., & Pereira, V., (2015). Culture Research in India: Critical Issues and Future Research Opportunities. In *Investigating Cultural Aspects in Indian Organizations* (pp. 185–197). Springer.

Malik, A., & Pereira, V., (Eds.)., (2016). *Indian Culture and Work Organisations in Transition.* Routledge.

Malik, A., Pereira, V., & Budhwar, P., (2020, in press). HRM in the Global Information Technology (IT) Industry: Towards Multivergent Configurations in Strategic Business Partnerships. *Human Resource Management Review*, 100743.

Malik, A., & Sanders, K., (2021). Managing Human Resources in Organisations during a Global Crisis. *British Journal of Management*, (1), 1–19.

Malik, A., Sinha, P., Pereira, V., & Rowley, C., (2019). Implementing Global-Local Strategies in a Post-GFC Era: Creating an Ambidextrous Context Through Strategic Choice and HRM. *Journal of Business Research*, 103, 557–569.

McPeek, R.W., Urquhart, C., Breiner, J.F., Holland, D.F., & Cavalleri, D., (2011). The Impact on Student Academic Performance and Attitudes of Psychological Type and its Introduction to the Classroom. *Journal of Psychological Type.* Center for Applications of Psychological Type, 71(3), 54–71.

Mendenhall, W., & Sincich, T., (2012). *A Second Course in Statistics: Regression Analysis.* Seventh Edition. Prentice Hall-Pearson.

Money Management, (2018). *The Royal Commission and the Future of Financial Advice.* Money Management. Retrieved on 13 November 2020 from https://www.moneymanagement.com.au/features/expert-analysis/royal-commission-and-future-financial-advice

Patel, P., Messersmith, J.G., & Lepak, D.P., (2013). Walking the Tightrope: An Assessment of the Relationship between High Performance Work Systems and Organisational Ambidexterity. *Academy of Management Journal*, 56(5), 1420–1442. Retrieved on 19 November 2017 from http://amj.aom.org/content/56/5/1420.abstract

Pereira, V., Budhwar, P., Temouri, Y., Malik, A., & Tarba, S., (2020). Investigating Investments in Agility Strategies in Overcoming the Global Financial Crisis-The Case of Indian IT/BPO Offshoring Firms. *Journal of International Management*, 100738.

Pereira, V., & Malik, A., (2015a). *Investigating Cultural Aspects in Indian Organizations.* Springer International Publishing: Imprint.

Pereira, V., & Malik, A., (2015b). Making Sense and Identifying Aspects of Indian Culture (s) in Organisations: Demystifying through Empirical Evidence. *Culture and Organization*, 21(5), 355–365.

Reserve Bank of Australia, (March 2018). Competition in the Financial System: Supplementary Submission to the Productivity Commission Inquiry. Page 2–5.

S&P Global, (2020). *Global Banking Country-By-Country Outlook Midyear 2020:More Or Less Resilient To COVID-19 Shocks.* Retrieved on 13 November 2020 from https://www.spglobal.com/_assets/images/ratings/pdf/global-banking-country-by-country-outlook-midyear-2020.pdf

Sekaran, U., & Bougie, R., (2013). *Research Methods for Business: A Skill Building Approach.* Sixth Edition. Wiley & Sons Ltd.

Senate Economic Committee, (2019). *Economics References Committee: Credit Hardship: Report of the Senate Inquiry into Credit and Financial Products Targeted at Australian's at Risk of Financial Hardship.* Senate Printing Unit, Parliament House Canberra Creative Commons Attribution-Non-Commercial-No-Derivs.

Sharma, N., Boyle, B., Mitchell, R., Malik, A., Gray, S., & O'Mahony, B., (2018). Leveraging the Common and Outsourcing the Distinct: Institutional Difference and Multinational Company Identity in Emerging Economies. *Social Identities*, 24(5), 564–581.

Tabachnick, B.G., & Fidell, L.S., (2007). *Using Multivariate Statistics.* Fifth Edition. Pearson Education.

The Banker, (2020). *Top 1000 World Banks 2020.* Retrieved on 13 November 2020 from https://top1000worldbanks.com/

Wu, T., (2020a). *AU Industry (ANZSIC) Report K6200: Finance in Australia.* IBIS-World Pty Ltd.

Wu, T., (2020b). *AU Industry (ANZSIC) Report K6221a: National and Regional Commercial Banks in Australia.* IBISWorld Pty Ltd.

Zikmund, W., D'Alessandro, S., Winzar, H., Lowe, B., & Babin, B., (2017). *Marketing Research.* 4th Asia-Pacific Edition. Cengage Learning Australia.

4 High performance in a large Australian financial institution – key findings

Introduction

Chapter 4 has five sections. The "Respondents' profile" section details the sample respondents' profiles. The "Preliminary analysis and assumption checking" section presents information surrounding the descriptive statistics and the outcomes of those statistics while the section discusses and presents the preliminary analysis of the data, including the tests of reliability and normality, factor analysis and further normality assumption checks that have been completed. The "Analysis results" section presents the analysis and results of a deep dive into the data, including discussing the hypotheses and outcomes pertaining to the relationships between the defined variables, along with potential moderating effects. The "Summary of findings" section provides a concise summary of the analysis, and the "Conclusion" section will provide a closing to the chapter.

Respondent profile

The data comes from productivity experts employed and qualified in productivity-based work at a large Australian financial services organisation. A total of 288 responses were collected, of which 263 were deemed usable.

Table 4.1 presents a summary of the sample demographic characteristics, which includes gender, age, education level, employment status, title, hours worked, productivity qualification, tenure with the organisation and the relevant business unit or division the sample respondents work for. The sample was female dominant, with women comprising 55% of the sample respondents. Age was symmetrically distributed, with sample respondents being 36–45 years old on average, which was also the median category and the mode of the sample, with 41.7% respondents falling into the 36–45 age category.

Sample respondents were employed predominately full-time (91%) and in productivity-based roles, meaning their main job roles and responsibilities were based around productivity projects, training and coaching and the four productivity habits (as identified earlier in Chapter 2). Regarding education level, respondents were typically tertiary educated (83%) and had completed a bachelor's degree on average, which was also the mode (43.4%). Sample respondents were more likely to be a manager of some sort (47%), with most sample respondents having been employed with the organisation for six-plus years (67%).

Regarding productivity qualification, 83% of respondents were Green Belt qualified in Lean Six Sigma, with the remainder being shared across Black Belt (12.3%) and Master Black Belt (4.7%) qualifications. Regarding qualification, 43% of sample respondents had one to two years of experience with their productivity qualification.[1]

The average number of productivity projects the productivity experts had active at the time of data collection was 1.3, with 34% having two-plus active projects on the go. Regarding the number of projects the productivity experts had completed in their career to date, sample respondents had completed two to five prior projects on average (also the mode at 43.2%), 21.4% had completed one project, 2.7% had completed 0 projects, 16.3% 6–10 projects, 9.3% 11–20 projects and 7% had completed 21 or more projects.

In summary, sample respondents were aged between 36 and 45 years old, tertiary qualified with a bachelor's degree and in full-time employment. The sample of individuals was an accurate representation of the population of individuals who are productivity-based experts in the banking and finance industry, the demographics of which have been outlined in Table 4.1 below.

In addition, general-employee profile data was requested from the data and analytics HR team at Organisation X to determine if the sample of respondents in this study was similar to the general-employee population at Organisation X. This would ascertain the extent to which the sample results were a reasonable representation of the employee population at Organisation X.

A series of pivot tables was used to analyse the spread of the data of the overall population at Organisation X and compare it to that of the sample as collected; the role types were the first to be reviewed. When they were compared to that

Table 4.1 Demographic Profile of Sample Respondents

Category	*Profile*
Gender	Male = 45% Female = 55%
Age	18–25 = 3% 26–35 = 25.6% 36–45 = 41.7% 46–55 = 25.6% 56–65 = 4% 66+ = 0%
Education level completed	Less than year 12 = 2.5% Year 12 (i.e. high school) = 13.6% Trade certificate = 1% TAFE (e.g. Associate Diploma Certificate II, III, IV or Advanced Diploma) = 13.6% Bachelors = 43.4% Masters = 24.7% Doctorate/PhD = 1%
Employment status	Full time = 91.1% Part time = 8.1% Casual/other = 0.8%

(*Continued*)

Category	*Profile*
Job title	Productivity Practitioner = 10% Productivity Specialist = 2.7% Productivity Analyst = 2.3% Manager Productivity = 3.1% Senior Manager Productivity = 9.2% Executive Manager Productivity = 4.2% Head of Productivity = 2.7% Specialist Process Improvement = 1.9% Manager Process Improvement = 3.1% Executive Manager Process Improvement = 0.8% Analyst = 11.9% Manager = 31.2% Executive Manager = 12.7% Other = 3.5%
Hours worked	1–30 hours = 3% 31–40 hours = 34% 41–50 hours = 50% 51+ hours = 13%
Productivity qualification	Green Belt = 83% Black Belt = 12.3% Master Black Belt = 4.7%
Tenure with the organisation	0–5 years = 29% 6–10 years = 34% 11–15 years = 16% 16–20 = 8% 21+ = 13%
Business unit	Division A = 12% Division B = 10% Division C = 1% Division D = 17% Division E = 6% Division F = 1% Division G = 1% Division H = 4% Division I = 3% Division J = 8% Division K = 15% Division L = 5% Division M = 10% Other = 7%
Years of productivity experience at the highest belt colour	Less than 1 year = 17.6% 1–2 years = 43.1% 3–5 years = 28.9% 6–10 years = 6.3% 11+ = 4.2%
Number of active productivity projects	0 = 38% 1 = 28% 2 = 21% 3+ = 13%
Number of productivity projects completed in career	0 = 2.7% 1 = 21.4% 2–5 = 43.2% 6–10 = 16.3% 11–20 = 9.3% 21+ = 7.0%

of the sample profile, the data showed that 95% of the individuals employed by Organisation X are at a manager level or below; by comparing this to the data spread obtained from this research it was revealed that approximately 80% of the sample respondents were, in fact, managers or ranked below based on their title. This indicates a broad similarity between the sample and general population at Organisation X in terms of role types.

The gender distribution in the sample saw 55% of sample respondents were female and 45% were male. This is similar to the general population employed at Organisation X, where 57% of Organisation X's employees are female, 42% identify as male and the rest have indicated 'unspecified' (1%). The results from the research suggest that the sample as collected is consistent with the overall population at Organisation X regarding gender.

Next, the divisional breakdown was reviewed for the overall population and the sample profile in Organisation X, which can be seen in Figures 4.1 and 4.2. The sample results generally reflect the overall population at Organisation X in this respect, indicating that the sample profile was broadly similar to the overall population for divisional breakdown.

Lastly, tenure of employees employed with Organisation X was reviewed in relation to the sample results. What can be seen in Figures 4.3 and 4.4 is that the majority of both groups fall in the 0–10 year range, 63% for the sample and 75% for Organisation X, with a tail that trails off before picking up slightly for 21+ years. The sample result mirrors the overall population at Organisation X in this respect, indicating that the sample profile was similar to the overall population for employee tenure.

In summary, the result of comparing the sample profile with that of overall population of Organisation X found a large degree of similarity for the employee demographics considered. On this basis, it is concluded that the survey sample is a reasonable reflection of the total population of Organisation X employees, which adds to the validity of the data collected for this research.

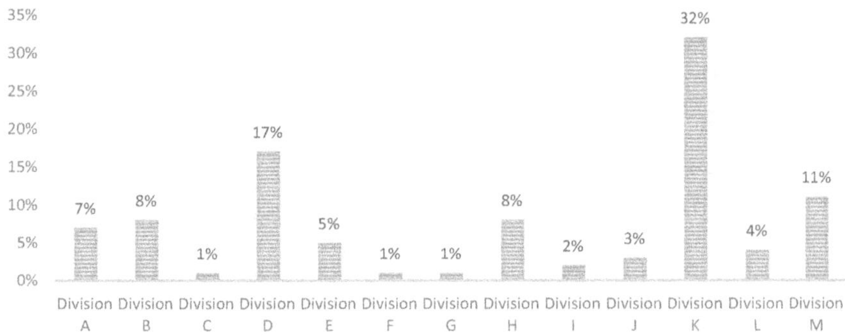

Figure 4.1 Total Population Broken Down by Division.

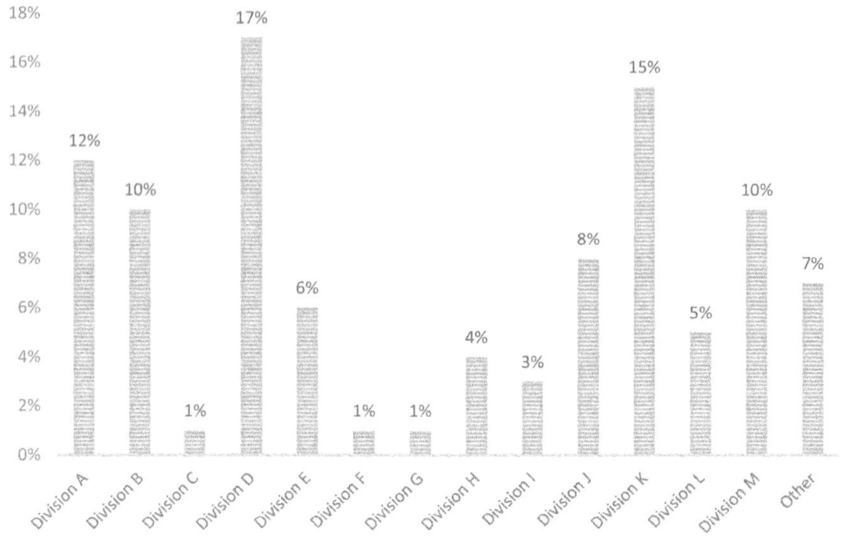

Figure 4.2 Sample Population Broken Down by Division.

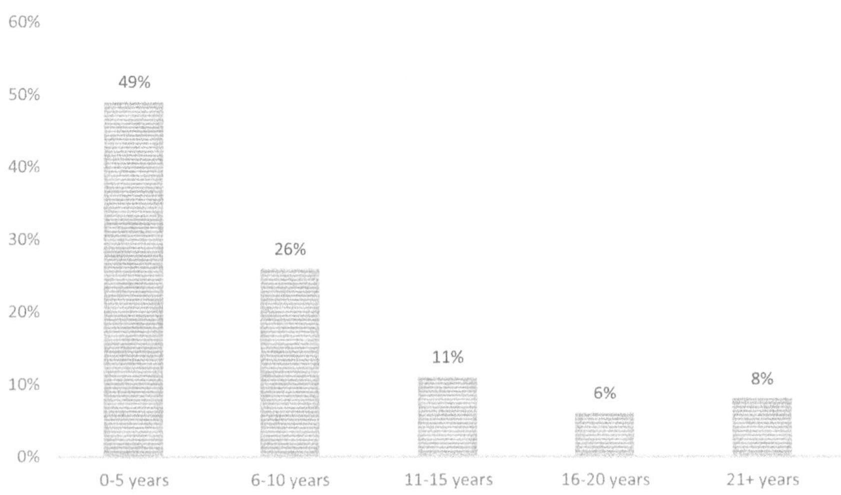

Figure 4.3 Total Population Tenure.

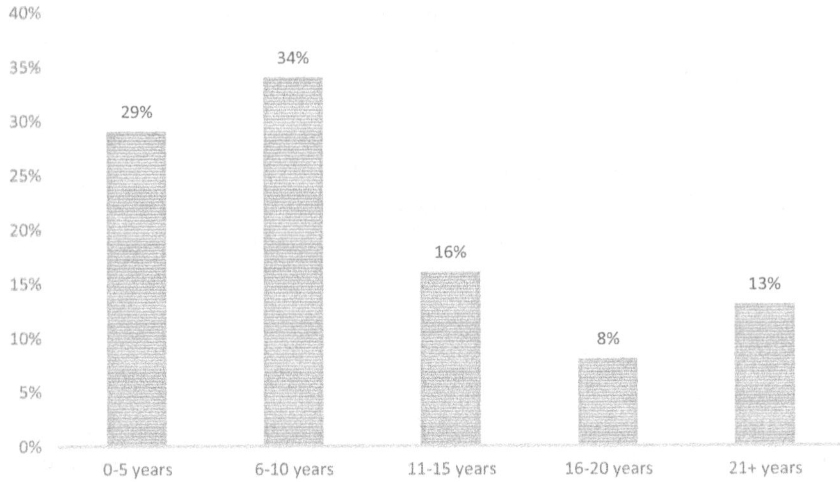

Figure 4.4 Sample Population Tenure.

Preliminary analysis and assumption checking

On completion of screening and cleaning of the data, a series of preliminary data-screening analyses were conducted using SPSS v24 before moving any further with the data analysis. Before assessing the proposed model, a number of preliminary checks were conducted including reliability analysis (Cronbach's alpha, composite reliability) and construct-validity tests (e.g. convergent validity using average variance extracted, or AVE), along with assumption checking for each technique used (e.g. normality checks). In summary, the Cronbach's alpha and composite-reliability results collectively suggest that the reliability of the multi-item reflective constructs used in this research was established. The results also indicate a satisfactory convergent validity was achieved. The assumption checking also suggested the data was suitable for analysis using the intended techniques. A detailed description of the screening process and assumption checking can be found in Appendix B1.

Analysis results

This part of the chapter will detail the analysis that was undertaken, focusing on the statistical analysis performed and findings, along with the research questions and their related hypotheses. The analysis techniques used to provide insights into the topics relating to the MBTI, productivity and HPWS include chi-square analysis, one-way ANOVA and multiple regression. Chi-square analysis examines two aspects; the first examines whether the data matches the population. The second type of chi-square test examines independence between two variables, usually in a contingency table to see whether the variables are related. A one-way ANOVA is used to determine whether there are any statistical differences between the means of two or more independent unrelated groups of data. Multiple regression predicts the value of a dependent (outcome) variable compared to the value of two or more other independent (antecedent) variables (Coakes, 2013). In addition, further analysis was conducted that provided insights into how Junior and Senior roles interact, the differences regarding productivity and non-productivity roles and the impact HPWS have on productivity-employed individuals.[2]

Personality profiling – MBTI

Sample respondents were asked to provide their MBTI 16 type as part of the survey for this research (section B); if the type was unknown, sample respondents were asked to complete their MBTI test prior to this research. There are four main types that underpin the Myers-Briggs personality profile. These four types are known as Analysts, Diplomats, Sentinels and Explorers, which are briefly described here (16Personalities.com, 2020).

- *Analysts* are known for their rational, impartial and intellectual nature and they are driven by intuition and thinking.
- *Diplomats* have a predisposition focused on caring, helping and connecting with people. They are often seen as kind and generous, and they prefer to cooperate than to compete. Diplomats have a preference towards deep conversation rather than small talk.
- *Sentinels* are seen as cooperative, practical and grounded, and they have a sense of awareness of whom they are and they take pride in their good character and their competence. They are seen as careful and consistent and often highly self-motivated.
- *Explorers* are seen as observant, prospecting personality types, and they are known for being spontaneous, genuine and flexible in their approach.

These types were compared against the general MBTI population to determine if the sample data differed. The results are presented in Table 4.2, where it is clear that the Organisation X sample differs from the general MBTI population. Several MBTI – 16 types that are significantly over- and under-represented include the ISFJs and ESFJs.

To complement this research, further investigation into the different MBTI types was undertaken to determine whether there was a preferred MBTI 'type' that would be best suited to productivity-based work. The profiles of the 16 types were reviewed in detail to understand their preferences, including what they enjoy and do not enjoy (16Personalities.com, 2017). What emerged is that there is a category of types who appear to have stronger preferences for

Table 4.2 Myers-Briggs Breakdown Population vs Survey Population Spread

MBTI Type	*Major Category*	*Population Spread (%)*	*Results from Survey (%)*	*Over- or Under-representation*
INTJ	Analysts	1.5	7.1	Over
INTP	Analysts	2.5	2.4	
ENTJ	Analysts	4.0	4.0	
ENTP	Analysts	4.5	2.0	Under
INFJ	Diplomats	1.0	4.0	Over
INFP	Diplomats	2.0	3.2	
ENFJ	Diplomats	4.0	5.9	
ENFJ	Diplomats	7.0	5.5	
ISTJ	Sentinels	8.5	5.9	
ISFJ	Sentinels	7.0	13.8	Over
ESTJ	Sentinels	13.0	5.9	Under
ESFJ	Explorers	12.0	27.7	Over
ISTP	Explorers	6.0	2.0	Under
ISFP	Explorers	6.0	1.6	Under
ESTP	Explorers	10.0	2.4	Under
ESFP	Explorers	11.0	6.7	Under

Note: Population Spread = general MBTI population as reported on 16personalities.com.

productivity work, the 'Sentinels'. Within the Sentinels category, there were two predominate types – ISFJ and ESFJ – who would be best placed to complete productivity-based work in light of their profile nature. The ESFJ type is profiled to be excellent managers of daily tasks, who thrive with structure and are great team players. In addition, ESFJs have a preference for project work and brainstorming to solve problems, and enjoy investigating solutions. In general, the general ESFJ profile suggests an affinity with most of the tasks/activities on the productivity tasks/activities list (see Appendix B2). The ISFJ is the introverted version of the same personality profile with almost identical characteristics; thus, these individuals are also deemed well-suited for productivity work due to the same characteristics shared with the ESFJs as noted.

Looking at the spread of the general MBTI population, the ESFJ and ISFJ types are estimated to comprise 12% and 7%, respectively, of the total MBTI population as reported on 16personalities.com (2017). Compared to the sample of sample respondents in this research, the results support this predisposition, as there is an approximate doubling of both ESFJs (27.7%) and ISFJs (13.8%) in productivity-work roles in Organisation X in comparison to the general MBTI population.

Organisation X does not use an MBTI-based recruitment tool to assist with managing their talent pipeline and employment practices as previously discussed. Therefore, this finding suggests that the organisation is unintentionally hiring these Sentinels for productivity-work roles. This could be seen to indicate that Organisation X has potentially seen a certain type of individual throughout the recruitment process who present as the best type for the role, and as such, they are hiring this type of individual. Alternatively, individuals who are of this type prefer productivity-based work and successfully complete the hiring process to achieve employment in these roles. Whatever the method is, the results show that there is a preference for a certain type of individual that is being employed organically.

To investigate differences in the overall profile of the 16 MBTI types, a series of chi-square goodness-of-fit tests were conducted. First, the sample was tested to see if there was a difference when equal proportions were specified for the 16 MBTI types, that is, each MBTI category was expected to have 15.8 responses (6.25%) for each type for the sample as analysed (n = 253). The statistically significant finding suggests that the sample does not feature equal proportions across the 16 MBTI categories.[3]

Second, the sample was tested to determine if the sample's 16 MBTI type proportions differed from the general population as reported on the 16personalities.com website (2017), which are reported in Table 4.5. A significant result would suggest that the general profile for the 16 MBTI types for the sample of financial services productivity specialists differs from that of the general population.

A chi-square goodness-of-fit test for unequal proportions was used. The general population's proportions for the 16 MBTI types reported by 16personalities.com (Table 4.5) were input as the reference values. A statistically significant result was found, which suggests that the sample's profile of 16 MBTI types differs significantly from the general MBTI population as reported by 16personalities.com.[4] In other words, the 16 MBTI types were not similarly distributed for the financial services productivity specialists in this study as for the general population reported by 16personalities.com. Specifically, the sample of financial services productivity specialists in this study featured a larger proportion of individuals in ISFJ and ESFJ categories.[5]

Research question one: personality type (MBTI) and HPWS (AMO)

Research Question 1 (RQ1): What influence does employee personality type have on employee HPWS, namely, ability, motivation and opportunity?

The first research question (RQ) is focused on understanding whether there is a relationship between an employee's personality type and the impact on HPWS (AMO). RQ1 is linked to several hypotheses, including H1a–c, H2a–d, H3a–d and H4a–d. The linked hypotheses are detailed below.

H1a–H1c: Personality type, as represented by the MBTI – 16, has an effect on (a) Motivation, (b) Opportunity and (c) Ability.

H2a–H2d: The MBTI – 4 dimensions of (a) Introvert/Extrovert, (b) Intuition/Sensing, (c) Thinking/Feeling and (d) Perceiving/Judging will have an influence on Motivation.

H3a–H3d: The MBTI – 4 dimensions of (a) Introvert/Extrovert, (b) Intuition/Sensing, (c) Thinking/Feeling and (d) Perceiving/Judging will have an influence on Opportunity.

H4a–H4d: The MBTI – 4 dimensions of (a) Introvert/Extrovert, (b) Intuition/Sensing, (c) Thinking/Feeling and (d) Perceiving/Judging will have an influence on Ability.

To analyse this group of hypotheses effectively, descriptive statistics, ANOVA (for H1a-c) and multiple regression analysis (for H2a–d, H3a–d and H4a–d) were used.

Descriptive statistics

The HPWS variables were analysed to understand the influence personality type has on employee outcomes, specifically the AMO model. To begin, the individual items were descriptively reviewed as depicted in Figure 4.5 and Tables 4.3 and 4.4.

The results show what the sample respondents feel positively and negatively in relation to their employment at the organisation, with the average around the mid-point (3) for nearly all questions. Some of the positive responses refer to their willingness to share their expertise and skills with co-workers. Productivity experts claim that they are willing to work harder to help the company succeed and that they encourage others to try new and effective ways to get their work done. Sample respondents also responded positively to statements regarding pay and performance. These themes saw a large proportion of sample respondents agree with the pay- and performance-related statements. Conversely, there was a negative sentiment regarding job security, with the majority of sample respondents

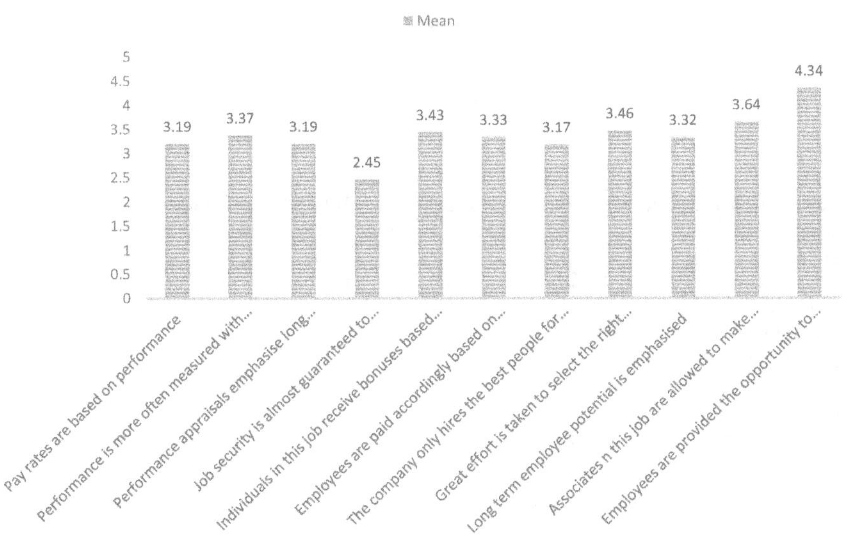

Figure 4.5 Descriptive Statistics Means.

Table 4.3 High-Performance Work Systems

Measurement/Statement	*Strongly Disagree*	*Disagree*	*Neither Agree Nor Disagree*	*Agree*	*Strongly Agree*	*Mean*
Motivation						
Pay raises are based on performance.	8%	23%	19%	40%	10%	3.19
Performance is more often measured with objective quantifiable results.	2%	24%	17%	49%	9%	3.37
Performance appraisals emphasise long-term and group-based achievement.	4%	27%	20%	40%	8%	3.19
Job security is almost guaranteed to employees.	22%	36%	20%	17%	4%	2.45
Individuals in this job receive bonuses based on the profit of the organisation.	7%	17%	16%	46%	13%	3.43
Employees are paid accordingly based on their individual/group performance.	6%	19%	20%	47%	8%	3.33
Ability						
The company hires only the very best people for this job.	4%	25%	26%	39%	6%	3.17

Table 4.4 High-Performance Work Systems

Measurement/Statement	*Strongly Disagree*	*Disagree*	*Neither Agree Nor Disagree*	*Agree*	*Strongly Agree*	*Mean*
Great effort is taken to select the right person for the job.	2%	18%	22%	45%	12%	3.46
Long-term employee potential is empathised.	3%	20%	26%	39%	10%	3.32
Opportunity						
Associates in this job are allowed to make important work-related decisions such as how the work is done or implementing new ideas.	2%	15%	10%	62%	11%	3.64
Employees are provided the opportunity to suggest improvements in the way things are done.	1%	12%	6%	46%	46%	4.34

disagreeing that job security is almost guaranteed to employees. This finding lends to future investigation to understand the drivers behind the respondents' dissatisfaction.

ANOVA: influence of MBTI – 16 on AMO

One-way ANOVA was used to examine the influence of MBTI – 16 profile as the IV (independent variable) on HPWS (Ability, Motivation and Opportunity scales) as the DVs (dependent variables). The ANOVA test was used to assess if one of the means for the MBTI – 16 groups was significantly different from the others for each DV.

To help illustrate the differences graphically, boxplots have been used. Boxplots plot the summary statistics, where the lower boundary of the box is the 25th percentile and the upper boundary is the 75th percentile. The horizontal line through the centre of the box represents the median. The 'whiskers' represent the smallest and largest values (Coakes, 2013). (For technical details on how the ANOVA analysis was run, please see Technical Appendix B3.)

MBTI – 16 ON MOTIVATION

After removing five potential outliers, a one-way ANOVA of the MBTI – 16 on Motivation was run. The boxplot analysing the MBTI – 16 and Motivation relationship is presented below in Figure 4.6.

A significant ANOVA result was found, with Motivation statistically significantly different for the MBTI – 16 groups. This result suggests at least one of the MBTI – 16 group means was different from the others, with the MBTI – 16 factor having a large effect in explaining the variability in Motivation. Therefore, hypothesis **H1a** is **supported**.

Follow-up pairwise comparisons were then conducted to identify where the differences existed. A planned contrast was run comparing the highest (ISFP) and lowest (INTP) Motivation scores. The Motivation score was found to be statistically significantly higher in the ISFP group (M = 3.8) compared to the INTP group (M = 2.6), with a mean difference of 1.2.

MBTI – 16 ON OPPORTUNITY

After removing five potential outliers, a one-way ANOVA of the MBTI – 16 on Opportunity was run. The boxplot analysing the MBTI – 16 and Opportunity relationship is presented below in Figure 4.7.

A significant ANOVA result was found, with Opportunity statistically significantly different for the MBTI – 16 groups. This result suggests at least one of the MBTI – 16 group means was different from the others, with the MBTI – 16 factor having a medium-to-large effect in explaining the variability in Opportunity. Therefore, hypothesis **H1b** is **supported**.

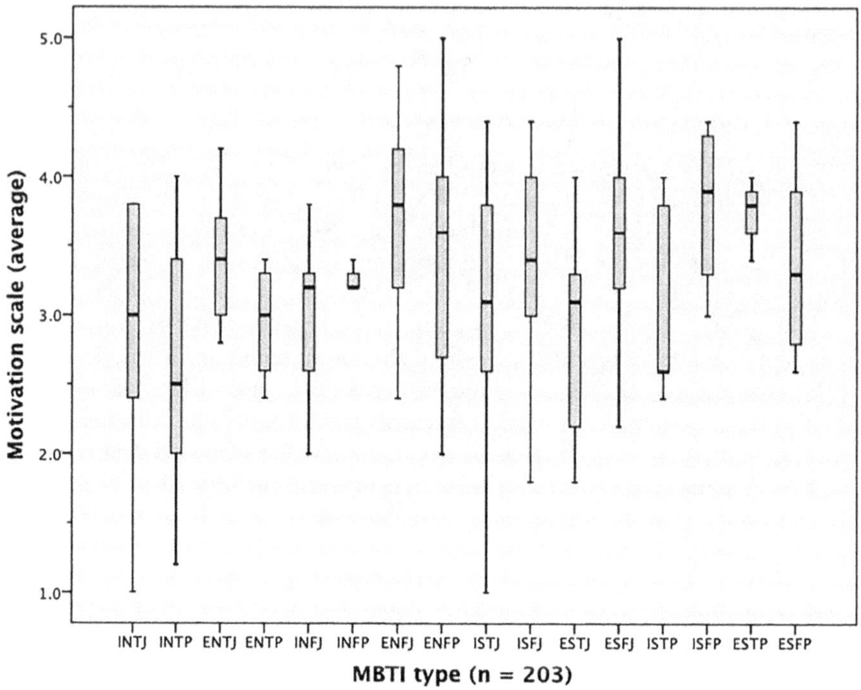

Figure 4.6 Boxplot: MBTI – 16 and Motivation.

Follow-up pairwise comparisons were then conducted to identify where the differences existed. A planned comparison between the (equal) highest (ISFP, ENTP) and lowest (ESTJ) Opportunity scores was conducted. The Opportunity score was statistically significantly higher in the (combined) ISFP and ENTP groups (M = 4.4) compared to the ESTJ group (M = 3.4), with a mean difference of 0.96.

MBTI – 16 ON ABILITY

After removing three potential outliers, a one-way ANOVA of the MBTI – 16 on Ability was run. The boxplot analysing the MBTI – 16 and Ability relationship is presented below in Figure 4.8.

A significant ANOVA result was found, with Ability being statistically significantly for the different MBTI – 16 groups. This result suggests at least one of the MBTI – 16 group means was different from the others, with the MBTI – 16 factor having a large effect size in explaining the variability in Ability. Therefore, hypothesis **H1c** is **supported**.

Follow-up pairwise comparisons were then conducted to identify where the differences existed. A planned contrast was conducted comparing the highest

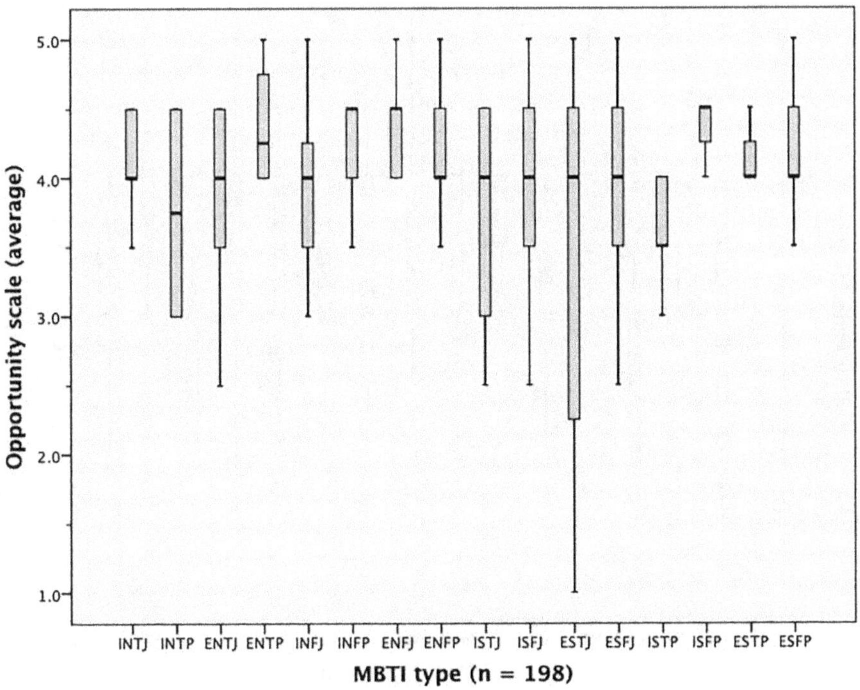

Figure 4.7 Boxplot: MBTI – 16 and Opportunity.

and lowest Ability scores. The Ability score was statistically significantly higher in the ENTP group (M = 4.0) compared to the ISTP group (M = 2.4), with a mean difference of 2.4.

This section has established the individual influence of MBTI – 16 on the HPWS variables of Motivation, Opportunity and Ability (H1a–c). The next section steps up the complexity by examining the discrete (individual) influence of the MBTI – 4 on the HPWS variables of Motivation, Opportunity and Ability in a multivariate approach using multiple regression.

Multiple regression analysis: MBTI – 4 on AMO

Multiple regression was used to determine the relationship between the MBTI (as the predictors) and HPWS (as the criterion or outcome), represented by Ability, Motivation and Opportunity. This was done by regressing the MBTI – 4 on each of the AMO elements separately using hierarchical regression, where the variables were entered in two sets (or steps). To control for respondent differences, age and gender were entered in step one of the regression. The four MBTI base pairs (MBTI – 4) were then entered in step 2. This approach allows the incremental influence of the MBTI – 4 in explaining changes in the criterion

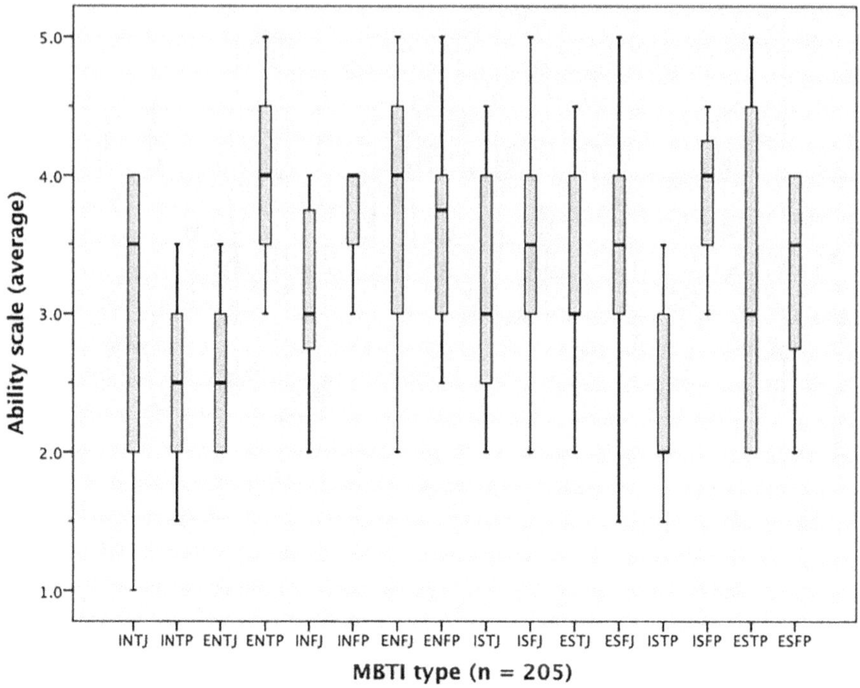

Figure 4.8 Boxplot: MBTI – 16 and Ability.

variable beyond that of the controls (age, gender) to be determined. (For technical details on how the MBTI – 4 multiple regression analysis was conducted, please see Technical Appendix B4.)

As presented in Table 4.5, the MBTI – 4 pair Thinking/Feeling had a statistically significant influence on each of the AMO outcomes. In contrast, the Introvert/Extrovert pair had a limited influence, only having a statistically significant influence on Motivation. The other MBTI – 4 base-pair influences were weak or negligible in magnitude, as well as statistically non-significant. When looking at the results in Table 4.5, positive relationships can be seen relating to the Introvert vs Extrovert dimension. In contrast, negative relationships are seen in all variables associated with Intuition vs Sensing and Thinking vs Feeling, the rest of the relationships vary from positive to negative relationships.

Next, the addition of the MBTI – 4 in the second step in each regression had a noticeable improvement in the explanatory power (R^2) of the model compared to only the control variables in the first step. The overall explanatory power of the MBTI – 4 model, when controlling for age and gender, performed the best for Motivation ($R^2 = 0.09$), followed by Opportunity ($R^2 = 0.06$) and then Ability ($R^2 = 0.05$), though all three R^2 values are modest in nature.

Table 4.5 Regression: Influence of the MBTI – 4 Base Pairs on AMO

		Motivation n = *196*	*Opportunity* n = *196*	*Ability* n = *197*
Step 1	Gender	0.01	−0.06	0.06
	Age	−0.08	0.10	−0.01
	R^2	0.01	0.01	0.004
Step 2	Gender	−0.04	−0.11#	0.02
	Age	−0.10#	0.10#	−0.02
	Introvert vs Extrovert	0.17*	0.03	0.08
	Intuition vs Sensing	−0.002	−0.04	−0.03
	Thinking vs Feeling	−0.20**	−0.21**	−0.19*
	Perceiving vs Judging	−0.003	0.04	0.01
	R^2	0.09	0.06	0.05
	R^2 change	0.08	0.04	0.04

Note: Standardised beta coefficients reported; regarding statistical significance, # = $p \leq 0.20$, ^ = $p \leq 0.10$, * = $p \leq 0.05$ ** = $p \leq 0.01$, *** = $p \leq 0.001$; sample size reported for each regression is the minimum pairwise *N*; MBTI – 4 dummy coding is as follows: Introvert = 0 and Extrovert = 1, Intuition = 0 and Sensing = 1, Feeling = 0 and Thinking = 1, Judging = 0 and Perceiving = 1.

Therefore, in relation to RQ1, on the basis of these findings, the hypotheses related to the MBTI – 4 influence of Introvert/Extrovert (**H2a**) and Thinking/Feeling (**H2c**, **H3c** and **H4c**) are **supported**, whilst **H2b**, **H2d**, **H3a**, **H3b**, **H3d**, **H4a**, **H4b** and **H4d** are **not supported**.

Research question two: MBTI and OCB and AOC

Research Question Two (RQ2): What influence does employee personality type have on organisational outcomes, namely, organisational citizenship behaviours (OCB) and affective organisational commitment (AOC)?

The second research question was developed to understand the relationships between an employee's personality type and the organisational citizenship behaviours and affective organisational commitment. RQ2 is linked to hypotheses H1d and H1e (ANOVA) and H5a–d and H6a–d (multiple regression), which cover both organisational citizenship behaviours and affective organisational commitment. The linked hypotheses are detailed below.

H1d: Personality type, as represented by the MBTI – 16, has an effect on OCB.
H5a–d: The MBTI – 4 dimensions of (a) Introvert/Extrovert, (b) Intuition/Sensing, (c) Thinking/Feeling and (d) Perceiving/Judging will have an influence on OCB.
H1e: Personality type, as represented by the MBTI – 16, has an effect on AOC.
H6a–H6d: The MBTI – 4 dimensions of (a) Introvert/Extrovert, (b) Intuition/Sensing, (c) Thinking/Feeling and (d) Perceiving/Judging will have an influence on AOC.

Table 4.6 AOC and OCB

Measure/Statement	*Strongly Disagree*	*Disagree*	*Neither Agree Nor Disagree*	*Agree*	*Strongly Agree*	*Mean*
Affective Organisational Commitment (AOC)						
I am willing to work harder to help this company succeed.	1%	1%	10%	52%	36%	4.06
Organisational Citizenship Behaviour (OCB)						
I encourage others to try new and effective ways of doing their job.	0%	0%	3%	47%	49%	4.43
I willingly share my expertise with my co-workers.	1%	1%	1%	31%	65%	4.58

Note: Five-point Likert scale used, where 1 = Strongly disagree, 2 = Disagree, 3 = Neither agree or disagree, 4 = Agree, 5 = Strongly agree; the numbers in each column are the percentage of the responses for that response option for that question.

Figure 4.9 Motivation.

Descriptive statistics, ANOVAs and multiple-regression analyses were completed to understand whether employee personality type has any influence on organisational outcomes, namely, OCB and AOC.

Descriptive statistics

To begin, descriptive statistics were run to analyse the spread, size and shape of the data for the two constructs. These are reported in Table 4.6. The means for all items for the two constructs were over 4.0 (see Figure 4.9) and fell into the 'agree' category (AOC) or 'strongly agree' category (OCB) of the five-point Likert scale used to measure the items. This indicates that respondents held positive AOC views and were willing to engage in OCBs.

ANOVA analysis: influence of MBTI – 16 on OCB and AOC

ANOVAs were conducted to analyse the relationship between the MBTI – 16 and OCB and AOC. The same procedures for running the analysis as detailed with the previous set of hypotheses were followed. (For technical details on how the ANOVA analysis was run, please see Appendix B5.)

MBTI – 16 ON OCB

After removing two potential outliers, a one-way ANOVA of the MBTI – 16 on OCB was run. The boxplot analysing the MBTI – 16 and OCB relationship is presented below in Figure 4.10.

A non-significant ANOVA result was found, with OCB not statistically significantly for the different MBTI – 16 groups. This result suggests that at least one of the MBTI – 16 group means was not different from the others at this omnibus level, although the MBTI – 16 factor had a small-to-medium effect size in explaining the variability in OCB.

However, given the suggestion of variability amongst the groups by the boxplot – and to try to better understand the non-significant result – it was decided to run a planned comparison between the lowest and highest OCB groups

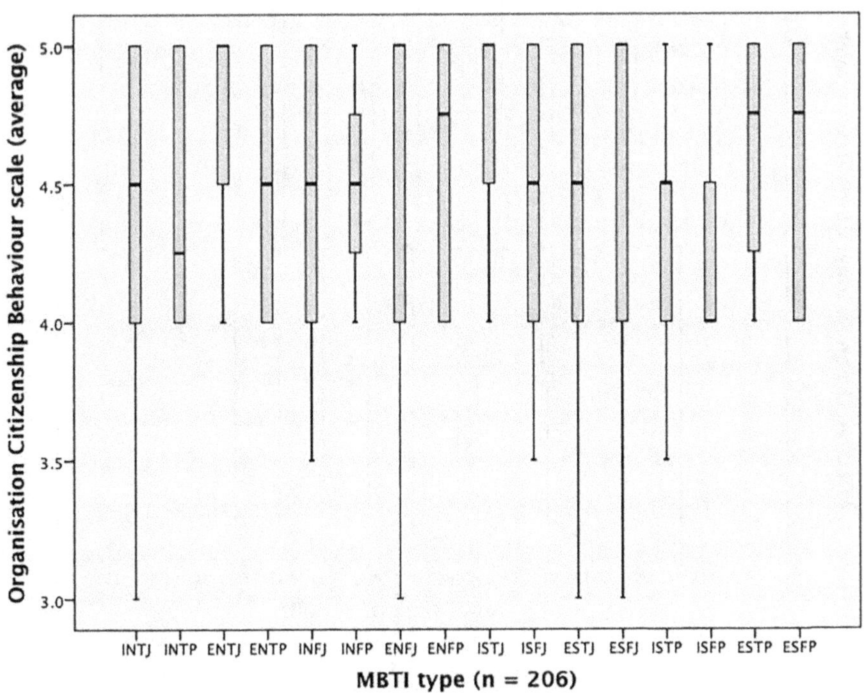

Figure 4.10 Boxplot: MBTI – 16 and Organisational Citizenship Behaviour.

as part of the analysis. A marginally statistically significant result was found, where the OCB score was higher in the ISTJ group ($M = 4.8$) compared to the ISFP group ($M = 4.3$, $SD = 0.50$), with a mean difference of 0.50.

In summary, the wide variation within groups (as seen in the boxplots in Figure 4.10), along with the small cell sizes for some groups, appears to be playing a role in the ANOVA not detecting a significant difference in OCB amongst the MBTI – 16 groups. Therefore, considering the marginally significant difference found, hypothesis **H1d** is **partially supported**.

MBTI – 16 ON AOC

After removing eight potential outliers, a one-way ANOVA of the MBTI – 16 on AOC was run. The boxplot analysing the MBTI – 16 and AOC relationship is presented below in Figure 4.11.

A non-significant ANOVA result was found, with AOC not statistically significantly for the different MBTI – 16 groups. This result suggests that at least one of the MBTI – 16 group means was not different from the others at this omnibus level, although the MBTI – 16 factor had a small effect size in explaining the variability in AOC.

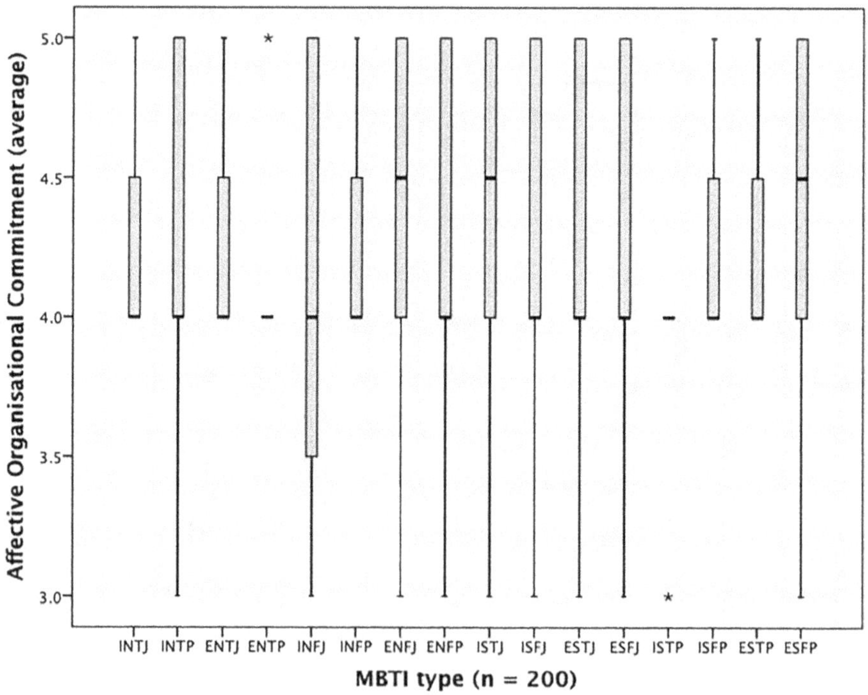

Figure 4.11 Boxplot: MBTI – 16 and Affective Organisational Commitment.

However, given the suggestion of variability amongst the groups by the boxplot – and to try to better understand the non-significant result – it was decided to run a planned comparison between the lowest and highest AOC groups as part of the analysis. A marginally statistically significant result was found, where the AOC score was higher in the ESFP group ($M = 4.4$) compared to the ISTP group ($M = 3.8$), with a mean difference of 0.64.

In summary, the wide variation within groups (as seen in the boxplots in Figure 4.11), along with the small cell sizes for some groups and the near-zero variance for two groups, appears to be playing a role in not detecting a significant difference in AOC amongst the MBTI – 16 groups. Therefore, considering the marginally significant result, hypothesis **H1e** is **partially supported**.

Multiple regression analysis: MBTI – 4 on OCB and AOC

To assess the combined influence of the four MBTI – 4 base pairs (as the predictors) on OCB and AOC (the outcome), hierarchical regression was used, where the variables were entered in two sets (or steps). To control for respondent differences, age and gender were entered in step one, and the MBTI – 4 base pairs were then entered in step two. (For technical details on how the MBTI – 4 multiple regression analysis was conducted, please see Appendix B6.)

As presented in Table 4.7, the MBTI – 4 pair Feeling/Thinking had the strongest influence of the four base pairs on both OCB and AOC, and was the only base pair to achieve at least a marginally significant influence on OCB and fell just short of a marginally significant influence on AOC. The other MBTI – 4 base-pair influences were weak or negligible in magnitude, as well as statistically non-significant.

Next, the addition of the MBTI – 4 in the second step in each regression had a noticeable improvement in the explanatory power (R^2) of the model compared to only the control variables in the first step. The overall explanatory power of the MBTI – 4 model, when controlling for age and gender, performed better for OCB ($R^2 = 0.056$) than for AOC ($R^2 = 0.044$), though both R^2 values are modest in nature.

Therefore, in relation to research question two, on the basis of these findings, hypotheses related to the MBTI – 4 influence of Thinking/Feeling (**H5c**) is **partially supported**, while **H5a**, **H5b**, **H5d**, **H6a**, **H6b**, **H6c** and **H6d** are **not supported**.

Research question three: MBTI and productivity

Research Question Three (RQ3): What influence does employee personality type have on productivity?

Table 4.7 Influence of the MBTI – 4 Base Pairs on OCB and AOC

		OCB n = *197*	*AOC* n = *194*
Step 1	Gender	−0.2	−0.13
	Age	0.08	0.04
	R^2	0.032	0.018
Step 2	Gender	−0.20**	−0.17*
	Age	0.08	0.04
	Introvert vs Extrovert	0.07	0.01
	Intuition vs Sensing	−0.002	0.08
	Thinking vs Feeling	−0.13^	−0.13#
	Perceiving vs Judging	−0.04	0.01
	R^2	0.056	0.044
	R^2 change	0.024	0.026

Note: Standardised beta coefficients reported; regarding statistical significance, # = $p \leq 0.20$, ^ = $p \leq 0.10$, * = $p \leq 0.05$ ** = $p \leq 0.01$, *** = $p \leq 0.001$; Sample size reported for each regression is the minimum pairwise *N*; MBTI – 4 dummy coding is as follows: Introvert = 0 and Extrovert = 1, Intuition = 0 and Sensing = 1, Feeling = 0 and Thinking = 1, Judging = 0 and Perceiving = 1.

RQ3 investigates whether there is a relationship between an individual's MBTI type and their work-related productivity levels, specifically enjoyment of tasks and the duration of tasks. As a result, RQ3 is linked to the hypotheses H1f and H1g (ANOVA) and H7a–d and H8a–d (multiple regression), which cover Task Enjoyment and Task Duration. The linked hypotheses are detailed below.

H1f: Personality type, as represented by the MBTI – 16, has an effect on Task Enjoyment.
H7a–H7d: The MBTI – 4 dimensions of (a) Introvert/Extrovert, (b) Intuition/Sensing, (c) Thinking/Feeling and (d) Perceiving/Judging will have an influence on Task Enjoyment.
H1g: Personality type, as represented by the MBTI – 16, has an effect on Task Duration.
H8a–H8d: The MBTI – 4 dimensions of (a) Introvert/Extrovert, (b) Intuition/Sensing, (c) Thinking/Feeling and (d) Perceiving/Judging will have an influence on Task Duration.

Descriptive statistics, ANOVA and multiple-regression analysis were conducted to analyse the relationships.

Descriptive statistics

This section will profile the types of productivity-based tasks and roles.

As part of the survey, sample respondents were provided a list of activities that pertain to productivity-based work and were asked to indicate whether they enjoyed or did not enjoy these activities; there was also a 'not applicable' response available, as some of the sample respondents might not complete some tasks. This question was asked to understand the drivers of task happiness or dissatisfaction.

The findings displayed in Table 4.8 showed themes whereby all sample respondents enjoyed problem solving; most sample respondents enjoyed root cause

Table 4.8 Tasks Productivity Experts 'Enjoy' and 'Do Not Enjoy'

Productivity Task	*Routine/ Non-routine*	*Hard/ Soft*	*Enjoy (%)*	*Do Not Enjoy (%)*	*Not Applicable (%)*
Problem solving	R	H	99	0	1
Data collection	R	H	52	44	4
Data analysis	R	H	86	13	1
Root cause analysis	R	H	94	4	2
Solution generation	R	H	98	1	1
Project management	R	H	64	26	10
Coaching	NR	S	82	5	13
Mentoring	NR	S	78	6	16
Training	NR	S	76	13	11
Facilitation of productivity syllabus	NR	S	34	16	50
Financial analysis	NR	H	56	32	12
Emails	R	H	46	53	1
Continuous improvement initiatives	NR	S	90	9	1
Huddles	R	S	80	20	0
VMB creation and management	R	H	71	26	3
SOP development and maintenance	R	H	41	55	4
Process and VSM mapping	R	H	68	23	7
Completion of presentation packs	R	H	60	39	1
Presentation of information to LT	NR	S	80	18	2
Tollgates	R	H	56	30	14
One-on-one with your manager	R	S	83	16	1
One-on-one with your direct reports	R	S	61	6	33
Workshopping	R	S	88	8	4
Preparation for workshops	R	S	69	25	6
Preparation for meetings	R	S	64	35	1
Development discussions	NR	S	74	22	4
Calendar maintenance	R	H	42	54	4
Governance forums	R	S	40	40	20
Dashboard metric creation and maintenance	NR	H	57	27	16

Note: R = Routine, NR = Non-routine, H = Hard, S = Soft.

Table 4.9 Productivity vs Non-productivity Roles

Title	*Proportion (%)*
Productivity	42
Non-productivity	58

analysis activities typically conducted in workshops and root cause analysis activities usually completed in a more creative environment, where innovative thinking and brainstorming could be conducted. Sample respondents also enjoyed solution generation, which is linked to root cause analysis, and they enjoyed continuous improvement initiatives.

The 'do not enjoy' categories showed that most sample respondents did not enjoy managing their emails, calendar maintenance and SOP creation and ongoing management; all of these tasks were poorly rated. SOPs were seen as a data-entry exercise, where no skills or qualifications are needed to execute the activity successfully, as a business-wide template existed that individuals filled in.

Looking at the 'do not enjoy' tasks, these tasks are repetitive and administrative in nature. No prior skills, education or qualifications are needed to successfully complete these activities; thus, no real intellectual thinking is needed to complete the tasks. Therefore, it is reasonable for knowledge workers to not enjoy these tasks.

The roles were also categorised into productivity and non–productivity-based roles depending on the title reported within the survey. This was to understand the split between those who were employed full-time as productivity experts. While an individual may not be employed as a full-time productivity expert, they would still be using their productivity knowledge and skills.

Table 4.9 depicts the breakdown in roles categorising all sample respondents as either working in productivity or non–productivity-based roles. The split between the two categories was fairly even, indicating that half of the sample respondents worked in core productivity roles.

ANOVA analysis: influence of MBTI – 16 on Task Enjoyment and Task Duration

A series of ANOVAs was completed to understand the relationship between the MBTI – 16 as the IV and the total number of tasks enjoyed (Task Enjoyment) and Task Duration as DVs. (For technical details on how the ANOVA analysis was run, please see Appendix B7.)

MBTI – 16 ON TASK ENJOYMENT

After removing three potential outliers, a one-way ANOVA of the MBTI – 16 on the total number of tasks enjoyed (Task Enjoyment) was conducted. The boxplot analysing the MBTI – 16 and Task Enjoyment relationship is presented below in Figure 4.12.

A marginally significant ANOVA result was found, with Task Enjoyment statistically marginally significantly for the different MBTI – 16 groups. This result suggests that at least one of the MBTI – 16 group means was marginally different from the others at this omnibus level, although the MBTI – 16 factor had a large effect size in explaining the variability in the total number of tasks enjoyed.

However, with the large effect size and given the suggestion of variability amongst the groups by the boxplot – and to try to better understand the marginally significant result – it was decided to run a planned comparison between the lowest and highest Task Enjoyment groups as part of the analysis. A statistically significant result was found, where the Task Enjoyment score was higher in the ENTP group (M = 23.0) compared to the INTP group (M = 14.7), with a mean difference of 8.3.

In summary, the wide variation within groups (as seen in the boxplots in Figure 4.12), along with the small cell sizes for some groups, appears to be playing a role in detecting only a marginally significant difference in Task Enjoyment amongst the MBTI – 16 groups. Therefore, also considering the significant planned-comparison result, hypothesis **H1f** is **partially supported**.

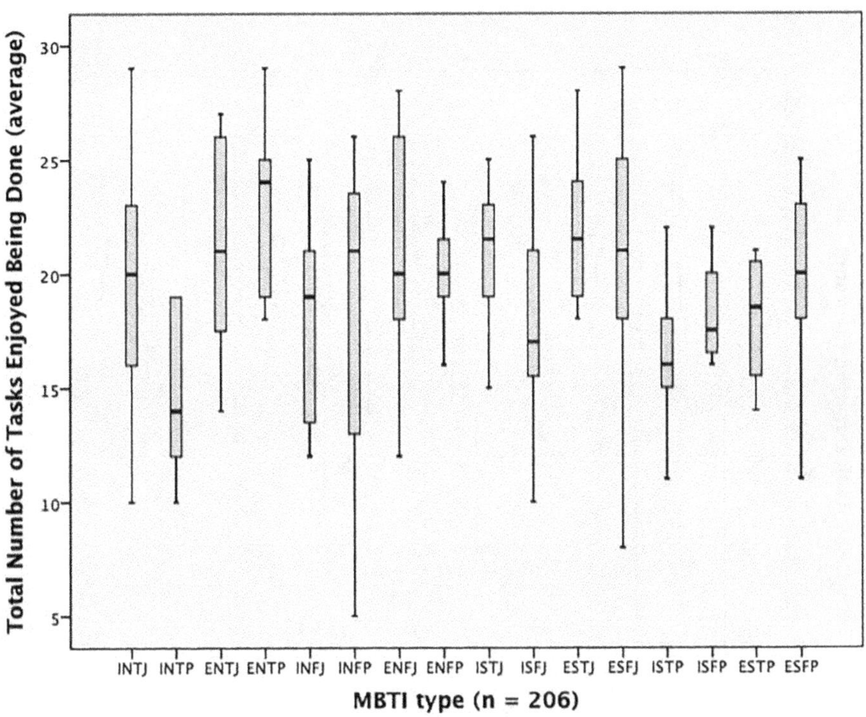

Figure 4.12 Boxplot: MBTI – 16 and Task Enjoyment.

MBTI – 16 ON TASK DURATION

After removing nine potential outliers, a one-way ANOVA of the MBTI – 16 on the Task Duration was conducted. The boxplot analysing the MBTI – 16 and Task Duration relationship is presented below in Figure 4.13. A significant ANOVA result was found, with Task Duration being statistically significantly for the different MBTI – 16 groups. This result suggests at least one of the MBTI – 16 group means was different from the others, with the MBTI – 16 factor having a medium-to-large effect size in explaining the variability in Task Duration. Therefore, hypothesis **H1g** is **supported**.

Follow-up pairwise comparisons were then conducted to identify where differences existed, with a planned comparison between the lowest and highest Task Duration groups as part of the analysis. The Task Duration score was statistically significantly higher in the ESTP group ($M = 4.6$) compared to the INFP group ($M = 2.9$), with a mean difference of 1.7.

Multiple regression analysis: MBTI – 4 on Task Enjoyment and Task Duration

To assess the combined influence of the four MBTI – 4 base pairs (as the predictors) on Task Enjoyment and Task Duration (the outcome), hierarchical

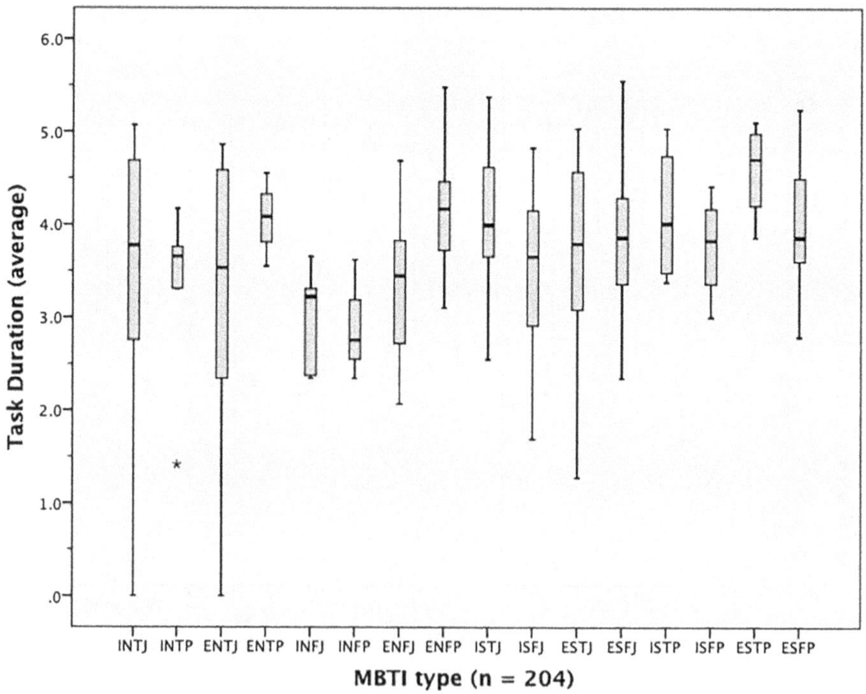

Figure 4.13 Boxplot: MBTI – 16 and Task Duration.

regression was used, where the variables were entered in two sets (or steps). To control for respondent differences, age and gender were entered in step one, and the MBTI – 4 base pairs were then entered in step two. The analysis examined all tasks undertaken, as well as when broken down into four types: Non-routine Tasks, Routine Tasks, Soft Tasks and Hard Tasks. The results are presented in Tables 4.10 and 4.11. (For technical details on how the MBTI – 4 multiple regression analysis was conducted, please see Appendix B8.)

MBTI – 4 ON TASK ENJOYMENT

As presented in Table 4.10, the MBTI – 4 pair Introvert/Extrovert had a statistically significant influence on Task Enjoyment – for all tasks and each of the task types (subgroupings). In contrast, Thinking/Feeling had a limited influence, only having a statistically significant influence on Non-routine Task Enjoyment. Similarly, Perceiving/Judging also had a limited influence, only having a statistically significant influence on Hard Task Enjoyment. The other MBTI – 4 base-pair influences were weak or negligible in magnitude, as well as statistically non-significant.

Next, the addition of the MBTI – 4 in the second step in each Task Enjoyment regression had a noticeable improvement in the explanatory power (R^2) of the

Table 4.10 Regression Analysis MBTI – 4 and Task Enjoyment

		Task Enjoyment – Total n = *197*	*Task Enjoyment – Soft Tasks* n = *196*	*Task Enjoyment – Hard Tasks* n = *197*	*Task Enjoyment – Routine Tasks* n = *197*	*Task Enjoyment – Non-routine Tasks* n = *197*
Step 1	Gender	0.03	0.03	0.04	0.05	-0.02
	Age	0.06	0.10#	-0.02	0.03	0.07
	R^2	0.004	0.01	0.002	0.004	0.01
Step 2	Gender	0.03	0.03	0.05	0.03	0.02
	Age	0.03	0.07	-0.04	0.01	0.05
	Introvert vs Extrovert	0.27***	0.30***	0.17*	0.22**	0.24***
	Intuition vs Sensing	-0.05	-0.02	-0.07	-0.05	-0.04
	Thinking vs Feeling	0.02	-0.01	0.10#	-0.08	0.16*
	Perceiving vs Judging	-0.11#	-0.06	-0.15*	-0.10#	-0.08
	R^2	0.079	0.10	0.051	0.07	0.075
	R^2 change	0.075	0.09	0.049	0.066	0.069

Note: Standardised beta coefficients reported; # = $p \leq .20$, ^ = $p \leq .10$, * = $p \leq .05$ ** = $p \leq .01$, *** = $p \leq .001$; Sample size reported for each regression is the minimum pairwise *N*; MBTI – 4 dummy coding is as follows: Introvert = 0 and Extrovert = 1, Intuition = 0 and Sensing = 1, Feeling = 0 and Thinking = 1, Judging = 0 and Perceiving = 1.

model compared to only the control variables in the first step. The overall explanatory power of the MBTI – 4 model, when controlling for age and gender, performed best for Soft Task Enjoyment ($R^2 = 0.10$), though all of the R^2 values are modest in nature.

Therefore, in relation to research question two, on the basis of these findings, the hypothesis related to the MBTI – 4 influence of Introvert/Extrovert (**H7a**) is **supported**. Given the significant influence for at least one task type (subgroup), hypotheses **H7c** (Thinking/Feeling) and **H7d** (Perceiving/Judging) are **partially supported**. Lastly, hypothesis **H7b** (Intuition/Sensing) is **not supported**.

MBTI – 4 ON TASK DURATION

As presented in Table 4.11, the MBTI – 4 pair Perceiving/Judging had a statistically significant influence on Task Duration – for all tasks and two of the task types (subgroupings), Soft Tasks and Routine Tasks. Next, Intuition/Sensing had a limited influence, only having a statistically marginally significant influence on the duration of all tasks, with a statistically significant influence on Soft Task Duration and Routine Task Duration. Similarly, Feeling/Thinking had a limited influence, only having a statistically marginally significant influence on the duration of all tasks, along with a statistically marginally significant influence on the duration of Soft Task Duration and Hard Task Duration. Lastly, Introvert/Extrovert also had a limited influence, only having a statistically significant influence on Non-routine Task Duration and a statistically marginally significant influence on Soft Task Duration. The other MBTI – 4 base-pair influences were statistically non-significant.

Next, the addition of the MBTI – 4 in the second step in each Task Duration regression had a noticeable improvement in the explanatory power (R^2) of the model compared to only the control variables in the first step. The overall explanatory power of the MBTI – 4 model, when controlling for age and gender, performed best for Soft Task Duration ($R^2 = 0.091$), though all of the R^2 values are modest in nature.

Therefore, in relation to research question two, on the basis of these findings, the hypothesis related to the MBTI – 4 influence of Perceiving/Judging (**H8d**) is **supported**. Next, given a marginally significant influence for all tasks, hypotheses **H8b** (Intuition/Sensing) and **H8c** (Thinking/Feeling) are **partially supported**. Finally, given at least a significant influence for at least one task type (subgroup), **H8a** (Introvert/Extrovert) is also **partially supported** (see Table 4.11).

Exploring the moderator potential of the MBTI – 4 base pairs

Having established that personality-profile types are an influence on employee attitudes and behaviours, we now seek to delve further and generate a more nuanced understanding of the MBTI – 4 effects. The deeper understanding

Table 4.11 Regression Analysis MBTI – 4 and Task Duration

		Duration – All Tasks n = *194*	*Duration – Soft Tasks* n = *192*	*Duration – Hard Tasks* n = *194*	*Duration – Routine Tasks* n = *193*	*Duration – Non-routine Tasks* n = *193*
Step 1	Gender	−0.07	−0.07	−0.11#	−0.03	−0.16*
	Age	−0.03	−0.04	0.002	−0.02	0.02
	R^2	0.01	0.01	0.01	0.002	0.03
Step 2	Gender	−0.02	−0.02	−0.07	0.02	−0.12#
	Age	−0.04	−0.05	−0.01	−0.03	0.01
	Introvert vs Extrovert	0.12#	0.14^	0.10#	0.09	0.15*
	Intuition vs Sensing	0.14^	0.18*	0.10#	0.18*	0.10
	Thinking vs Feeling	0.14^	0.14^	0.13^	0.12#	0.12#
	Perceiving vs Judging	0.15*	0.19**	0.11#	0.23**	0.05
	R^2	0.061	0.091	0.050	0.080	0.063
	R^2 change	0.056	0.084	0.037	0.078	0.038

Note: Standardised beta coefficients reported; # = $p \leq .20$, ^ = $p \leq .10$, * = $p \leq .05$ ** = $p \leq .01$, *** = $p \leq .001$; Sample size reported for each regression is the minimum pairwise *N*; MBTI – 4 dummy coding is as follows: Introvert = 0 and Extrovert = 1, Intuition = 0 and Sensing = 1, Feeling = 0 and Thinking = 1, Judging = 0 and Perceiving = 1.

sought relates to the potential moderating influence of the MBTI – 4, which was investigated through running subgroup analysis.

Moderation can help us to understand how a process operates if the moderator places constraints on how or when that process can function (Hayes, 2009). The importance of moderators arises from their ability to enhance understanding of the relationship between relevant independent variables and dependent variables, as well as seemingly established relationships (Walsh, Evanschitzky & Wunderlich, 2008), such as that between AMO and OCB.

This section presents the subgroup (moderation) analysis that details the relationships between MBTI – 4 base pairs and the influence of AMO and the AOC relationship, along with the OCB relationship and the influence of AMO on the OCB relationship along with Task Duration and Task Enjoyment.

To do this, the model was first run on its own for the full sample using hierarchical regression as in previous analyses, along with assessing model basics (e.g. outliers). This formed the baseline. Next, a second run was then done using the SPSS feature of 'Organise output by groups' to generate the subgroup analysis, with the results assessed for each MBTI – 4 base pair. Due to the varying sample sizes, which can affect the power in determining coefficients of a certain size are significant (Coakes, 2013), attention is focused here on both the magnitude of the coefficients, including the difference in magnitude in a pair, as well as their statistical significance. (See Appendix B9 for technical details related to the analyses.)

Moderating the A-M-O → AOC relationship

To begin with, the varying effects of the individual MBTI – 4 base pairs on the AMO → AOC relationship was evident (see Table 4.12), where differences were observed in both the pattern of coefficients of the predictor IVs and the explanatory power of the model (R^2).

Table 4.12 presents the effects the MBTI – 4 base pairs have on the A-M-O → AOC relationship. For the full sample, Opportunity and Ability have a statistically significant influence on AOC. In contrast, Motivation's influence is negligible and not statistically significant.

Looking across the MBTI – 4 subgroups, Opportunity retains its statistically significant influence for the most part (excepting for the Extrovert subgroup), though the strength of its influence does vary from moderately weak (Extrovert) to moderately strong (Intuition). A similar consistency is evident for Ability's influence across the subgroups. Finally, Motivation retains its negligible-to-weak influence for the most part, though there does look to be something happening in the Thinking subgroup, where its influence is noticeably stronger.

Next, the addition of A-M-O variables in the second step had a noticeable improvement in the explanatory power (R^2) of the model in explaining variation in AOC compared to only the control variables in the first step. Looking across the MBTI – 4 subgroups, we see some variability in the model's explanatory power, ranging from a high of explaining 41% of the variation (i.e. $R^2 = 0.41$) for Intuition and 27% for Introvert to a low of explaining 10% of the variation for Sensing.

Collectively, the results of the subgroup analysis are supportive of MBTI – 4 having a moderating influence on the AMO → AOC relationship, supporting the moderating effect of personality type. Additionally, the varying influence of gender is something that could be investigated as part of future research to understand the impact gender has in relation to the MBTI – 4 base pairs.

Moderating the A-M-O → OCB relationship

To begin with, the varying effects of the individual MBTI – 4 base pairs on the AMO → OCB relationship was evident (see Table 4.13), where differences were observed in both the pattern of coefficients of the predictor IVs and the explanatory power of the model (R^2).

Table 4.13 presents the effects the MBTI – 4 base pairs have on the A-M-O → OCB relationship. For the full sample, only Opportunity has a statistically significant influence on OCB. In contrast, Ability and Motivation both have a weak influence on OCB that is not statistically significant.

Looking across the MBTI – 4 subgroups, Opportunity retains its statistically significant influence for the most part (excepting for the Perceiving subgroup),

Table 4.12 Moderating Effect of MBTI – 4 on A-M-O → AOC Relationship

		AOC	*AOC*	*AOC*	*AOC*	*AOC*	*AOC*	*AOC*	*AOC*	*AOC*
		Full Sample n = *195*	*Introvert* n = *71*	*Extrovert* n = *124*	*Intuition* n = *64*	*Sensing* n = *131*	*Feeling* n = *138*	*Thinking* n = *57*	*Judging* n = *141*	*Perceiving* n = *54*
Step 1	Gender	−0.143*	−0.091	−0.173^	−0.237^	−0.111	−0.188*	−0.092	−0.223**	0.116
	Age	0.039	0.124	−0.004	−0.089	0.102	−0.023	0.194#	0.001	0.159
	R^2	0.021	0.022	0.030	0.062	0.020	0.036	0.046	0.05	0.040
Step 2	Gender	−0.141*	−0.069	−0.16^	−0.247*	−0.106	−0.169*	−0.043	−0.203*	0.06
	Age	0.016	−0.001	0.009	−0.067	0.061	−0.032	0.154#	0.004	0.01
	Motivation	−0.008	−0.124	0.083	0.062	−0.052	0.054	**−0.209**#	−0.005	0.001
	Opportunity	0.249**	**0.452*****	0.122	**0.49*****	0.147#	0.196*	**0.418***	0.194*	**0.465****
	Ability	0.214**	0.181#	**0.207***	0.106	**0.22***	0.174^	0.237^	**0.243****	0.033
	R^2	0.166	**0.265**	0.136	**0.406**	0.095	0.145	**0.255**	0.178	0.245
	R^2 change	0.145	0.243	0.106	0.344	0.075	0.109	0.209	0.128	0.205

Note: Standardised beta coefficients reported; # = $p \leq 0.20$, ^ = $p \leq 0.10$, * = $p \leq 0.05$ ** = $p \leq 0.01$, *** = $p \leq 0.001$; Sample size reported for each regression is the minimum pairwise *N*; Coefficient or R^2 difference 0.10 or greater in size for a base pair features the larger value in bold.

Table 4.13 Moderating Effect of MBTI – 4 on the A-M-O → OCB Relationship

		OCB	*OCB*	*OCB*	*OCB*	*OCB*	*OCB*	*OCB*	*OCB*	*OCB*
		Full Sample n = *197*	*Introvert* n = *72*	*Extrovert* n = *125*	*Intuition* n = *64*	*Sensing* n = *133*	*Feeling* n = *139*	*Thinking* n = *58*	*Judging* n = *143*	*Perceiving* n = *54*
Step 1	Gender	−0.16*	−0.229^	−0.123#	−0.342**	−0.074	−0.145^	−0.229^	−0.250**	0.073
	Age	0.084	0.202^	0.025	−0.023	0.124#	0.034	0.174#	0.031	0.253^
	R^2	0.032	0.087	0.015	0.117	0.019	0.022	0.082	0.063	0.070
Step 2	Gender	−0.15*	−0.225*	−0.109#	−0.344***	−0.043	−0.119#	−0.192^	−0.219**	0.034
	Age	0.049	0.087	0.026	0.016	0.056	-0.007	0.15#	0.019	0.191#
	Motivation	0.06	-0.039	**0.138#**	**0.159#**	-0.04	-0.031	**0.194#**	0.004	**0.18**
	Opportunity	0.42***	0.432***	0.378***	0.439***	0.441***	0.355***	0.426**	**0.477*****	0.164
	Ability	0.078	**0.21^**	-0.002	**0.207^**	-0.022	0.106	0.042	**0.102#**	-0.002
	R^2	0.269	**0.366**	0.231	**0.572**	0.188	0.171	**0.424**	**0.336**	0.143
	R^2 change	0.237	0.279	0.216	0.455	0.169	0.149	0.342	0.274	0.073

Note: Standardised beta coefficients reported; # = $p \leq 0.20$, ^ = $p \leq 0.10$, * = $p \leq 0.05$ ** = $p \leq 0.01$, *** = $p \leq 0.001$; Sample size reported for each regression is the minimum pairwise *N*; Coefficient or R^2 difference 0.10 or greater in size for a base pair features the larger value in bold.

though the strength of its influence does vary from moderately weak (Extrovert) to moderately strong (Intuition). However, there is greater variability for Ability, with the strength of its influence ranging from almost zero (Extrovert) to moderate (Introvert). A similar range in variability is also evident for Motivation's influence across the subgroups. There were also some pronounced differences across the base pairs.

Next, the addition of A-M-O variables in the second step had a noticeable improvement in the explanatory power (R^2) of the model in explaining variation in OCB compared to only the control variables in the first step. Looking across the MBTI – 4 subgroups, we see some variability in the model's explanatory power, ranging from a high in explaining 57% of the variation (i.e. $R^2 = 0.57$) for Intuition and 37% for Introvert to a low of explaining 14% of the variation for Perceiving. Between pairs, the R^2 was meaningfully higher for Introvert, Intuition, Thinking and Judging in their respective pairs.

Collectively, the results of the subgroup analysis are supportive of MBTI – 4 having a moderating influence on the AMO → OCB relationship, supporting the moderating effect of personality type. Additionally, the varying influence of gender is something that could be investigated as part of future research to understand the impact gender has in relation to the MBTI – 4 base pairs.

Moderating the AOC + OCB → Task Duration relationship

To begin with, the varying effects of the individual MBTI – 4 base pairs on the AOC + OCB → Task Duration relationship was evident (see Table 4.14), where differences were observed in both the pattern of coefficients of the predictor IVs and the explanatory power of the model (R^2).

Table 4.14 presents the effects the MBTI – 4 base pairs have on the AOC + OCB → Task Duration relationship. For the full sample, only OCB has a statistically significant influence on Task Duration. In contrast, AOC has a moderately weak influence on Task Duration that is not statistically significant.

Looking across the MBTI – 4 subgroups, OCB retains its statistically significant influence for five of the eight subgroups (significant for four and marginally significant for one), though the strength of its influence does vary from strong (Thinking) to weak (Feeling). AOC also shows some variability – though not to the same extent/range as OCB – with the strength of its influence ranging from weak (Feeling) to moderately strong (Thinking). There were also some pronounced differences across the base pairs.

Next, the addition of AOC + OCB variables in the second step had a noticeable improvement in the explanatory power (R^2) of the model in explaining variation in Task Duration compared to only the control variables in the first step. Looking across the MBTI – 4 subgroups, we see some variability in the model's explanatory power, ranging from a high in explaining 28% of the variation (i.e. $R^2 = 0.28$) for Thinking and 15% for Intuition to a low of explaining 1.3% for Perceiving. Between pairs, the R^2 was meaningfully higher for Introvert, Intuition and Thinking in their respective pairs.

Table 4.14 Moderating Effect of MBTI – 4 on AOC + OCB → Task Duration (Overall) Relationship

		Duration	*Duration*	*Duration*	*Duration*	*Duration*	*Duration*	*Duration*	*Duration*	*Duration*
		Full Sample n = *194*	*Introvert* n = *71*	*Extrovert* n = *123*	*Intuition* n = *62*	*Sensing* n = *131*	*Feeling* n = *138*	*Thinking* n = *56*	*Judging* n = *141*	*Perceiving* n = *53*
Step 1	Gender	−0.067	−0.157#	−0.013	−0.077	−0.074	−0.059	−0.033	−0.047	−0.065
	Age	−0.027	0.038	−0.074	−0.089	0.006	0.024	−0.133	−0.001	−0.092
	R^2	0.005	0.025	0.006	0.013	0.005	0.004	0.019	0.002	0.013
Step 2	Gender	−0.041	−0.068	−0.015	0.052	−0.076	−0.055	0.103	0.012	−0.053
	Age	−0.043	−0.027	−0.077	−0.098	0.004	0.022	−0.200	−0.011	−0.09
	OCB	0.277***	**0.531*****	0.087	**0.476*****	0.173^	0.067	**0.688*****	**0.324*****	0.181
	AOC	−0.132#	**−0.206**	−0.09	−0.154	−0.152#	−0.026	**−0.349**#	−0.114	**−0.265**#
	R^2	0.058	**0.207**	0.013	**0.146**	0.033	0.007	**0.282**	0.074	0.066
	R^2 change	0.053	0.182	0.007	0.133	0.028	0.003	0.263	0.072	0.053

Note: Standardised beta coefficients reported; # = $p \leq 0.20$, ^ = $p \leq 0.10$, * = $p \leq 0.05$ ** = $p \leq 0.01$, *** = $p \leq 0.001$; Sample size reported for each regression is the minimum pairwise *N*; Coefficient or R^2 difference 0.10 or greater in size for a base pair features the larger value in bold.

Collectively, the results of the subgroup analysis are supportive of MBTI – 4 having a moderating influence on the AOC + OCB → OCB relationship, supporting the moderating effect of personality type.

Moderating the AOC + OCB → Task Enjoyment relationship

To begin with, the varying effects of the individual MBTI – 4 base pairs on the AOC + OCB → Task Enjoyment relationship was somewhat evident (see Table 4.15), where some differences were observed in both the pattern of coefficients of the predictor IVs and the explanatory power of the model (R^2).

Table 4.15 presents the effects the MBTI – 4 base pairs have on the AOC + OCB → Task Enjoyment relationship. For the full sample, neither OCB nor AOC has a statistically significant influence on Task Enjoyment.

Looking across the MBTI – 4 subgroups, AOC only achieves marginal statistical significance for Feeling, though the strength of its influence does vary from moderate (Intuition) to weak (Sensing). OCB also shows some variability – though not to the same extent/range as OCB – with the strength of its influence ranging from very weak (Extrovert) to moderate (Intuition). There were also a couple of pronounced differences across the base pairs.

Next, the addition of AOC + OCB variables in the second step had a small to negligible improvement in the explanatory power (R^2) of the model in explaining variation in Task Enjoyment compared to only the control variables in the first step. Looking across the MBTI – 4 subgroups, we see modest, limited variability in the model's explanatory power, ranging from a high in explaining 7.2% of the variation (i.e. $R^2 = 0.072$) for Perceiving to a low of 1.3% for Extrovert. Between pairs, the R^2 was somewhat higher for Intuition and Perceiving in their respective pairs. Overall, there is still a noticeable improvement in the R^2 for Intuition, Thinking and Perceiving over the baseline, albeit these are still modest values.

Collectively, while there is not a lot happening in the subgroup regressions for this combination of predictors and outcome, the results of the subgroup analysis do offer some tentative support for MBTI – 4 having a moderating influence on the AOC + OCB → Task Enjoyment relationship, thus supporting the moderating effect of personality type. Additionally, the varying influence of gender is something that could be investigated as part of future research to understand the impact gender has in relation to the MBTI – 4 base pairs.

Differences in Junior and Senior roles

Some further analyses were completed to understand the role split of individuals in Junior and Senior roles and the impact on Organisation X. (See Appendix B10 for details.) This information was taken from the roles that the individuals indicated in the survey (i.e. their title), from which they were categorised into being either Junior or Senior. To ensure consistency, the following classification was applied: all specialists, analysts and managers were deemed Junior roles, whilst

Table 4.15 Moderating Effect of MBTI – 4 on AOC + OCB → Task Enjoyment Relationship

		Enjoyment	*Enjoyment*	*Enjoyment*	*Enjoyment*	*Enjoyment*	*Enjoyment*	*Enjoyment*	*Enjoyment*	*Enjoyment*
		Full Sample n = *196*	*Introvert* n = *71*	*Extrovert* n = *125*	*Intuition* n = *63*	*Sensing* n = *133*	*Feeling* n = *138*	*Thinking* n = *58*	*Judging* n = *143*	*Perceiving* n = *53*
Step 1	Gender	0.044	0.046	0.053	–0.089	0.120#	–0.023	0.133	–0.031	0.233^
	Age	0.038	–0.054	0.048	0.168#	–0.042	0.03	0.054	0.021	0.089
	R^2	0.003	0.005	0.005	0.038	0.015	0.001	0.021	0.001	0.064
Step 2	Gender	0.058	0.063	0.064	–0.09	0.131#	0.017	0.159	–0.012	0.221#
	Age	0.031	–0.073	0.047	0.183#	–0.060	0.028	0.062	0.018	0.074
	OCB	0.042	0.028	0.019	**–0.161**	0.115	0.051	0.138	0.032	0.006
	AOC	0.069	0.087	0.075	**0.224#**	0.029	0.168^	**–0.202**	0.060	0.090
	R^2	0.013	0.015	0.013	0.065	0.032	0.039	0.044	0.008	0.072
	R^2 change	0.01	0.01	0.008	0.027	0.017	0.038	0.023	0.007	0.008

Note: OCB = Organisation Citizenship Behaviour, AOC = Affective Organisational Commitment; Standardised beta coefficients reported; # = $p \leq 0.20$, ^ = $p \leq 0.10$, * = $p \leq 0.05$ ** = $p \leq 0.01$, *** = $p \leq 0.001$; Sample size reported for each regression is the minimum pairwise *N*; Coefficient or R^2 difference 0.10 or greater in size for a base pair features the larger value in bold.

senior managers, executive managers and general managers were deemed Senior roles. This categorisation was used, as this is how the organisation categorises its staff. Table 4.16 shows the distribution between Junior and Senior roles, and the results suggest that the categories are fairly evenly distributed.

Table 4.17 shows the MBTI – 16 type, the percentage split of Junior and Senior roles and the overall population of the MBTI type. In further analysis, the profile of MBTI – 16 types for each group of sample respondents in Junior or Senior roles were found not to be similarly distributed for the financial services productivity specialists in this study as the general population reported by 16personalities.com. In other words, the Junior and Senior groups' MBTI – 16 profiles were statistically different from that of the general MBTI population.

Lastly, the Junior and Senior roles were examined with respect to the MBTI – 4 base pair categories regarding the expected proportions. The proportions for each pair were statistically significantly different from the 50% test proportion except for the Extrovert and Introvert category for Junior roles.

Table 4.16 Junior vs Senior Role Categorisation

Title	*Count (%)*
Junior	57
Senior	43

Table 4.17 MBTI – 16 – Comparing Junior and Senior Roles

MBTI Type	*Junior (%)*	*Senior (%)*	*General MBTI Population (%)*
INTJ	10.5	6.7	1.5
INTP	3.5	0.96	2.5
ENTJ	2.1	6.7	4.0
ENTP		4.8	4.5
INFJ	4.2	2.8	1.0
INFP	4.2	1.9	2.0
ENFJ	10.5	3.8	4.0
ENFP	2.8	7.6	7.0
ISTJ	5	7.6	8.5
ISFJ	13.5	14.4	7.0
ESTJ	6.4	5.7	13.0
ESFJ	28.5	25	12.0
ISTP	2.1	1.9	6.0
ISFP	2.1	0.96	6.0
ESTP	2.1	2.8	10.0
ESFP	7.1	5.7	11.0

Note: The general population profile for the 16 MBTI types is that as reported by 16personalities.com. The cell for ENTP types had zero responses for Junior roles (ENTP), so this category was combined with an adjacent category (ENTJ) to facilitate the analysis.

Summary of findings

Therefore, based on the results from within this chapter, it can confidently be concluded that there are relationships between the different variables. More specifically, it can be determined that there are relationships between an employee's personality type and the employee outcomes, being HPWS (AMO). In addition, personality type has an influence on organisational outcomes, specifically organisational citizenship behaviour and affective organisational commitment displayed. Lastly, it can also be stated that there is a relationship between personality type and productivity levels in the workplace specifically Task Enjoyment and Task Duration (Figure 4.14 and Table 4.18).

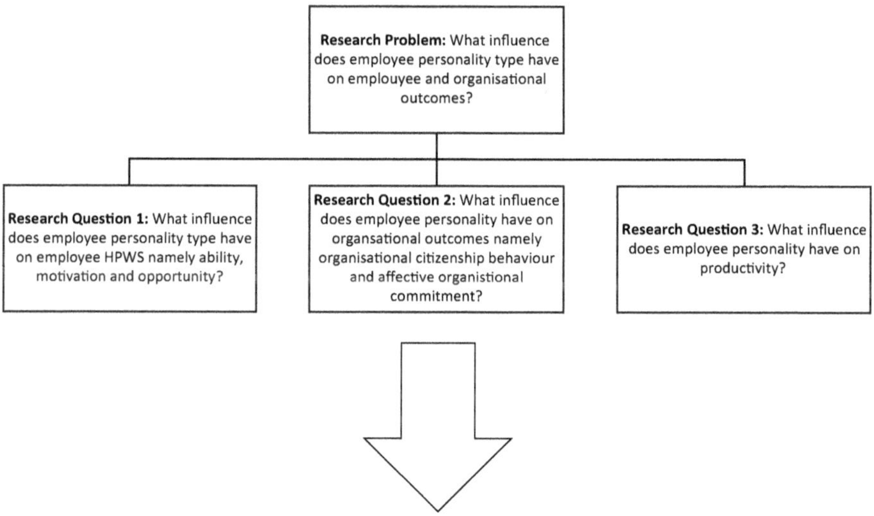

Figure 4.14 Research Problem and Questions.

Table 4.18 Summary of Hypothesis Outcomes

Hypothesis	*Detail*	*RQ Link*	*Outcome*
Personality type, as represented by the MBTI – 16, has an effect on …			
H1a	… Motivation.	RQ1	Supported
H1b	… Opportunity.	RQ1	Supported
H1c	… Ability.	RQ1	Supported
H1d	… OCB.	RQ2	Partially supported
H1e	… AOC.	RQ2	Partially supported
H1f	… Task Enjoyment.	RQ3	Partially supported
H1g	… Task Duration.	RQ3	Supported
H2a	The MBTI – 4 dimension of Introvert/Extrovert will have an influence on Motivation.	RQ1	Supported

Hypothesis	*Detail*	*RQ Link*	*Outcome*
H2b	The MBTI – 4 dimension of Intuition/Sensing will have an influence on Motivation.	RQ1	Not supported
H2c	The MBTI – 4 dimension of Thinking/Feeling will have an influence on Motivation.	RQ1	Supported
H2d	The MBTI – 4 dimension of Perceiving/Judging will have an influence on Motivation.	RQ1	Not supported
H3a	The MBTI – 4 dimension of Introvert/Extrovert will have an influence on Opportunity.	RQ1	Not supported
H3b	The MBTI – 4 dimension of Intuition/Sensing will have an influence on Opportunity.	RQ1	Not Supported
H3c	The MBTI – 4 dimension of Thinking/Feeling will have an influence on Opportunity.	RQ1	Supported
H3d	The MBTI – 4 dimension of Perceiving/Judging will have an influence on Opportunity.	RQ1	Not supported
H4a	The MBTI – 4 dimension of Introvert/Extrovert will have an influence on Ability.	RQ1	Not supported
H4b	The MBTI – 4 dimension of Intuition/Sensing will have an influence on Ability.	RQ1	Not supported
H4c	The MBTI – 4 dimension of Thinking/Feeling will have an influence on Ability.	RQ1	Supported
H4d	The MBTI – 4 dimension of Perceiving/Judging will have an influence on Ability.	RQ1	Not supported
H5a	The MBTI – 4 dimension of Introvert/Extrovert will have an influence on OCB.	RQ2	Partially supported
H5b	The MBTI – 4 dimension of Intuition/Sensing will have an influence on OCB.	RQ2	Partially supported
H5c	The MBTI – 4 dimension of Thinking/Feeling will have an influence on OCB.	RQ2	Partially supported
H5d	The MBTI – 4 dimension of Perceiving/Judging will have an influence on OCB.	RQ2	Partially supported
H6a	The MBTI – 4 dimension of Introvert/Extrovert will have an influence on AOC.	RQ2	Partially Supported
H6b	The MBTI – 4 dimension of Intuition/Sensing will have an influence on AOC.	RQ2	Partially supported
H6c	The MBTI – 4 dimension of Thinking/Feeling will have an influence on AOC.	RQ2	Partially supported
H6d	The MBTI – 4 dimension of Perceiving/Judging will have an influence on AOC.	RQ2	Partially supported
H7a	The MBTI – 4 dimension of Introvert/Extrovert will have an influence on Task Enjoyment.	RQ3	Supported
H7b	The MBTI – 4 dimension of Intuition/Sensing will have an influence on Task Enjoyment.	RQ3	Not supported
H7c	The MBTI – 4 dimension of Thinking/Feeling will have an influence on Task Enjoyment.	RQ3	Partially supported
H7d	The MBTI – 4 dimension of Perceiving/Judging will have an influence on Task Enjoyment.	RQ3	Partially supported
H8a	The MBTI – 4 dimension of Introvert/Extrovert will have an influence on Task Duration.	RQ3	Partially Supported
H8b	The MBTI – 4 dimension of Intuition/Sensing will have an influence on Task Duration.	RQ3	Partially supported
H8c	The MBTI – 4 dimension of Thinking/Feeling will have an influence on Task Duration.	RQ3	Partially supported
H8d	The MBTI – 4 dimension of Perceiving/Judging will have an influence on Task Duration.	RQ3	Supported

Conclusion

To conclude, this chapter presents the results and findings of the research, which include the demographic details and the descriptive statistical analysis of the sample collected, analysis of the reliability and validity of the constructs, as well as the primary data analysis. The primary data analysis addressed the research questions and their related hypotheses as related to the focal topics of interest for this research, with the findings of the analysis presented. To do this, one-way ANOVA and hierarchical multiple regression were used, with additional insights generated through the use of chi-square analysis and binomial analysis. Following on from the hypothesis testing, further examination of the data was conducted using sub-group analysis involving multiple regression, where the sub-groups were the MBTI – 4 base pairs, in order to provide a rich robustness to the data analysis and interpretation component of this research.

The key findings and insights to emerge were the influence of personality type at the construct level (MBTI – 16) with significant results found for H1a (Motivation), H1b (Opportunity) and H1c (Ability). The more discrete analysis (MBTI – 4 influence) saw mixed support, with significant influence of Introvert/Extrovert (H2a, Motivation) and Thinking/Feeling (H2c, Motivation; H3c, Opportunity, H4c, Ability).

Related to RQ2, partial support was found for the MBTI – 16 influence for H1d (OCB) and H1e (AOC), with partial support for all MBTI – 4 pairs for H5a–d (OCB) and H6a–d (AOC).

Related to RQ3, partial support was found for the MBTI – 16 influence for H1f (Task Enjoyment) and H1g (Task Duration), with partial support for all MBTI – 4 pairs for H7a–d (Task Enjoyment) and H8a–d (Task Duration).

Finally, further analysis was conducted into the potential moderating effects of personality type, with subgroup analysis run in regression using the MBTI – 4 base pairs as the group basis. The results suggest that there is something happening moderation wise, with notable differences emerging between a number of the base pairs for the different models examined. Further analysis also explored the relationship between Junior-Senior roles and personality type. The next, and final, chapter discusses the key findings of this research.

Notes

1 The mean being Green Belts and the median also being Green Belts.

2 When reporting the statistical significance of hypothesis testing, p-values ≤ 0.05 were considered to be 'significant' and those that were > 0.05 and ≤ 0.10 were considered to be 'marginally significant'. A result of statistical significance was the basis for a hypothesis to be 'supported' and a result of marginal significance was deemed to be 'partially supported'.

3 Using a chi-square goodness-of-fit test, a significant result was found (Chi-square = 253.625, $df = 15$, $p < 0.001$).

4 A chi-square goodness-of-fit test for unequal proportions was used, with a significant result found (Chi-square = 197.997, $df = 15$, $p < 0.001$).

5 To understand the MBTI profiles better, a series of binomial tests were conducted to analyse the MBTI – 4 base pairs. The binomial test assessed whether the observed proportions differed from a specification of equal proportions (i.e. a 50/50 split for each base pair). The results showed that the actual proportion for each base pair was statistically (i.e. significantly) different from the expected 50/50 proportion. This suggests that the greater proportions of Extrovert (60%), Sensing (66%), Feeling (68%) and Judging (74%) observed in the sample were not what would be expected in a random event (i.e. a 50% occurrence). See Technical Appendix B3 for the full test results.

References

16personalities.com, (2017). *Personality Types.* Retrieved on 19 November 2017 from https://www.16personalities.com/personality-types

16personalities.com, (2020). *Personality Types.* Retrieved on 4 December 2020 from https://www.16personalities.com/personality-types

Coakes, S.J., (2013). *SPSS Version 24 for MAC, Analysis without Anguish.* John Wiley & Sons.

Hayes, A.F., (2009). Beyond Baron and Kenny: Statistical Mediation Analysis in the New Millennium. *Communication Monographs, 76*(4), 408–420.

Walsh, G., Evanschitzky, H., & Wunderlich, M., (2008). Identification and Analysis of Moderator Variables: Investigating the Customer Satisfaction - Loyalty Link. *European Journal of Marketing,* 42(9/10), 977–1004.

5 Key learnings for practice and future directions

Introduction

The aim of this research was to review what influence employee personality type had on an employee and organisational outcomes, more specifically to address whether there were any relationships between an individual's personality type (in this case the MBTI), and the linkages to productivity and the HPWS within a given organisation. The study itself took place in the banking and finance industry at a financial services organisation. Following the introduction to the research project which was established in Chapter 1, Chapter 2 conducted a comprehensive review of the literature pertinent to the topics of personality profiling (the MBTI), productivity and HPWS, drawing on previous literature and outlining the gaps in the current literature and research.

In order to address this problem and understand the relationships between personality preferences (specifically the MBTI), productivity and HPWS, three overarching research questions (RQs) were developed: first, *what influence does employee personality type have on employee HPWS, namely, Ability, Motivation and Opportunity?* Second, *what influence does employee personality type have on organisational HPWS outcomes, namely, organisational citizenship behaviours and affective organisational commitment?* Third, *what influence does employee personality type have on productivity?*

To address the information needs of the research problem and questions discussed, a number of hypotheses have been examined as part of this research. These hypotheses consider personality types and their effects on Motivation, Opportunity and Ability, along with the considerations of the MBTI dimensions and the relationships between these dimensions.

This chapter will discuss the findings associated with this research. The structure of this chapter will be a detailed discussion of the results, including the contributions of the research, specifically including the theoretical contributions and the implications for practice. Next, it will detail the limitations and the recommendations on future direction of research as obtained within this study. The conceptual model considers Myers-Briggs personality profiling and the relationships with high-performance workplace systems, individual and organisational behaviours and productivity outcomes (Figure 5.1).

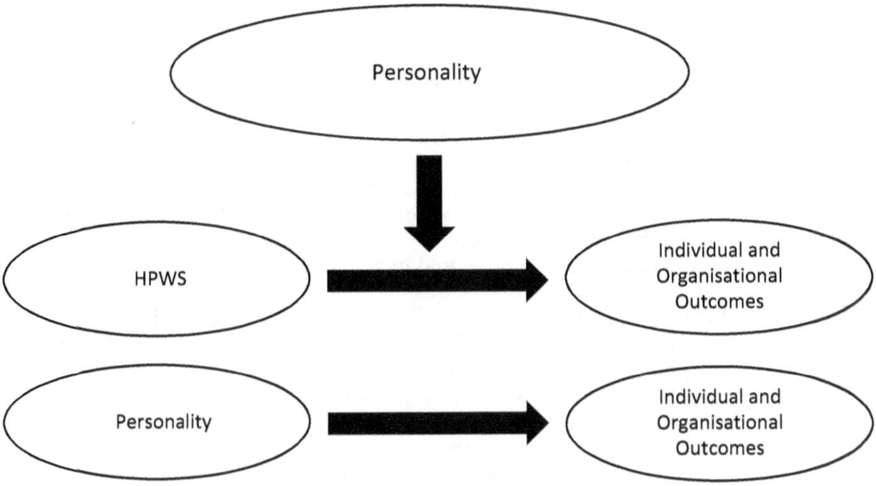

Figure 5.1 Simple Conceptual Model.

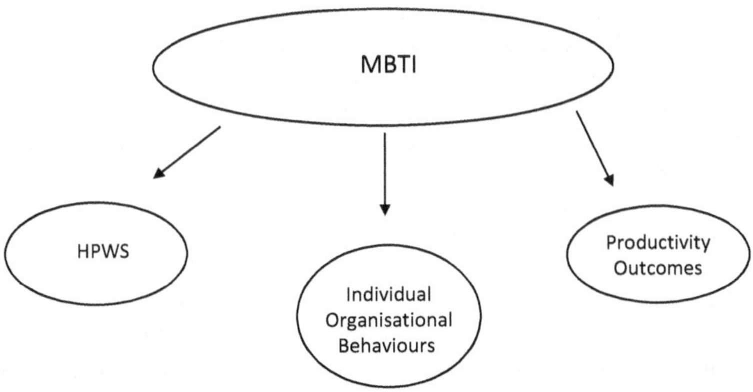

Figure 5.2 Moderation Effects.

Please note that arrows represent relationships between variables. Note: For clarity of presentation, the Personality direct influences on the constructs in the model are not shown (Figure 5.2).

Section Simple Conceptual Model and its subsection provide an overview of the results and detailed discussion surrounding the outcomes of the study. This section will also review the results and discuss them in greater detail (Table 5.1).

The first group of hypotheses were designed to analyse whether there is a relationship between HPWS and the AMO (Ability, Motivation and Opportunity)

Table 5.1 Research Questions and Hypothesis Outcomes

Hypothesis	*Detail*	*RQ Link*	*Outcome*
H1a	Personality type, as represented by the MBTI – 16, has an effect on Motivation.	RQ1	Supported
H1b	Personality type, as represented by the MBTI – 16, has an effect on Opportunity.	RQ1	Supported
H1c	Personality type, as represented by the MBTI – 16, has an effect on Ability.	RQ1	Supported
H1d	Personality type, as represented by the MBTI – 16, has an effect on OCB.	RQ2	Partially Supported
H1e	Personality type, as represented by the MBTI – 16, has an effect on AOC.	RQ2	Partially Supported
H1f	Personality type, as represented by the MBTI – 16, has an effect on Task Enjoyment.	RQ3	Partially Supported
H1g	Personality type, as represented by the MBTI – 16, has an effect on Task Duration.	RQ3	Supported

model when compared to the MBTI type. There was an expectation that a significant relationship would be present, based on findings from prior research. For hypotheses H1a, H1b and H1c, personality type (specifically the MBTI – 16 dimensions) was analysed with respect to Motivation, Opportunity and Ability (the AMO model) and whether there was a relationship between the variables. Literature on personality profiling has discussed the MBTI in detail and the importance of understanding how an individual's attitude is presented and how it operates in the external world (Boult, Thompson & Schaubhut, 2017; Quenk, 2009). In the AMO literature, it is argued that if managers want to enhance their staff performance, then they need to seek to positively influence the three parts of the AMO model (Hughes, 2007; Robbins & Barnwell, 2002). The results of this study showed that there were supported relationships between these variables. Specifically, it was found that personality type, in the guise of the MBTI – 16, has a significant relationship with each AMO variable, which is consistent with prior studies in this area (Quenk, 2009; Stahl et al., 2012). This finding expands our understanding of the influence of the relationship between these variables. A relationship between MBTI and AMO was expected and was established once tested, therefore resulting in hypotheses **H1a, H1b and H1c** being **supported**.

The second group of hypotheses were developed to analyse whether there was a relationship between an individual's personality type and the level of organisational commitment they hold.

Regarding hypotheses H1d and H1e a marginally significant difference was found when examining MBTI and OCB and MBTI and AOC, therefore resulting in hypotheses **H1d and H1e** being **partially supported**. Hypotheses H1d, H1e, H1f and H1g considered personality type (MBTI – 16) and OCB and AOC, along with Task Enjoyment and Task Duration, respectively, and whether there was a relationship between these variables. The literature states that for an organisation to achieve high performance among employees there must be an interaction between Task Enjoyment and Task Duration in relation to daily tasks.

Research suggests that organisations need to focus on OCB and AOC and in turn they will see increased organisational performance in the form of increased and improved profitability, productivity, customer satisfaction, quality of deliverables and, lastly, growth of market share (Patel, Messersmith & Lepak, 2013).

Hypotheses H1d, H1e, H1f and H1g were deemed partially supported, meaning there were marginal relationships between the variables; these outcomes extended our understanding of the influence that MBTI type has against OCB, AOC, Task Enjoyment and Task Duration.

H1a, H1b, H1c, H1d, H1e, H1f and H1g: recap

Hypotheses H1a, H1b and H1c were designed to analyse whether there is a relationship between MBTI – 16 dimensions and whether there was a relationship to the AMO (Ability, Motivation and Opportunity) model. A relationship between MBTI and AMO was expected based on findings from prior research and was established once tested, therefore resulting in hypotheses **H1a, H1b and H1c** being **supported**.

Hypotheses H1d, H1e, H1f and H1g were developed to analyse whether there was a relationship between MBTI – 16 dimensions and whether there was a relationship with OCB, AOC, Task Enjoyment and Task Duration, respectively.

Hypotheses H1d, H1e and H1f were partially supported, whereas H1g was fully supported (Table 5.2).

H2a, H2b, H2c and H2d: results and discussion

The MBTI – 4 dimensions, which are Introvert/Extrovert, Intuition/Sensing, Thinking/Feeling and Perceiving/Judging were tested against the Motivation component of the AMO model, as represented in hypotheses H2a, H2b, H2c and H2d, respectively, using multiple regression. The literature in this area suggests organisations that are able to focus on the three elements of the AMO model can achieve increased organisational performance in the form of increased and improved profitability, productivity, customer satisfaction, quality of deliverables and, lastly, market share (Patel, Messersmith & Lepak, 2013). In addition, when the AMO model is used accordingly, combined with personality profiling, personality type can drive competitive advantage for the organisation, representing a more successful organisation and a greater competitive advantage focus. The results found that the MBTI – 4 dimensions showed a relationship with the AMO model. More specifically, the MBTI – 4 dimensions Introvert/Extrovert and Thinking/Feeling had a significant influence on motivation, thus supporting H2a. In contrast, Intuition/Sensing and Perceiving/Judging did not show a significant relationship with motivation, therefore resulting in H2b and H2d not being supported.

Table 5.2 Research Questions and Hypothesis Outcomes

Hypothesis	*Detail*	*RQ Link*	*Outcome*
H2a	The MBTI – 4 dimension of Introvert/ Extrovert will have an influence on Motivation.	RQ1	Supported
H2b	The MBTI – 4 dimension of Intuition/ Sensing will have an influence on Motivation.	RQ1	Not supported
H2c	The MBTI – 4 dimension of Thinking/ Feeling will have an influence on Motivation.	RQ1	Supported
H2d	The MBTI – 4 dimension of Perceiving/ Judging will have an influence on Motivation.	RQ1	Not supported
H3a	The MBTI – 4 dimension of Introvert/ Extrovert will have an influence on Opportunity.	RQ1	Not supported
H3b	The MBTI – 4 dimension of Intuition/ Sensing will have an influence on Opportunity.	RQ1	Not supported
H3c	The MBTI – 4 dimension of Thinking/ Feeling will have an influence on Opportunity.	RQ1	Supported
H3d	The MBTI – 4 dimension of Perceiving/ Judging will have an influence on Opportunity.	RQ1	Not supported
H4a	The MBTI – 4 dimension of Introvert/ Extrovert will have an influence on Ability.	RQ1	Not supported
H4b	The MBTI – 4 dimension of Intuition/ Sensing will have an influence on Ability.	RQ1	Not supported
H4c	The MBTI – 4 dimension of Thinking/ Feeling will have an influence on Ability.	RQ1	Supported
H4d	The MBTI – 4 dimension of Perceiving/ Judging will have an influence on Ability.	RQ1	Not supported
H5a	The MBTI – 4 dimension of Introvert/ Extrovert will have an influence on OCB.	RQ2	Partially supported
H5b	The MBTI – 4 dimension of Intuition/ Sensing will have an influence on OCB.	RQ2	Partially supported
H5c	The MBTI – 4 dimension of Thinking/ Feeling will have an influence on OCB.	RQ2	Partially supported
H5d	The MBTI – 4 dimension of Perceiving/ Judging will have an influence on OCB.	RQ2	Partially supported
H6a	The MBTI – 4 dimension of Introvert/ Extrovert will have an influence on AOC.	RQ2	Partially supported
H6b	The MBTI – 4 dimension of Intuition/ Sensing will have an influence on AOC.	RQ2	Partially supported
H6c	The MBTI – 4 dimension of Thinking/ Feeling will have an influence on AOC.	RQ2	Partially supported
H6d	The MBTI – 4 dimension of Perceiving/ Judging will have an influence on AOC.	RQ2	Partially supported
H7a	The MBTI – 4 dimension of Introvert/ Extrovert will have an influence on Task Enjoyment.	RQ3	Supported

H2c represented Feeling/Thinking, which showed the strongest negative influence (–0.197), and H2a depicted Introvert/Extrovert dimensions, which showed the second strongest positive influence (0.171), whereas Intuition/Sensing and Perceiving/Judging displayed the third strongest relationships with a negative influence (–0.002 and –0.003 respectively).

These findings expand our understanding of this relationship which provides a new insight for the literature in this domain. In general, the results support the general influence of the MBTI – 4 on motivation. More specifically, the influence of the Introvert/Extrovert and Thinking/Feeling MBTI – 4 dimensions on motivation is consistent with prior studies in this area (Bong-Chang & Gurbaxani, 2012; Drucker, 1999; Jabbour, 2013; Kasman, Kasman, Ayhan & Torun, 2013). However, the non-significant influence of Intuition/Sensing and Perceiving/Judging on motivation is contrary to previous research and literature. This may be due to the nature of the productivity work examined at Organisation X which was focused on knowledge-based productivity-focused work, and it may also be due to the specific industry which was examined within this research, which was the Australian Banking and Finance industry.

H2a, H2b, H2c and H2d: recap

In relation to hypotheses H2a, H2b, H2c and H2d, that is, the relationships between MBTI – 4 dimensions and Motivation, H2a and H2c showed supported outcomes, meaning there were relationships between the constructs, whereas H2b and H2d showed no relationship, meaning there was a relationship seen between Thinking/Feeling and Perceiving/Judging and Motivation, and no relationship between Intuition/Sensing and Perceiving/Judging and Motivation.

H3a, H3b, H3c and H3d: results and discussion

Next hypotheses H3a, H3b, H3c and H3d analysed the MBTI – 4 dimensions and their influence on Opportunity; the results showed no support for hypothesised relationships H3a, H3b and H3d and support for H3c, which examined MBTI – 4 dimensions against Thinking/Feeling. Literature relating to MBTI and Opportunity suggested there would be no relationships between the variables and this was confirmed; thus, these findings were consistent with prior research (Bong-Chang & Gurbaxani, 2012; Drucker, 1999; Jabbour, 2013; Kasman, Kasman, Ayhan & Torun, 2013). However, the results showed support for hypothesis H3c, which examined the relationship between the MBTI dimension of Thinking/Feeling and the Ability component of the AMO model. The literature depicted four principal psychological functions by which humans experience the world; two of these were stated to be Feeling and Thinking. In addition, literature discussed that these two functions are dominant for a person most of the time (Boult, Thompson & Schaubhut, 2017; Quenk, 2009). The results for Thinking/Feeling dimension showed support for the hypotheses and showed consistent outcomes, thus expanding our understanding of the MBTI – 4 dimensions and their relationship with the Opportunity segment of the AMO model.

H3a, H3b, H3c and H3d: recap

In relation to hypotheses H3a, H3b, H3c and H3d and whether there was a relationship between the MBTI – 4 dimensions and the Opportunity segment of the AMO model, the results showed no support for hypotheses H3a, H3b and H3d, meaning there was no relationship present. However, Thinking/Feeling showed a positive relationship, meaning there was a relationship shown.

H4a, H4b, H4c and H4d: results and discussion

Hypotheses H4a, H4b, H4c and H4d analysed the MBTI – 4 dimensions and their relationship to the Ability component of the AMO model. The results were similar to those found with H3a–H3d, whereby no relationship was found between the variables, namely, MBTI – 4 dimensions and the Ability section of the AMO model, and thus did not support hypotheses H4a, H4b and H4d, which was consistent with prior research and literature on the topics of MBTI and AMO (Bong-Chang & Gurbaxani, 2012; Drucker, 1999; Jabbour, 2013; Kasman, Kasman, Ayhan & Torun, 2013). However, similarly to H3c, there was a positive relationship between the MBTI dimension of Thinking/Feeling and its influence on Ability, thus supporting hypothesis H4c and expanding our understanding of the MBTI – 4 dimensions and the Ability segment of the AMO model.

H4a, H4b, H4c and H4d: recap

Hypotheses H4a, H4b, H4c and H4d reviewed the relationship between the MBTI – 4 dimensions and the Ability segment of the AMO model. The outcomes showed that H4a, H4b and H4d were not supported, meaning no relationship was seen between Introvert/Extrovert, Intuition/Sensing, Perceiving/Judging and Motivation; however, there was a relationship seen between Thinking/Feeling and the Ability section of the AMO.

H5a, H5b, H5c and H5d: results and discussion

Hypotheses H5a, H5b, H5c and H5d examined the relationship between the MBTI – 4 dimensions and organisational citizenship behaviour (OCB), with the outcomes of the variables partially supporting the hypotheses.

Literature on the topics states that for employees to display a certain type of behaviour that benefit the organisation, the organisation should attempt to engage employees in activities that make them feel like they are helping the organisation be successful. This may lead to new capabilities or skills through training and increasing knowledge and talents used on the job (Boxall & Purcell, 2008; Robbins & Barnwell, 2002; Robbins, Judge, Millett & Waters-Marsh, 2008). Research suggests if organisations are able to focus on these elements they may, in turn, achieve increased organisational performance in the form of increased and improved profitability, productivity, customer satisfaction, quality of deliverables and, lastly, growth of market share (Patel, Messersmith & Lepak, 2013). The findings from the relationships provided expected outcomes relating to these topics, meaning a relationship was expected and was subsequently seen relating to these topics.

H5a, H5b, H5c and H5d: recap

Hypotheses H5a, H5b, H5c and H5d analysed whether there was a relationship between MBTI – 4 dimensions and OCB. The findings showed partially supported outcomes, meaning there were partial relationships seen between Introvert/Extrovert, Intuition/Sensing, Thinking/Feeling and Perceiving/Judging and OCB.

H6a, H6b, H6c and H6d: results and discussion

Hypotheses H6a, H6b, H6c and H6d analysed the relationship between the MBTI – 4 dimensions and affective organisational commitment (AOC). H6a, H6b, H6c and H6d were partially supported by the outcomes relating to these variables, that is, the hypotheses were partially supported. Literature on the topics states that for employees to display an interaction with AOC organisations should focus on performance-related pay, various employee communication means, training and team-based work which are said to be mutually reinforcing and to generate superior organisational commitment and, in turn, organisational performance (Boxall & Purcell, 2008; Robbins, Judge, Millett & Waters-Marsh, 2008). Advocates of HPWS argue that improvements in organisational performance are generated because these practices enhance employee discretion which, in turn, can flow into an improved attitude towards the work undertaken by employees (Boxall & Purcell, 2008; Robbins, Judge, Millett & Waters-Marsh, 2008). The hypotheses were partially supported by the outcomes, expanding our knowledge in these areas.

H6a, H6b, H6c and H6d: recap

Hypotheses H6a, H6b, H6c and H6d analysed whether there was a relationship between MBTI – 4 dimensions and AOC. The findings showed partially supported outcomes, meaning there were partial relationships seen between Introvert/Extrovert, Intuition/Sensing, Thinking/Feeling and Perceiving/Judging and AOC (Table 5.3).

Table 5.3 Research Questions and Hypothesis Outcomes

Hypothesis	*Detail*	*RQ Link*	*Outcome*
H7b	The MBTI – 4 dimension of Intuition/ Sensing will have an influence on Task Enjoyment.	RQ3	Not supported
H7c	The MBTI – 4 dimension of Thinking/ Feeling will have an influence on Task Enjoyment.	RQ3	Partially supported
H7d	The MBTI – 4 dimension of Perceiving/ Judging will have an influence on Task Enjoyment.	RQ3	Partially supported
H8a	The MBTI – 4 dimension of Introvert/ Extrovert will have an influence on Task Duration.	RQ3	Partially supported
H8b	The MBTI – 4 dimension of Intuition/ Sensing will have an influence on Task Duration.	RQ3	Partially supported
H8c	The MBTI – 4 dimension of Thinking/ Feeling will have an influence on Task Duration.	RQ3	Partially supported
H8d	The MBTI – 4 dimension of Perceiving/ Judging will have an influence on Task Duration.	RQ3	Supported

H7a, H7b, H7c and H7d: results and discussion

Hypotheses H7a, H7b, H7c and H7d reviewed whether there were any relationships between the MBTI – 4 dimensions and the enjoyment relating to tasks and activities. Similarly to H5a–H5d and H6a–H6d the hypotheses were partially supported by the outcomes, meaning that there were some relationships seen between the variables.

Literature on these topics displayed insights that innovative workplace practices are often responded to with employee enjoyment and these practices are said to be linked to complementary human resource practices and performance (Andreeva & Sergeeva, 2016; Beltran-Martin & Roca-Puig, 2013; Smith, Tucker & Pitt, 2011).

H7a was fully supported; however, H7c and H7d were partially supported, meaning, as expected, there were relationships between MBTI – 4 dimensions and enjoyment. The findings have provided an expansion on the knowledge associated with these topics.

H7a, H7b, H7c and H7d: recap

Hypotheses H7a H7b, H7c and H7d analysed whether there was a relationship between MBTI – 4 dimensions and enjoyment. The findings showed that except H7a, which was fully supported, all other hypotheses were partially supported, meaning there were partial relationships seen between Introvert/Extrovert, Intuition/Sensing, Thinking/Feeling and Perceiving/Judging and enjoyment.

Lastly, **H8a, H8b, H8c and H8d** analysed the relationship between Task Duration and the MBTI – 4 types, with Junior/Senior roles as IVs. The findings showed that except H8d which was fully supported, all other hypotheses were partially supported. Each of these hypotheses and their respective outcomes will be discussed in greater detail in the "Hypotheses" section.

Conceptual model

This research developed and empirically tested a theoretical model as outlined in Chapter 2 of this book, in order to facilitate a discussion concerning what influence employee personality type had on employee and organisational outcomes in Organisation X, one of the largest Australian financial services institutions. The critical review of the literature showed that there was extant research regarding personality profiling, productivity and HPWS as individual topics (Fahy, Farrelly & Quester, 2002; Matson & Prusak, 2010; Mladkova, 2011; Stahl et al., 2012). However, this critical review also identified gaps in the literature that warranted research to address them, namely, to determine whether there were direct linkages among personality preferences, productivity and HPWS (Argote & Ingram, 2000; Chowhan, 2016; Smith, Tucker & Pitt, 2011).

The review concluded that there was a lack of understanding regarding the impact an individual's personality type had on their individual productivity in the workplace and the HPWS they are part of, which also formed part of the justification and the objective of this research, i.e. examining the influence of each topic individually and jointly (Macky &Boxall, 2007, 2009, 2014). Given the stated aim, a research problem was formulated to concisely capture the topic at hand, 'What influence does employee personality type have on employee and organisational outcomes?'

From this overarching research problem came the development of three research questions (RQs) that shaped the focus of this research and the resulting empirical investigation.

RQ1: What influence does employee personality type have on employee HPWS, namely, Ability, Motivation and Opportunity?

RQ2: What influence does employee personality type have on organisational outcomes, namely, organisational citizenship behaviour and affective organisational commitment?

RQ3: What influence does employee personality have on productivity?

As each of these research questions developed, so too did the linked eight supporting hypotheses, which were developed to identify and examine each of the topic areas in greater detail. Guided by the research questions and resulting hypotheses, data was collected to enable testing of the hypotheses. Adopting a positivist, quantitative research method, an anonymous self-administered web based questionnaire was used. As detailed in Chapter 3, data was collected from 288 productivity experts in the banking and finance industry at the largest financial-services organisation within Australia (Deshpandé, 1983). Data was analysed using descriptive statistics, cross tabulations, ANOVAs, Pearson's correlations, chi-square analysis, pairwise comparisons, phi coefficient, biserial correlations and multiple regression to understand the relationships between each of the variables. The results as detailed in Chapter 4 show that all three of the research problems and subsequently eight of the hypotheses tested were primarily supported or partially supported. These results showed that there were relationships present between most of the variables, including MBTI, productivity and HPWS (specifically the AMO model).

Research questions

The first research question analysed was what influence does employee personality type have on employee HPWS, namely, Ability, Motivation and Opportunity? the second, what influence does employee personality type have on organisational outcomes, namely, organisational citizenship behaviour and affective organisational commitment? and the third, what influence does employee personality have on productivity?

Hypotheses

RQ1 linked to hypotheses group one

This group of hypotheses were designed to analyse whether there is a relationship between HPWS (Ability, Motivation and Opportunity) and MBTI type; it was expected that a significant relationship would be present based on prior research. Prior literature argues that not only does HPWS have an impact on employees, but employees are also motivated through other ways such as by work processes and also through the environment they are working in, as it is believed that it is easier to perform when a company is successful (Boxall & Macky, 2009; Boxall & Purcell, 2008; Macky & Boxall, 2007). Per available research on the topic personality types in an organisational context has been explored in terms of the relationship between psychological type and the motivation of workers (Barbuto, Fritz, Lim & Xu, 2008), contributing to maximising knowledge worker productivity levels (Maruta, 2012) and boosting productivity of knowledge workers (Matson & Prusak, 2010; Mladkova, 2011).

Further to this, the AMO framework was explored as the basis for conceptualising a high-performance workplace system. Using the AMO model it was theorised that the HPWS of a large organisation has an impact it has on an individual's level of performance along with their personality type (Boxall & Purcell, 2008; Robbins, Judge, Millett & Waters-Marsh, 2008).

It has been argued that for the AMO framework to work it must positively affect employee abilities, motivations and opportunities, in order for them to contribute to the organisation (Boxall & Purcell, 2008; Robbins, Judge, Millett &

Waters-Marsh, 2008). Further, rewards are a direct attempt to enhance Motivation, which may also be improved through empowerment of information and knowledge (Boxall & Macky, 2009).

Advocates of high-performance work systems have argued that improvements in organisational performance is generated because these practices enhance employee discretion which, in turn, can flow into an improved attitude towards the work undertaken by employees (Boxall & Purcell, 2008; Robbins, Judge, Millett & Waters-Marsh, 2008; see hypotheses in the "Introduction" section).

A relationship between MBTI and AMO was expected and if the relationship was seen once tested it was considered **supported**. Hypotheses **H1a, H1b, H1c** were **supported**. Therefore, in relation to research question one, on the basis of these findings, hypotheses related to the MBTI – 4 influence of Introvert/Extrovert (**H2a**) and Thinking/Feeling (**H2c**, **H3c** and **H4c**) were **supported**, whilst **H2b**, **H2d**, **H3a**, **H3b**, **H3d**, **H4a**, **H4b** and **H4d** were **not supported**. Therefore, it is clear that this thesis supports the argument that aspects of an individual's personality (MBTI – 16) are vital for achieving high performance especially when it moderates the relationship between an organisation's Ability, Motivation and Opportunity through enhancing practices as part of its human resources practices and productivity.

RQ2 linked to hypotheses group two

The second group of hypotheses were developed to analyse whether there was a relationship between an individual's personality type and the level of organisational commitment they hold. All of these factors are part of the thinking surrounding organisational commitment, and it can be argued that organisational commitment is seen through the level of motivation an individual has and that the knowledge they hold and their productivity levels feed into their commitment. Studies have found that personality types are an important factor in successful team performance, which again is linked to the level of commitment one displays (Bradley & Hebert, 1997; Kasman, Kasman, Ayhan & Torun, 2013; Ones & Dilchert, 2009). Further to this and more recently, research has found linkages between personality preferences and learning environments (Chesborough, 2005), happiness (Francis & Jones, 2000), coping styles (Genco, 2006) sunk costs and outsourcing (Jabbour, 2013), as well as the fit between type and roles (Herk, 2011), which strengthens the concept that personality profiling (specifically the MBTI) has a relevancy in understanding an individual's preferences or behaviours but more than relevancy MBTI has a presence and place in understanding why an individual behaves as they do (Boxall & Purcell, 2008; Robbins & Barnwell, 2002; Robbins, Judge, Millett & Waters-Marsh, 2008). Therefore, it was expected that a relationship would be seen between the individual's personality type and the levels of commitment they display in the workplace.

Looking at affective organisational commitment (AOC) is looking at how committed an individual is to their place of employment or how they emotionally feel about their organisation. In order to understand the AOC an individual possesses the AMO model should be reviewed. Studies have found for the AMO framework to work it must positively affect employee abilities, motivations and opportunities in order for them to contribute to the organisation. Improvements in knowledge enhance Ability, whilst empowerment and information enhance the Opportunity to contribute (Boxall & Purcell, 2008; Robbins, Judge, Millett & Waters-Marsh, 2008).

High-performance work systems include performance-related pay, various employee communication means, training and team-based work which are said to be mutually reinforcing and to generate superior organisational performance (Boxall & Purcell, 2008; Robbins, Judge, Millett & Waters-Marsh, 2008). Advocates of HPWS argue that improvements in organisational performance are generated because these practices enhance employee discretion which, in turn, can flow into an improved attitude towards the work undertaken by employees (Boxall & Purcell, 2008; Robbins, Judge, Millett & Waters-Marsh, 2008). Therefore, one could assume that with an improved attitude towards work undertaken is the linkage needed to foster the right level of commitment and engagement for the individual. Further, research suggests organisations that are able to focus on the three elements of the AMO model can achieve increased organisational performance in the form of increased and improved profitability, productivity, customer satisfaction, quality of deliverables and, lastly, growth of market share (Patel, Messersmith & Lepak, 2013). That said, a relationship was expected between MBTI and affective organisational commitment displayed by employees (see hypotheses in the "Introduction" section).

Considering the marginally significant difference found, hypotheses **H1d, H1e** and **H1f** were **partially supported**. Therefore, in relation to research question two, hypotheses related to the MBTI – 4 influence of Thinking/Feeling (**H5c**) were **partially supported**, as well as **H5a**, **H5b**, **H5d**, **H6a**, **H6b**, **H6c** and **H6d** are also **partially supported**.

Therefore, it is clear that this thesis supports the argument that aspects of an individual's personality (MBTI – 16) are vital for achieving high performance. In particular, when it moderates the relationship between an organisation's Ability, Motivation and Opportunity through enhancing practices as part of its human resources practices and productivity.

RQ3 linked to hypotheses group three

The third group of hypotheses cover productivity outcomes which, for the purpose of this study, includes Task Enjoyment linked to satisfaction and Task Duration.

This group of hypotheses were built to determine whether personality type has an impact on employee enjoyment within the workplace. The factors used as part of these hypotheses were MBTI type and how satisfied an individual is in the workplace; in order to understand this, individuals at the case organisation provided insights into the activities they enjoyed and did not enjoy as part of their jobs.

Considering the HPWS concept is the AMO model, which is concerned with the individual's performance when they have Ability, Motivation and Opportunity present. Literature argues that if managers want to enhance their staff performance they need to influence the three. Underpinning this hypothesis is the HPWS concept, which is aimed at building individual and organisation performance (Chowhan, 2016). As discussed earlier in Chapter 2, for the AMO framework to work effectively it needs to positively affect employee abilities, motivations and opportunities in order for them to contribute to the organisation.

In addition, and along with the AMO model, HPWS include performance-related pay, various employee communication means, training and team-based work, which are said to be mutually reinforcing and to generate superior organisational performance (Boxall & Purcell, 2008; Robbins, Judge, Millett & Waters-Marsh, 2008). Some of the advocates of HPWS argue that improvements in organisational performance are generated because these practices enhance employee discretion which, in turn, can flow into an improved attitude towards the work undertaken by employees (Boxall & Purcell, 2008; Robbins, Judge, Millett & Waters-Marsh, 2008).

With this in mind, it was expected that if the AMO model was followed closely and successfully executed a relationship would be found between an individual's MBTI and their enjoyment within the workplace. Linked to the idea of enjoyment is the thought process centred on satisfaction. For example, early research found that personality types are an important factor affecting successful team performance (Bradley & Hebert, 1997; Kasman, Kasman, Ayhan & Torun, 2013; Ones & Dilchert, 2009). The conceptual model of high-involvement work processes was examined as part of this literature review; specifically, the indirect path as part of that model was referenced. The indirect path is said to focus on employee motivation and satisfaction with an effort to lower turnover rates; this path is important in ensuring staff want to solve work-related problems and their continued responsibility for doing so remains at the forefront of their mind (Boxall & Purcell, 2008; Robbins & Barnwell, 2002). Therefore, it was expected that a relationship would be found between personality type, enjoyment and employee satisfaction in the workplace.

The final group of hypotheses linked to this RQ were created to understand whether personality type has an effect on the duration of tasks completed (by productivity experts).

In order to understand the relationship between MBTI and Task Duration the AMO model should be examined more closely. Abilities are the level of physical, financial, cognitive, emotional or social resources a person can apply to perform a specific task (Boxall & Purcell, 2008; Robbins, Judge, Millett & Waters-Marsh, 2008).

Motivation is the needs and wants of an individual and how these may influence them to behave in a certain way; it is the encouragement for behaviour (Boxall & Purcell, 2008; Robbins & Barnwell, 2002; Robbins, Judge, Millett & Waters-Marsh, 2008).

Opportunity is the relevant restrictions, such as the availability of time and resources that also enable behaviour; generally speaking, employees seek opportunities to complete a task that will result in a benefit for them or for others (Boxall & Purcell, 2008; Robbins, Judge, Millett & Waters-Marsh, 2008).

For employees, Motivation is provided by incentives and rewards for the type of expected behaviour and outcomes that benefit the organisation. Opportunities, for example, engage employees in activities that make them feel like they are helping the organisation be successful. This may lead to new capabilities or skills through training and increasing knowledge and talents used on the job (Boxall & Purcell, 2008; Robbins & Barnwell, 2002; Robbins, Judge, Millett & Waters-Marsh, 2008).

Research suggests organisations that are able to focus on these three elements can achieve increased organisational performance in the form of increased and improved profitability, productivity, customer satisfaction, quality of deliverables and, lastly, growth of market share (Patel, Messersmith & Lepak, 2013).

With this in mind, if an organisation can effectively tap into the potential of the parts of the AMO model they can increase organisational performance through greater productivity; that said, one can assume that an individual would complete more tasks in a shorter timeframe with greater quality attached to those deliverables. Therefore, it is expected that a positive relationship should be ascertained between MBTI and Task Duration (see hypotheses in the "Introduction" section).

Hypothesis **H1f** was **partially supported**, whereas **H1g was fully supported**, and research question three and the appropriate linked hypotheses were **partially supported**. This thesis supports the argument that aspects of an individual's personality (the MBTI – 16) are vital for achieving better productivity outcomes in terms of Task Duration and Task Enjoyment.

Contribution of the research

This study has explored some previously researched topics surrounding HPWS, productivity and personality type, and none of these terms are new. However, this research has connected the three topics to analyse the relationships between the topics in question and the impact they have on each other; some of this research has provided great insights into the topics, adding depth to this literature. Most of the findings have been significant and proven; some of the relationships are significant and therefore provide real insights. However, potential learnings are always present, and as with these relationships future research options should explore other ways to review and analyse these topics.

Theoretical contributions

The distinctive contribution that this study offers is by analysing the role personality profiling plays in better understanding of the relationship between HPWS and productivity. In addition, the contribution extends into how aspects of personality impact each of the terms of HPWS and productivity separately and finally how aspects of personality impact each of the two attitudinal variables of AOC and OCB. It is important to note that no prior studies and research have done this in the context of the Australian Banking and Finance industry.

As discussed in Chapter 1, from an academic perspective, personality profiling (specifically MBTI) is an older mechanism for determining individual preferences and behaviours. Significant prior research has been completed reviewing MBTI along with a large amount of preferences, behaviours and intentions.

As detailed earlier, significant literature exists regarding personality profiling and the variety of tools and instruments available to the individual or organisation seeking more introspective information, and the MBTI instrument is one of the primary tools an individual can use to understand their behavioural preferences. The MBTI was the chosen tool for this research as a depth and abundance of available information and documentation exist on the tool; in addition, the instrument has been utilised for a significant time now, with further iterations on the tool being developed to ensure it remains current and usable with today's times and expectations (Quenk, 2009). The contribution relating to productivity is grounded in the operational definitions that have been designed to document the topic along with the in-depth literature review which highlighted that knowledge-based productivity is a complex and poorly investigated topic that requires future research and deliberation. This research has highlighted there are some significant relationships as outlined in the discussion above (Quenk, 2009).

Second, the term productivity is not a new one; productivity in the manufacturing or operational sense has been present for many years. Productivity was said to be grounded in the production environment, and it was understood in its simplest form to look at *items in* against *items out* in a factory-based setting. However, according to the literature in recent times productivity has been shifted out of the factory and has been applied to all companies or firms across every industry (George, Rowlands, Price & Maxey, 2005; Sye, 2004).

Literature argues that in an environment where a company is turning over items the translation is simple; there is a focus on the volume of *items in* against that of *items out* which depict how productive a workforce is. However, the real challenge comes when productivity is applied in knowledge-based environments with individuals whose skills are concentrated in academic or more knowledge-based roles; even today the translation isn't clear and there continues to be challenges with how to apply productivity in large knowledge-based companies, which was the focus of this research (Sye, 2004). The contribution of this research to productivity is providing robustness to the knowledge-based productivity space where literature and research is uncommon. It is recommended that future research continue to explore this area more to ensure the growth and evolution of the topics.

The final topic is HPWS, which is similar to productivity in the sense that there is significant research that has been conducted on the topic; however, more interestingly HPWS have not been examined with regard to productivity and personality testing.

There is a large volume of literature in this area; however, there are very few studies that have examined the impact of high-performance work systems on the company's employees, therefore necessitating further research on the topic. In addition, the main feature of high-performance work systems is understood as a change from a 'Tayloristic' work organisation to a more holistic work organisation (Boxall & Purcell, 2008; Robbins, Judge, Millett & Waters-Marsh, 2008).

This study took a closer look at the AMO model and discovered that abilities are the level of physical, financial, cognitive, emotional or social resources a person can apply to perform a specific task (Boxall & Purcell, 2008; Robbins, Judge, Millett & Waters-Marsh, 2008). Motivation is the needs and wants of an individual and how these may influence them to behave in a certain way; it is the encouragement for behaviour (Boxall & Purcell, 2008; Robbins, Judge, Millett & Waters-Marsh, 2008). Opportunities are the relevant restrictions, such as the availability of time and resources that also enable behaviour; employees seek opportunities to complete a task that will result in a benefit for them or for others (Boxall & Purcell, 2008; Robbins, Judge, Millett & Waters-Marsh, 2008).

Research has shown that an organisation that is able to focus on these three elements can achieve increased organisational performance in the form of increased and improved profitability, productivity, customer satisfaction, quality of deliverables and, lastly, growth of market share (Patel, Messersmith & Lepak, 2013).

Not only this study provide a massive contribution when considering these topics individually, but it also provides a contribution to a space that hasn't been researched before, and this takes us back to the research problem which is focused on understanding the influence an employee's personality type (MBTI type) has on their and the organisation's outcomes.

Implications for practice

Implications for practice revolve around four major themes. The first relates to the creation of a formal mechanism to define productivity experts using personality profiling; until this research there has been no way for the case organisation to identify their productivity experts within the organisation and bring them together as a unified community. This research has provided a formal tangible mechanism for this activity. The case organisation can now better manage their relationship with the individuals who are highly skilled in the productivity knowledge-based environment.

Second, this research has defined productivity expert's roles and responsibilities; until this research there was no way to define the tasks and activities, how often these are completed and the level of enjoyment associated with the activities. This research has now developed a framework around the formal definition of these activities which can be updated regularly as an inventory of information. This information can also be stored in a central location for all of the productivity workers, enabling organisation-wide access.

The third is the idea surrounding the talent pipeline as detailed in Chapter 2 within this research; as mentioned earlier talent recruitment has been managed in differing ways with little consistency and alignment across the organisation, and this research has now developed a formal mechanism for the management of talent. This includes the following formula: a hiring manager is recommended to look into three facets. The first is the MBTI profile of the individual which identifies MBTI profiles that are most suitable to productivity-based roles; second, their past performance as defined by their last two performance reviews and third, the interview process which explores the education, exposure and experience model. This threefold model can now be used to manage new recruits and succession planning for existing employees within the case organisation. This is now a concept that can be formalised into a set of tools hiring managers can download and utilise in the talent management process; future recommendations can be made to formally capture this information off the back of this study.

The fourth is the concept around the business understanding their competitive advantage and the best way to maximise their competitive advantage; as discussed at great length one of the key problems facing organisations today is not only how to remain locally or regionally competitive but also to become globally competitive (Argote & Ingram, 2000; Chowhan, 2016; Smith, Tucker & Pitt, 2011). It is important to study personality profiling, productivity and HPWS together to enable firms and companies to create and monitor their competitive advantage in a tangible manner in an ever-changing and highly competitive business market. This advantage can be the difference between success and failure especially in an industry like the one being analysed, the banking and financial services industry, where the product offerings are commodities. This is important because as a consumer, the products offered by all of the financial institutions are all the same, and there is little that really differentiates these organisations in this market; thus, a well-built and monitored personnel framework and talent pipeline can be the difference an organisation needs to be better than its competitors. That said, companies and firms should exhibit an interest in obtaining more information on competitive advantage.

Limitations and directions for future research

Despite making important contributions to the literature, as with all cases of research, there are limitations associated with this research. It is important to consider limitations with regard to this research for transparency and deliberation. The limitations take several different forms, with the first being that this research is conducted in only one case organisation; second, limitations regarding the use of surveys; third, a smaller sample size; fourth, self-reported results; fifth, that the sample considered mostly managers with little representation of upper management; and, lastly, environmental factors.

The first limitation is associated with this research being conducted in only one financial services organisation, and therefore the sample profile representing the information from only that organisation. This might limit the generalisability of the results beyond this organisation. Despite this potential issue, the sample did satisfy the theory development methodology of the study (Calder, Phillips & Tybout, 1981). The support for this study is that it is expected that productivity experts in similar organisations would make similar decisions, have similar preferences and perform in similar ways, therefore enabling the results to be generalised. Future directions for research could look at the conceptual model that was developed, and carrying out research in other organisations to understand whether behaviours and preferences are consistent with that of the current case organisation or whether they are representative of the Australian Banking and Finance industry; this view could take into consideration the local, regional and global markets to understand whether there are any differences in the way businesses operate on different scales, starting with a micro view and moving on to a macro perspective.

The second limitation is regarding the use of surveys. There is a potential issue of measurement error when researchers collect data using surveys as the primary method. For example, using a self-administered survey can cause error due to several factors, the first being question wording and interpretation, the order the questions are presented in, the timing of the survey, missing data and the response options of the questions (Bryman & Bell, 2011). In addition, there are concerns focused on inaccuracy of the responses which could, in turn, impact and affect data quality and subsequently data analysis (Bryman & Bell, 2011). That said, the survey was designed in the best possible manner to minimise and avoid these potential issues from being present, as outlined in Chapter 3 of this book. Future research could focus on using other techniques to gain insights into behaviours and preferences potentially in the form of focus groups or the use of a control environment to determine if there are any consistencies in the results or whether they are an actual representation of behaviours and preferences.

The third limitation is focused on the sample size, as a smaller sample size is said to limit the results and the usability of the results (Malhotra, 2010). This study had a sample size of 288 sample respondents overall post data cleaning and screening. Although the sample size satisfied the requirements of the assumptions and sample size requirements outlined in Chapter 3, there are still concerns regarding the ability of achieving a sample size that is representative of enough of the population. Future research should focus on obtaining a larger sample size to ensure that the results remain consistent (Malhotra, 2010).

Looking into the sample size further the analyses related to multiple regression satisfy the minimum requirements for the recommended approaches for the full sample used in the testing of the hypothesised relationships. However, in the further sub-group analysis, some of the MBTI – 4 base-pair models do not achieve the recommended minimums based on the formula approaches; while they do satisfy the recommended minimum ratios of the number of observations to predictors. The result is that the power of the affected regressions can be affected, with this attenuation also linked to a reduced ability to detect small effect sizes, i.e. small R^2 values (VanVoorhis & Morgan, 2007). Therefore, the limitation of a small sample size should be reviewed and future researchers should try to attract a larger sample size if they are using the same response characteristics.

Future research could simply look to increase the sample size associated with the research to determine if there are any changes in the profile or findings.

A further recommendation would be to investigate the talent pipeline further by profiling other roles within the banking and finance industry, potentially looking at more operational roles or more unique knowledge-based roles to determine if there are any relationships between MBTI preferences, productivity levels and HPWS associated with other roles.

The fourth limitation is based on the self-reported nature of the results of both the MBTI component and the survey for this research, meaning this survey might not be a complete representative of the productivity experts in the banking and finance industry in the Australian market. There is a possibility that the findings might be biased by reflecting subjective personal views and opinions about the experiences being investigated than the actual experiences (Bryman & Bell, 2011; Malhotra, 2010). It is determined that as the information was collected involuntarily from individuals who had been made aware of the anonymity of their participation the information collected is accurate and reflective of the situation at hand. Future research could look into the self-reported nature of the survey and whether that can be standardised or controlled in a more formal environment to eliminate bias of the individual responding, through, again, the use of focus groups or the development of a controlled environment.

The fifth limitation is based on the fact that the research results obtained were mostly based on managers in the case organisation and there were little responses from higher management, therefore meaning the information is a decent representative sample of managers within the organisation but the results may differ or vary with individuals who hold different roles and responsibilities within the organisation. There is a recommendation for future research to review different roles within the same location or context but looking at different individual role types and whether there are any major differences associated with more highly ranked individuals. Future research could analyse different role levels within the productivity expert space to determine whether there are any major differences in the roles and responsibilities they undertake; as the sample is representative of managers it would be useful to understand executive managers and general managers in the knowledge-based environment to understand whether there are any major differences. Further to this, no entry-level roles were included in the sample, that is, the individuals who were included in the research were all experts in the productivity field with considerable experience in their roles. Future research could expand the sample to determine whether there are differences between productivity experts and productivity 'beginners'; this would enable a comparison to be made to understand if there are any major differences between the different types of individuals.

The sixth and final limitation is focused on the environmental factors at play regarding the completion of the self-administered survey, as each individual would take the survey in a different location geographically at a different time within the day, on different days in the week and in a variety of different environments. Some sample respondents took the survey early in the morning before core business hours, during core business hours, later at night, working from home, working from one of their offices around Sydney, or nationally and internationally. Therefore, it would be safe to conclude that there would be a variety of environmental factors that may have impacted the individual participating in the study and this may have introduced some level of bias dependent on where they were. Again, future research could look at implementation of a different method to capture insights or development of a more controlled environment to eliminate bias from responses.

Conclusion

In closing this study offers insight into the relationship between employee personality type and employee and organisational outcomes. This study has expanded on prior topics in personality profiling, productivity and HPWS, adding theoretical findings and details on each topic individually and as a collective. While the majority of the hypotheses were supported, there were still some relationships that were only partially supported and these partially supported learnings could evolve into future research areas for researchers to develop and explore. Based on the results of this study, there is a need for further research on the mechanisms outlined to draw firm conclusions regarding the linkages between personality type and employee and organisational outcomes. Future research would benefit from a larger sample of respondents that would represent each of the 16 dimensions of the MBTI.

References

Andreeva, T., & Sergeeva, A., (2016). The More the Better....Or Is It? The Contradictory Effects of HR Practices on Knowledge Sharing Motivation and Behaviour. *Human Resource Management Journal*, 26(2), 151–171.

Argote, L., & Ingram, P., (2000). Knowledge Transfer: A Basis for Competitive Advantage in Firms. *Organisation Behavior and Human Decisions Processes*, 82(1), 150–169.

Barbuto, J.E., Fritz, S.M., Lim, J.C.S., & Xu, Y., (2008). Using the MBTI Instrument and the Motivation Sources Inventory to Test the Relationships between Jung's Psychological Types and Sources of Motivation. *Journal of Psychological Type,* Center for Applications of Psychological Type, 105, 1155–1158. Retrieved on 19 November 2017 from http://journals.sagepub.com/doi/pdf/10.2466/pms.105.4.1155-1158

Beltran-Martin, I., & Roca-Puig, V., (2013). Promoting Employee Flexibility Through HR Practices. *Human Resource Management,* Wiley Periodicals, 52(5), 645–674. Retrieved on 19 November 2017 from http://onlinelibrary.wiley.com/doi/10.1002/hrm.21556/abstract

Bong-Chang, Y., & Gurbaxani, V., (2012). Information Technology Outsourcing, Knowledge Transfer and Firm Productivity: An Empirical Analysis. *MIS Quarterly,* 36(4), 1043–1063.

Boult, M.J.L., Thompson, R.C., & Schaubhut, N.A., (2017). Well-Being and MBTI Personality Type in the Workplace. An International Comparison. CPP White Paper, Asia Pacific, 1–33.

Boxall, P., & Macky, K., (2009). Research and Theory on High Performance Work Systems: Progressing the High Involvement Stream. *Human Resource Management Journal,* Blackwell Publishing Ltd, 2(6), 177–185. Retrieved on 19 November 2017 from http://www.sciepub.com/reference/83569

Boxall, P., & Macky, K., (2014). High Involvement Work Processes, Work Intensification and Employee Well-Being. *Sage Publications*, 28(6) 3–23. Retrieved on 19 November 2017 from http://journals.sagepub.com/doi/abs/10.1177/0950017013512714

Boxall, P., & Purcell, J., (2008). *Strategy and Human Resource Management.* Second Edition. Palgrave Macmillan.

Bradley, J.H., & Hebert, F.J., (1997). The Effect of Personality Type on Team Performance. *Journal of Management Development*, 16(5), 337–353. Retrieved on 19 November 2017 from http://www.emeraldinsight.com/doi/abs/10.1108/02621719710174525

Bryman, A., & Bell, E., (2011). *Business Research Methods.* Third Edition. Oxford University Press.

Calder, B., Phillips, L., & Tybout, A., (1981). Designing Research for Application. *Journal of Consumer Research*, 8(2), 197–207.

Chesborough, S., (2005). Do Athletes Learn Differently? Implications for Improving the Learning Environments for Athletes. *Journal of Psychological Type.* Center for Applications of Psychological Type, 64(4), 31–40. Retrieved on 19 November 2017 from https://www.capt.org/research/psychological-type-journal.htm

Chowhan, J., (2016). Unpacking the Black Box: Understanding the Relationship between Strategy, HRM Practices, Innovation and Organisational Performance. *Human Resource Management Journal*, 26(2) 112–133. Retrieved on 19 November 2017 from http://onlinelibrary.wiley.com/doi/10.1111/1748-8583.12097/abstract

Deshpandé, R., (1983). Paradigms Lost: On Theory and Method in Research in Marketing, *Journal of Marketing*, 47(Fall), 101–110.

Drucker, P., (1999). Knowledge-Worker Productivity: The Biggest Challenge, *California Management Review* 41(2), 76–156.

Fahy, J., Farrelly, F., & Quester, P., (2002). Competitive Advantage through Sponsorship: A Conceptual Model and Research Propositions. *European Journal of Marketing*, 38(8), 1013–1030.

Francis, L.J., & Jones, S.H., (2000). Psychological Type and Happiness: A Study among Adult Churchgoers. *Journal of Psychological Type,* Center for Applications of Psychological Type, 54, 36–41. Retrieved on 19 November 2017 from https://www.capt.org/research/psychological-type-journal.htm

Genco, J.T., (2006). Relationships between MBTI Personality Types and Coping Styles: A Pilot Study. *Journal of Psychological Type,* Center for Applications of Psychological Type, 66(6). Retrieved on 19 November 2017 from https://www.capt.org/research/psychological-type-journal.htm

George, M.L., Rowlands, D., Price, M., & Maxey, J., (2005). *The Lean Six Sigma Pocket Toolbook.* McGraw-Hill.Herk, N.A., (2011). Ethnic and Gender Differences in Best-Fit Type. *Journal of Psychological Type,* Center for Applications of Psychological Type, 71(4). Retrieved on 19 November 2017 from https://www.capt.org/research/article/JPT_Vol71_01_1211.pdf

Hughes, J., (2007). *The Ability – Motivation – Opportunity Framework for Behavior Research in IS. 40th Hawaii International Conference on System Sciences,* 1–9.

Jabbour, L., (2013). Market Thickness, Sunk Costs, Productivity and the Outsourcing Decision: An Empirical Analysis of Manufacturing Firms in France. *Canadian Journal of Economics,* Canada, 46(1), 103–134. Retrieved on 19 November 2017 from http://onlinelibrary.wiley.com/doi/10.1111/caje.12007/abstract

Kasman, A., Kasman, S., Ayhan, D., & Torun, E., (2013). Total Factor Productivity and Convergence Evidence from Old and New EU Member Countries Banking Sectors. *Journal of Business Economics and Management,* 14(1), 13–35.

Macky, K., & Boxall, P., (2007). The Relationship between 'High Performance Work Practices' and Employee Attitudes: An Investigation of Additive and Interaction Effects. *The International Journal of Human Resource Management,* Australia, 18(4), 537–567. Retrieved on 19 November 2017 from http://www.tandfonline.com/doi/abs/10.1080/09585190601178745

Malhotra, N.K., (2010). Marketing Research: An Applied Orientation. Pearson United States of America, Prentice Hall, chapter 3 and 5.

Maruta, R., (2012). Maximising Knowledge Work Productivity: A Time Constrained and Activity Visualised PDCA Cycle. *Knowledge and Process Management,* 19(4), 203–214,. Retrieved on 19 November 2017 from http://onlinelibrary.wiley.com/doi/10.1002/kpm.1396/full

Matson, E., & Prusak, L., (2010). Boosting the Productivity of Knowledge Workers. *EBSCOhost,* 41(2) 79–94. Retrieved on 19 November 2017 from http://www.mckinsey.com/business-functions/organisation/our-insights/boosting-the-productivity-of-knowledge-workers

Mladkova, L., (2011). Knowledge Management for Knowledge Workers. *Electronic Journal of Knowledge Management,* 9(3) 260–267. Retrieved on 19 November 2017 from http://connection.ebscohost.com/c/articles/78296183/knowledge-management-knowledge-workers

Ones, D., & Dilchert, S., (2009). Personality Tests in the Workplace. In the black. *ABI/INFORM Complete,* 60(4), 995–1027. Retrieved on 19 November 2017 from http://onlinelibrary.wiley.com/doi/10.1111/j.1744-6570.2007.00099.x/abstract

Patel, P., Messersmith, J.G., & Lepak, D.P., (2013). Walking the Tightrope: An Assessment of the Relationship between High Performance Work Systems and Organisational Ambidexterity. *Academy of Management Journal,* 56(5), 1420–1442. Retrieved on 19 November 2017 from http://amj.aom.org/content/56/5/1420.abstract

Quenk, N.L., (2009). *Essentials of Myers Brigg's Type Indicator Assessment.* Second Edition. John Wiley & Sons.

Robbins, S.P., & Barnwell, N., (2002). *Organisational Theory.* Fourth Edition. Pearson Education Australia, Prentice Hall.

Robbins, S.P, Judge, T.A., Millett, B., & Waters-Marsh, T., (2008). *Organisational Behaviour.* Fifth Edition. Pearson Education Australia.

Smith, A., Tucker, M., & Pitt, M., (2011). Healthy, Productive Workplaces: Towards a Case for Interior Plantscaping. *Facilities,* 29(5/6), 209–223.

Stahl, G., Björkman, I., Farndale, E., Morris, S.S., Paauwe, J., Stiles, P., Trevor, J., & Wright, P., (2012). Six Principles of Effective Global Talent Management. *Sloan Management Review,* 53(2), 25–42.

Sye, G.L., (2004). *Process Mastery with Lean Six Sigma.* Second Edition. Soarent Vision.

VanVoorhis, C.R., & Morgan, L.B., (2007). Understanding Power and Rules of Thumb for Determining Sample Sizes. *Tutorials in Quantitative Methods for Psychology,* 3(2), 43–50.

Technical Appendix A

Appendix A1

This technical appendix provides details for the interested reader about the methodology and analytical procedures employed in this research. This appendix presents supplementary materials for the "Survey instrument development and measures used" section.

Appendix A – survey instrument

Q1 What is your job role?

1 Productivity Practitioner
2 Productivity Specialist
3 Productivity Analyst
4 Manager Productivity
5 Senior Manager Productivity
6 Executive Manager Productivity
7 Head of Productivity
8 Specialist Process Improvement
9 Manager Process Improvement
10 Executive Manager Process Improvement
11 Analyst
12 Manager
13 Executive Manager
14 Other ______________________________

Q3 How long have you been with the organisation?

1 0–5 years
2 6–10 years
3 11–15 years
4 16–20 years
5 21+ years

Q4 What is your employment status?

1 Full time
2 Part time
3 Casual
4 Other____

Q5 How many hours do you work per week?

1 1–10 hours
2 11–20 hours
3 21–30 hours
4 31–40 hours
5 41–50 hours
6 51+ hours

Q6 The (Lean Six Sigma) belt colour of the highest level that you hold is _______________.

1 Green Belt
2 Black Belt
3 Master Black Belt
4 Not applicable

Q7 What is the number of years of experience at that level (belt colour)?

1 Less than 1 year
2 1–2 years
3 3–5 years
4 6–10 years
5 11+ years
6 Not applicable

Q8 How many productivity projects do you have active right now?

1 0
2 1
3 2
4 3
5 4
6 5
7 6
8 7+

Q9 How many productivity projects have you completed in your career?

1 0
2 1
3 2–5
4 6–10
5 11–20
6 21+

Q10 In this section, we would like to know your **Myers-Briggs personality type**. If you know it, please select from one of the following types. If you have not done it before, please complete the test here: https://www.16personalities.com/free-personality-test before continuing. *The Myers-Briggs Type Indicator (MBTI) is an introspective, self-report questionnaire designed to indicate psychological preferences in how people perceive the world around them and make decisions. The MBTI works on the approach that there are four principal psychological functions by which humans experience the world – sensation, intuition, feeling, and thinking – and that one of these four functions is dominant for a person most of the time.*

Q11 Please select your MBTI 'type'.

1 INTJ
2 INTP
3 ENTJ
4 ENTP
5 INFJ
6 INFP
7 ENFJ
8 ENFP
9 ISTJ
10 SFJ
11 ESTJ
12 ESFJ
13 ISTP
14 ISFP
15 ESTP
16 ESFP

Q13 How Long Does It Take to Complete Each of the Tasks?	*Not Done (1)*	*A Month, Four Weeks or Longer (2)*	*Two to Three Weeks (3)*	*One Week (4)*	*Two to Four Days (5)*	*One Full Working Day (6)*	*Less Than One Full Working Day (7)*
1 Problem solving	○	○	○	○	○	○	○
2 Data collection	○	○	○	○	○	○	○
3 Data analysis	○	○	○	○	○	○	○
4 Root cause analysis	○	○	○	○	○	○	○
5 Solution generation	○	○	○	○	○	○	○
6 Project Management	○	○	○	○	○	○	○
7 Coaching	○	○	○	○	○	○	○
8 Mentoring	○	○	○	○	○	○	○
9 Training	○	○	○	○	○	○	○
10 Facilitation of productivity syllabus (e.g. Green Belt or Black Belt training)	○	○	○	○	○	○	○
11 Financial analysis (e.g. cost vs benefit)	○	○	○	○	○	○	○
12 Emails (responding to and sending)	o	o	o	o	o	o	o
13 Continuous improvement initiatives	○	○	○	○	○	○	○
14 Huddles	○	○	○	○	○	○	○
15 Visual management board creation and management	○	○	○	○	○	○	○
16 Development and maintenance of standard operating procedures	○	○	○	○	○	○	○
17 Process/ value stream mapping and maintenance	○	○	○	○	○	○	○
18 Completion of presentation packs (e.g. PowerPoint packs)	○	○	○	○	○	○	○

Q13 How Long Does It Take to Complete Each of the Tasks?	*Not Done (1)*	*A Month, Four Weeks or Longer (2)*	*Two to Three Weeks (3)*	*One Week (4)*	*Two to Four Days (5)*	*One Full Working Day (6)*	*Less Than One Full Working Day (7)*
19 Presentation of information to your leadership team/other management individuals	○	○	○	○	○	○	○
20 Tollgates (planned and ad hoc)	○	○	○	○	○	○	○
21 One-on-ones with your manager	○	○	○	○	○	○	○
22 One-on-ones with your direct reports	○	○	○	○	○	○	○
23 Workshopping	○	○	○	○	○	○	○
24 Preparation for workshopping	○	○	○	○	○	○	○
25 Preparation for meetings	○	○	○	○	○	○	○
26 Development discussions	○	○	○	○	○	○	○
27 Calendar maintenance	○	○	○	○	○	○	○
28 Governance forums	○	○	○	○	○	○	○
29 Dashboard/ metric creation and maintenance	○	○	○	○	○	○	○

Q14 Please Indicate Which of the Tasks You Enjoy Doing?	*Enjoy Doing (1)*	*Do Not Enjoy Doing (2)*	*Not Applicable (3)*
1 Problem solving	○	○	○
2 Data collection	○	○	○
3 Data analysis	○	○	○
4 Root cause analysis	○	○	○
5 Solution generation	○	○	○
6 Project management	○	○	○
7 Coaching	○	○	○
8 Mentoring	○	○	○
9 Training	○	○	○
10 Facilitation of productivity syllabus (e.g. Green Belt or Black Belt training)	○	○	○
11 Financial analysis (e.g. cost vs benefit)	○	○	○
12 Emails (responding to and sending)	○	○	○
13 Continuous improvement initiatives	○	○	○
14 Huddles	○	○	○
15 Visual management board creation and management	○	○	○
16 Development and maintenance of standard operating procedures	○	○	○

	Q14 Please Indicate Which of the Tasks You Enjoy Doing?	*Enjoy Doing (1)*	*Do Not Enjoy Doing (2)*	*Not Applicable (3)*
17	Process/value stream mapping and maintenance	○	○	○
18	Completion of presentation packs (e.g. PowerPoint packs)	○	○	○
19	Presentation of information to your leadership team/other management individuals	○	○	○
20	Tollgates (planned and ad hoc)	○	○	○
21	One-on-ones with your manager	○	○	○
22	One-on-ones with your direct reports	○	○	○
23	Workshopping	○	○	○
24	Preparation for workshopping	○	○	○
25	Preparation for meetings	○	○	○
26	Development discussions	○	○	○
27	Calendar maintenance	○	○	○
28	Governance forums	○	○	○
29	Dashboard/metric creation and maintenance	○	○	○

Q15 Please answer the following questions about the workplace systems in your organisation taking into consideration the following statements.

1 = Strongly disagree
2 = Disagree
3 = Neither agree or disagree
4 = Agree
5 = Strongly agree

		1 = Strongly Disagree	*2 = Disagree*	*3 = Neither Agree or Disagree*	*4 = Agree*	*5 = Strongly Agree*
1	Pay raises are based on performance.	○	○	○	○	○
2	Associates in this job are allowed to make important work-related decisions such as how the work is done or implement new ideas.	○	○	○	○	○
3	The company hires only the very best people for this job.	○	○	○	○	○
4	I am willing to work harder to help this company succeed.	○	○	○	○	○
5	I encourage others to try new and effective ways of doing their job.	○	○	○	○	○

		1 = Strongly Disagree	*2 = Disagree*	*3 = Neither Agree or Disagree*	*4 = Agree*	*5 = Strongly Agree*
6	I willingly share my expertise with my co-workers.	○	○	○	○	○
7	Great effort is taken to select the right person for the job.	○	○	○	○	○
8	Long-term employee potential is empathised.	○	○	○	○	○
9	Performance is more often measured with objective quantifiable results.	○	○	○	○	○
10	Performance appraisals emphasis long-term and group-based achievement.	○	○	○	○	○
11	Job security is almost guaranteed to employees.	○	○	○	○	○
12	Individuals in this job receive bonuses based on the profit of the organisation.	○	○	○	○	○
13	Employees are paid accordingly based on their individual/group performance.	○	○	○	○	○
14	Employees are provided the opportunity to suggest improvements in the way things are done.	○	○	○	○	○

Appendix A2: time dimensions and sample size

This appendix presents supplementary materials for the "The design for this research" section, focusing on time dimensions and sample size. Similar to other studies completed on these topics (Gupta & Sahu, 2013; Shaker & Basem, 2010), this study adopted a cross-sectional design framework and collected data from the sample population at a single point in time (Sekaran & Bougie, 2013; Zikmund et al., 2017). This was due to time-and-resource constraints, along with access restrictions imposed by Organisation X, whereby only one data-collection round was allowed.

Typically, the sample size needs to consider the objective of the research, the extent of precision needed, the acceptable risk in predicting that level of precision, the amount of variability in the population, cost and time constraints and the overall population itself (Bryman & Bell, 2011; Malhotra, 2010; Sekaran & Bougie, 2013; Zikmund et al., 2017). Based on the expected interest in the research topic by the target population, a conservative response rate of 25% was anticipated to yield around 200 responses. A sample of 200 would be sizeable enough to provide a suitable representation of the target population the sample respondents were drawn from, as well as sufficiently large for analysis purposes.

With regard to ANOVA (analysis of variance), the sample size meets the basic requirements for conducting one-way ANOVA for the MBTI – 16 as the independent variable. Using G*Power 3.1.9.6 (Faul et al., 2007), a total sample size of $n = 192$ was calculated. As the usable sample across all one-way ANOVA tests exceeded 192, this requirement was satisfied.[1]

The sample size also needed to consider the multiple-regression analyses used in this research. There are several approaches for arriving at a minimum recommended sample size for regression analysis. In the first approach, the recommended minimum sample size is 50 or higher (VanVoorhis & Morgan, 2007). The second approach is to use at least five times more cases than independent variables, with a preferred ratio of 10–20 times more cases than the number of independent variables (Coakes, 2013; Malhotra, 2010). In the regression analysis conducted for this study, the number of independent variables (which includes both the focal variables plus the two controls of age and gender) ranged from four to seven, with the minimum sample sizes being 53 (for the sub-group, moderating analysis) to 191 (MBTI – four base-pair analysis), yielding a minimum ratio of 10.6 for the sub-group, moderating analysis and 31.8 for the MBTI – Four base-pair analysis (Coakes, 2013; Malhotra, 2010).

The third approach for the minimum required regression sample size uses the formulae recommended by Tabachnick and Fidell (2013) and VanVoorhis and Morgan (2007) for testing (1) the overall regression model and (2) the individual predictors in the regression model. (See Technical Appendix A for the calculations based on the formulae.) Following Tabachnick and Fidell (2013), the minimum sample size using this approach ranges from 82 to 106 for testing the overall model and from 108 to 111 for testing the individual predictors in the regression model. Following VanVoorhis and Morgan (2007), the minimum sample size ranges from 54 to 55 for the regression models with four or five independent variables.

In summary, the sample size in the regression analyses satisfies the minimum requirements for all recommended approaches for the full sample used in testing the hypothesised relationships. In the further sub-group analysis, some of the MBTI – Four base-pair models do not achieve the recommended minimums based on the formulae approaches; however, they do satisfy the recommended minimum ratios of the number of observations to predictors. The result is that the power of the affected regressions can be affected, with this attenuation also linked to a reduced ability to detect small effect sizes, i.e. small R^2 values (VanVoorhis & Morgan, 2007).

Regression sample size calculations

This appendix presents supplementary materials for the "Data screening and cleaning" section.

In the regression analysis conducted for this study, the number of independent variables (which includes both the focal variables plus the two controls of age and gender) ranged from four to seven, with the minimum sample sizes being 53 (for the sub-group, moderating analysis) to 192 (MBTI – Four base-pair analysis), yielding a minimum ratio of 10.6 for the sub-group, moderating analysis and 32 for the MBTI – Four base-pair analysis (Coakes, 2013; Malhotra, 2010).

The third approach for the minimum required regression sample size (N) uses the formulae recommended by Tabachnick and Fidell (2013) for testing (1) the overall regression model and (2) the individual predictors in the regression model. First, to test the overall regression model is the formula, $N \geq 50 + 8(m)$, and second, to test the individual predictors in the model is the formula, $N > 104 + m$, where m = the number of independent variables. Alternatively, for models with five or fewer independent variables, $N > m + 50$ is also a recommendation (cf. VanVoorhis & Morgan, 2007). The number of predictors in the regression models varies from four to seven. Using these formulae yields the following.

Overall model: $N \geq 50 + 8(4) = 50 + 32 = 82$
Individual predictors: $N > 104 + 4 = 108$
Overall model: $N \geq 50 + 8(7) = 50 + 56 = 106$
Individual predictors: $N > 104 + 7 = 111$
$N > 50 + 4 = 54$
$N > 50 + 5 = 55$

Therefore, following Tabachnick and Fidell (2013), the minimum sample size using this approach ranges from 82 to 106, for testing the overall model, and from 108 to 111 for testing the individual predictors in the regression model. Following VanVoorhis and Morgan (2007), the minimum sample size ranges from 54 to 55 for the regression models with four or five independent variables.

Appendix A3: data screening and cleaning procedure

This appendix presents supplementary materials for the "Data screening and cleaning" section. The data from the 288 responses was input into SPSS v24 for review and preliminary analysis. To screen the data, incompletes were removed along with responses completed so quickly as to indicate inadequate time for considered reading of the survey questions, resulting in a usable sample of 263 responses. A one-way ANOVA check of the remaining sample showed no significant differences amongst duration groups (coded into ten groups based on quickness of completion) for any of the focal constructs of interest ($p \geq 0.377$).

Next a respondent ID was assigned to each of the responses. For questions with options for an open-ended response, such as the individual's role/title, open-ended answers were reviewed and assigned to one of the existing categories as appropriate. For example, one participant reported that their job role was as a 'Process Improvement Consultant', which was then coded as 'Specialist Process Improvement'. Following this, to allow analysis to be undertaken relating to roles and responsibilities, each participant was subsequently classified into having (1) a Productivity or Non-productivity–based role and (2) a Junior or Senior role based on the titles presented in the survey. Additionally, the data was cleaned to show how individuals felt about productivity-related tasks, the findings displayed that most of the activities were deemed enjoyable, there were no activities or tasks that were not enjoyed by the sample respondents.

Next, further recoding was undertaken to disaggregate the combined, four-character MBTI personality profile sample respondents reported (with 16 MBTI profiles possible, MBTI – 16 hereafter) into four new dichotomous variables representing the four MBTI – four base pairs (i.e. Introverted vs Extroverted, Sensing vs Intuition, Feeling vs Thinking, Perceiving vs Judging). For example, a participant indicating that their combined MBTI profile was 'INFP' would then be coded as being Introverted-Intuition-Feeling-Perceiving in the four new variables.

Finally, the data was reviewed to determine whether the dependent variables (e.g. affective commitment, organisation citizenship behaviours) were deemed to be normally distributed or not, as this is typically a requirement for the parametric techniques used (*t*-test, ANOVA, multiple regression). Using basic descriptive statistics and the SPSS Explore procedure suggested that the distribution of the data was approximately normal and suitable for the planned analysis techniques.

Note

1 The G*Power settings used were as follows: ANOVA: Fixed effects, omnibus, one-way test, effect size $f = 0.40$, α error probability = 0.05, Power ($1-\beta$) error probability = 0.95 and number of groups = 16.

References

Gupta, A., & Sahu, G., (2013). Factors Influencing Adoption of Relationship Marketing Practices for Overall Growth of Firm an ISM-Based Model Validation. *International Journal of Electronic Customer Relationship Management*, 7(1) 21–44.

Malhotra, N. K., (2010), *Marketing Research: An Applied Orientation*. Pearson United States of America, Prentice Hall chapter 3 and 5.

Shaker, T.I. & Basem, Y.A., (2010). Relationship marketing and organizational performance indicators. *European Journal of Social Sciences*, 12, 545–557.

Sekaran, U., & Bougie, R., (2013). *Research Methods for Business: A Skill Building Approach*. Sixth Edition. Wiley & Sons Ltd.

Bryman, A., & Bell, E., (2011). *Business Research Methods.* Third Edition. Oxford University Press.

Zikmund, W., D'Alessandro, S., Winzar, H., Lowe, B., & Babin, B., (2017). *Marketing Research.* 4th Asia-Pacific Edition. Cengage Learning Australia.

Faul, F., Erdfelder, E., Lang, A.-G., & Buchner, A., (2007). G*Power 3: A Flexible Statistical Power Analysis Program for the Social, Behavioral, and Biomedical Sciences. *Behavior Research Methods*, 39, 175–191. Retrieved from https://www.psychologie.hhu.de/arbeitsgruppen/allgemeine-psychologie-und-arbeitspsychologie/gpower.html

VanVoorhis, C.R., & Morgan, L.B., (2007). Understanding Power and Rules of Thumb for Determining Sample Sizes. *Tutorials in Quantitative Methods for Psychology*, 3(2), 43–50.

Coakes, S., (2013). *SPSS: Analysis without Anguish version 12.0 for Windows.* John Wiley & Sons.

Tabachnick, B.G., & Fidell, L.S., (2007). *Using Multivariate Statistics.* Fifth Edition. Pearson Education.

Technical Appendix B

Appendix Bl: preliminary analysis and assumption checking

This appendix presents supplementary materials for the "Preliminary analysis and assumption checking" section. Upon completion of screening and cleaning of the data, a series of preliminary data-screening analyses were conducted using SPSS v24 before moving any further with the data analysis. First, basic checks were undertaken on the data, which included reviewing the data to ensure the responses were complete and captured correctly in the raw data file, and the data was sorted by 'time to complete', which enabled a view of those individuals who had taken considerably less time and those who took a considerably longer time to complete the survey. Those that were deemed too fast in completion were removed; 'too fast' was determined through completing the survey using a 'test' identifier, who completed the survey as fast as possible with as little error as possible. It was determined that any responses completed in 75 seconds or less were too fast for the responses to be accurate; therefore, these responses were removed from the sample. All other incomplete sample respondents who dropped out without providing responses past section B of the survey (at or around the MBTI question) were also removed, as they also provided little to no real substance.

Second, before assessing the proposed model, a number of preliminary checks were conducted including reliability analysis (Cronbach's alpha, composite reliability) and construct-validity tests (average variance extracted, or AVE), along with assumption checking for each technique used (e.g. normality checks).

Reliability

To ensure that the instruments utilised were able to measure what they were intended to measure, a focus on minimum error and with as much reliability as possible, tests were used to check the internal consistency of the indicators. Reliability, simply put, is the extent to which measures are free from random error (Malhotra, 2010; Sekaran & Bougie, 2013). The reliability checks were initially completed using coefficient alpha, otherwise known as Cronbach's alpha, which looks at the average of all possible split-half coefficients resulting from different ways of splitting the scale items (Malhotra, 2010). The Cronbach's alpha tests were conducted using SPSS v24. When the value of Cronbach's alpha is

Table B1 Reliability

Construct	*Number of Items*	*Cronbach's Alpha (α)*	*Composite Reliability (CR)*
Organisational citizenship behaviour	2	0.744	0.89
Ability	2	0.752	0.89
Opportunity	2	0.654	0.86
Motivation	5	0.794	0.86

larger than 0.70, the measurement items are considered to be reliable (Malhotra, 2010). The Cronbach's alpha values are summarised in Table 4.2, and they came in at 0.744 or higher for three of the reflective multi-item scales, with the fourth (Opportunity) close at 0.654. Cronbach's alpha is a measure of internal consistency; it shows how closely related items are in a set of data. Cronbach's alpha is generally used to measure the reliability of a scale and it can show the dimensions of a specific measure (Coakes, 2013).

Cronbach's alpha can be low when there are a smaller number of items in a scale, where inter-item correlations of 0.2–0.4 are acceptable (Pallant, 2007). As the inter-item correlation for the Opportunity items was 0.497, this suggests an acceptable level for the two-item Opportunity scale. Therefore, the overall Cronbach's alpha result for the four reflective scales below was deemed an acceptable level, indicating good reliability and consistency; this is outlined in Table B1 above.

Composite reliability was also used to examine the reliability of the reflective scales. In exploratory research, composite-reliability values of 0.60–0.70 are acceptable, with values ranging from 0.70 to 0.90 deemed satisfactory for more advanced research (Nunnally & Bernstein, 1994). SPSS does not feature a routine to determine composite reliability; therefore, the composite-reliability scores were calculated in Excel based on the factor loadings of each item (see Table B2). The composite-reliability scores (see Table B1) were greater than 0.85 for the reflective constructs, thus suggesting good reliability. In summary, the Cronbach's alpha and composite-reliability results collectively suggest that the reliability of the multi-item reflective constructs used in this research has been established.

Construct validity

Construct validity investigates the question of what construct or characteristic the scale is measuring; when assessing construct validity, the researcher looks to answer theoretical questions about why the scale works and what deductions can be made concerning the underlying theory (Malhotra, 2010). To establish construct validity of this research, the items for each multi-item scale were examined regarding the inter-item correlation and item-total scale correlation to each other for each construct, establishing that these measured the construct distinctly from other constructs (Bryman & Bell, 2011; Malhotra, 2010).

To evaluate the convergent validity of the latent reflective constructs, factor analysis was used to generate factor loadings of the indicators for each reflective construct, and the average variance extracted (AVE) for each reflective construct was then computed. The AVE measures the amount of variance that is captured by a construct in relation to the volume of variance due to measurement error (Malhotra, 2010; O'Leary, 2004). The AVE was calculated for Motivation, Opportunity, Ability and Organisation Citizenship Behaviour.

To generate the factor loadings used for calculating the AVE, each of the reflective multi-item constructs was assessed individually using a principal-component factor analysis in SPSS. The results (see Table B2) showed that each construct returned one clean factor with an eigenvalue greater than 1.0, and with all but one item loading strongly at 0.699 or higher. The one weak item was the job-security item for Motivation, which had a loading of 0.366. As the AVE for Motivation fell just short of the 0.50 threshold with this item in the scale (at 0.474), and in consideration of the weaker inter-item correlations with the other items in the scale, this item was dropped from the scale.

This resulted in all items for the reflective constructs satisfying the recommended benchmark of 0.50 or higher for factor loadings (Coakes, 2013; Malhotra, 2010), as well as the AVE for these constructs exceeding the recommended 0.5 threshold (Fornell & Larker, 1981). These results indicate a satisfactory convergent validity, meaning the latent constructs account for between 55% and 80% of the variance in the observed variables (Malhotra, 2010; Robbins & Barnwell, 2002); this is detailed in Table B2 below.

Table B2 Factor Loadings and Average Variance Extracted (AVE)

Statement	*Factor Loading*
Organisational Citizenship Behaviour, AVE = 0.80	
I encourage others to try new and effective ways of doing their job.	0.89
I willingly share my expertise with my co-workers.	0.89
Ability, AVE = 0.80	
Great effort is taken to select the right person for the job.	0.90
The company hires only the very best people for this job.	0.90
Opportunity, AVE = 0.75	
Employees are provided the opportunity to suggest improvements in the way things are done.	0.87
Associates in this job are allowed to make important work-related decisions such as how the work is done or implement new ideas.	0.87
Motivation, AVE = 0.55	
Employees are paid accordingly based on their individual/group performance.	0.80
Performance appraisals emphasise long-term and group-based achievement.	0.75
Pay raises are based on performance.	0.72
Performance is more often measured with objective, quantifiable results.	0.72
Individuals in this job receive bonuses based on the profit of the organisation.	0.72
Job security is almost guaranteed to employees.*	–

Note: * = item dropped during reliability and validity checks; AVE = average variance extracted.

Normality assumption checks

A normality assessment of the interval-scaled data was completed as part of the basic assumption checking for multiple regression and ANOVA. Normality checking included visual examination as well as establishing that the differences among the obtained and predicted construct scores were normally distributed (Malhotra, 2010; Sekaran & Bougie, 2013). Summated means for each multi-item scale (i.e. the average of the scale items) were assessed for normality using the Explore feature in SPSS.

Multiple regression assumption checks

Multiple regression has a number of assumptions that need to be fulfilled when using it as a statistical analysis technique (Coakes, 2013; Malhotra, 2010). These assumptions include ratio of cases to the independent variables, outliers, multicollinearity and singularity and, lastly, the normality, linearity, homoscedasticity and independence of residuals (Coakes, 2013; Malhotra, 2010).

The number of cases required can vary due to the type of regression model that will be used (Coates, 2013; Malhotra, 2010). The minimum of cases is at least five times more cases than independent variables, with a preferred ratio of 10–20 times more cases than the number of independent variables (Coates, 2013; Malhotra, 2010). In the regression analysis conducted for this study, the number of independent variables ranged from a maximum of five (for the sub-group analysis) to six (for the influence of the MBTI – 4 base pairs), with minimum sample sizes being 53 (for the sub-group analysis) to 192 (MBTI – 4 base-pair analysis), yielding a minimum ratio of 10.6 for the sub-group analysis and 32 for the MBTI – 4 base-pair analysis. Therefore, this assumption was satisfied (Coates, 2013; Malhotra, 2010; VanVoorhis & Morgan, 2007). Regarding the formula approaches for sample size, the sample size satisfies the minimum requirements for all recommended approaches for the full sample used in testing the hypothesised relationships. However, some of the MBTI – 4 base-pair models do not achieve the recommended minimums in the further sub-group analysis. (The potential limitations of this are discussed in Chapter 5, "Contribution of the research" section.)

Extreme outliers have a considerable impact on the regression solution and should be deleted or modified to reduce their influence (Coates, 2013; Malhotra, 2010). In the multiple regression analysis, the standardised residuals were evaluated, with outliers greater than ±3 standard deviations evaluated for removal with the aim of improving model fit. The decision to remove the outliers was made with extreme care to ensure deletion of results did not generate additional outlying cases in the data (Coates, 2013; Malhotra, 2010).

Multicollinearity assesses the high correlations among the independent variables, whereas singularity occurs when there are perfect correlations among independent variables. Multicollinearity problems impact how to understand the relationships between the IVs and DVs, and were evaluated by assessing

Table B3 Construct Correlation Matrix

Variable	*Mean*	*SD*	*1.*	*2.*	*3.*	*4.*	*5.*	*6.*	*7.*	*8.*	*9.*	*10.*	*11.*	*12.*	*13.*
1 Motivation	3.30	0.80	1												
2 Ability	3.32	0.90	0.44**	1											
3 Opportunity	3.99	0.73	0.48**	0.37***	1										
4 AOC	4.20	0.75	0.23***	0.29***	0.38***	1									
5 OCB	4.51	0.59	0.30***	0.25***	0.49***	0.56***	1								
6 Task Duration	3.63	1.08	0.04	0.16*	0.14*	0.02	0.14*	1							
7 Task Enjoyment	19.87	4.77	0.20**	0.22***	0.14*	0.09	0.09	0.26***	1						
8 Introvert vs Extrovert	0.60	0.49	0.19**	0.11#	0.06	0.04	0.10#	0.10#	0.25***	1					
9 Intuition vs Sensing	0.66	0.48	0.05	0.02	−0.02	0.05	0.03	0.08	0.002	0.13*	1				
10 Feeling vs Thinking	0.32	0.47	−0.21**	−0.20**	−0.20**	−0.11#	−0.09#	0.05	−0.04	−0.21***	−0.21***	1			
11 Perceiving vs Judging	0.26	0.44	0.02	0.01	0.07	0.05	−0.01	0.12^	−0.09	0.05	−0.21***	0.03	1		
12 Age	3.02	0.89	−0.08	−0.01	0.10#	0.05	0.08	−0.03	0.06	0.10#	0.02	−0.03	−0.001	1	
13 Gender	1.55	0.50	−0.01	0.06	−0.03	−0.12^	−0.16*	−0.04	0.03	−0.02	0.06	−0.26**	−0.14*	0.04	1

Note: Significance (two-tailed): # = $p \leq 0.20$, ^ = $p \leq 0.10$, * = $p \leq 0.05$ ** = $p \leq 0.01$, *** = $p \leq 0.001$.
Hard/soft and routine/non-routine are subsets of the main variables in this table and therefore excluded from the table above.

the construct-correlation matrix, and the variance inflation factor (VIF) scores (Coates, 2013; Malhotra, 2010). Most correlations were below 0.50 and all below 0.65. The VIF scores were 2.1 or smaller in size, well below the recommended more stringent threshold of 5 (Hair et al., 2014). This suggests that multicollinearity was not present (Coates, 2013; Malhotra, 2010). A construct correlation matrix was completed that showed correlation values no greater than 0.56 (see Table B3), which also supports a lack of multicollinearity.

An assessment of residual scatterplots allows the final assumptions to be examined (Coates, 2013; Malhotra, 2010). It is expected that the differences between the obtained and predicted dependent variable scores are normally distributed. Further, it is assumed that the residuals have a linear relationship with the predicted dependent variable scores and that the variance of the residuals is the same for all predicted scores (Coates, 2013; Malhotra, 2010). Normal p-plots of the standardised regression residuals and bivariate scatter plots were assessed for linear relationships. The evaluation of the standardised residual plots suggested that these assumptions have been successfully satisfied (Coates, 2013; Malhotra, 2010).

ANOVA assumption checking

ANOVA assumption checking is concerned with five major themes, the first being population normality, whereby the sample as drawn should be normal regarding skewness, with the Explore procedure used to ensure this assumption was met (Coakes, 2013). In addition, the test of homogeneity of variance, whereby the scores in each group should have homogeneous variances, was carried out. Levene's test was used to determine if the variances were equal, with the relevant test statistic used accordingly (Coakes, 2013). Second, as significant outliers can have a disproportionate effect on the ANOVA results (Laerd Statistics, 2017), using the Explore procedure in SPSS, boxplots were used to identify potential outliers, with those cases being more than 1.5 box-lengths from the edge of the box evaluated for omission (Laerd Statistics, 2017). The third theme relates to the type of variable, in that a continuous dependent variable (i.e. interval or ratio scaled) for the dependent variable was used in the ANOVA analysis. Fourth, the independent variable was categorical with two or more independent groups. Finally, as the fifth theme, there was an independence of observations.

Chi-square assumption checking

There are two different types of chi-square tests, the first of which is the chi-square test for the goodness of fit, which is used when the analysis of a single categorical variable is required. The other test is the chi-square test for independence or relatedness, which applies to the analysis of the relationship between two categorical variables (Coakes, 2013; Kumar & Weber, 2005). There are three assumptions that underpin the chi-square, the first of which relates to observations being randomly sampled from the population of all possible observations. The second assumption is related to the independence of observations, which means each observation should be generated by a different subject and no subject is counted twice (Coakes, 2013). A limitation of the chi-square analysis technique is that the chi-square is sensitive to very small or very large data sets and hence should be treated with care in such instances to avoid issues with data interpretation (Coakes, 2013).

Appendix B2: productivity tasks and their descriptions

This appendix presents supplementary materials for the "Personality profiling – MBTI" section and contains a description of key productivity tasks.

- **Problem solving:** this refers to solving issues/concerns/problems that are either found or presented to you. Problem solving refers to problems of all sizes (e.g. small to large).
- **Data collection:** the collection/collation of data on projects or initiatives.
- **Data analysis:** this refers to dissecting and analysing the data to arrive at conclusions after you have collected your data.
- **Root cause analysis:** identifying pain points and completing root cause analysis on them to arrive at the root cause of the problem. This can be done using 5 whys, fishbone, FMEA and other tools.
- **Solution generation:** once root causes are identified solutions are generated to solve the problem.
- **Project management:** the process of managing projects from inception to conclusion.
- **Coaching:** coaching of Green Belts, Black Belts or MBBs while projects are underway
- **Mentoring:** refers to one-on-one sessions you complete in a mentoring environment with another individual.
- **Training:** any formal programs you facilitate or attend.
- **Facilitation of productivity syllabus** (e.g. Green belt and black belt training): formal training of the productivity syllabus, for example Lean Six Sigma, Productivity Essentials, The Four Productivity Habits, Green Belt, Black Belt or Master Black Belts.
- **Financial analysis** (e.g. cost vs benefit): financial analysis of costs and benefits relating to projects and initiatives.
- **Emails:** (responding to and sending) email management, monitoring your inbox and responding to work-related emails.
- **Continuous improvement initiatives:** from the exceptionally small to the large continuous improvement initiatives. Managing the CI initiatives of your team or project.

- **Huddles:** physical huddles where your team comes together to review progress, discuss improvement opportunities and assign future work.
- **Visual management board creation and management:** the development and ongoing management of visual management boards for your team or project.
- **Development and maintenance of SOPs:** creation and ongoing management of SOPs relating to your team or project.
- **Process/VSM mapping and maintenance:** process mapping or VSM mapping to understand and manage processes.
- **Completion of presentation packs** (e.g. PowerPoint packs): time spent working on presentations packs relating to BAU or projects.
- **Presentation of information** (to your LT/Other management individuals): time spent presenting information to leadership teams or other Senior groups across the bank.
- **Tollgates (planned and ad hoc):** formal tollgates relating to your projects at define, measure, analyse, improve or control.
- **One-on-ones with your manager:** time spent in 1-1s with your manager discussing your performance or work-related priorities.
- **One-on-ones with your direct reports:** time spent in 1-1 environments with direct reports.
- **Workshopping**: formal or informal workshops relating to projects or problems.
- **Preparation for workshopping:** time spent preparing for workshop.
- **Preparation for meetings:** time spent preparing for daily meetings.
- **Development discussions:** any other development discussions.
- **Calendar maintenance:** time spent managing your day/calendar appointments.
- **Governance forums:** formal management of governance forums.
- **Dashboard/metric creation and maintenance:** creation and ongoing management of dashboard for business or project consumption.

Appendix B3: further analysis – binomial tests

This appendix presents supplementary materials for the "Personality profiling – MBTI" section. To understand the MBTI profiles better, a series of binomial tests were conducted to analyse the MBTI – 4 base pairs by assessing whether the observed proportions differed from a specification of equal proportions (i.e. a 50/50 split for each base pair). The results showed that the actual proportion for each base pair (see Table B4) differed significantly from the expected 50/50 split ($n = 253$, $p \leq 0.002$). This suggests that the greater proportions of Extrovert (60%), Sensing (66%), Feeling (68%) and Judging (74%) observed in the sample were not what would be expected in a random event (i.e. a 50% occurrence).

Table B4 Binomial Test – MBTI – 4 Base Pairs

Category	*Expected Proportion*	*Actual Proportion*	p-*Value*
Introvert	0.50	0.40	0.002
Extrovert	0.50	0.60	
Intuition	0.50	0.34	0.000
Sensing	0.50	0.66	
Thinking	0.50	0.32	0.000
Feeling	0.50	0.68	
Judging	0.50	0.74	0.000
Perceiving	0.50	0.26	

Notes: N = 253; p-values ≤ 0.05 are statistically significant.

Appendix B4: ANOVA – influence of MBTI – 16 on AMO

This appendix presents supplementary materials for the "ANOVA – influence of MBTI – 16 on AMO" section. A one-way ANOVA was used to examine the influence of MBTI – 16 profile as the IV (independent variable) and HPWS (Ability, Motivation and Opportunity scales) as the DVs. To conduct the analysis, the one-way ANOVA routine in SPSS was used in preference to the General Linear Model (GLM) – Univariate Routine in SPSS, due to its ability to conduct non-equal variance tests (Laerd Statistics, 2017). The GLM Routine was run to generate the partial eta squared (η^2) statistic for how well the MBTI – 16 factor explained variability in the dependent variable.

MBTI – 16 on Motivation

Regarding Motivation, five potential outliers were identified in the starting pool of sample respondents: one each for ENTP (ID = 233) and ISFJ (ID = 99) and three for ESFJ (IDs = 129, 248, 17). In the first round, three sample respondents (IDs = 233, 99, 17) were omitted, with two outliers remaining for ESFJ when the analysis was rerun (IDs = 129, 248). ID = 248 was omitted and the analysis rerun, with ID = 129 still showing as an outlier and thus omitted, with a final check showing no remaining outliers ($n = 203$).

The one-way ANOVA test was then run on this reduced group. There was homogeneity of variances, as assessed by Levene's test for equality of variances ($p = 0.116$). A significant ANOVA result was found, with Motivation statistically significantly different for different MBTI – 16 groups ($n = 203$), $F(15, 187) = 2.189$, $p = 0.008$, partial eta squared (η^2) = 0.149.[1] This result suggests at least one of the MBTI – 16 group means was different from the others, with the MBTI – 16 factor explaining 14.9 per cent of the variability in Motivation for the sample, which would be considered a large effect size (Cohen, 1988).[2]

Follow-up pairwise comparisons were then run to identify where differences existed. As the homogeneity-of-variances assumption was not violated, the Tukey's honestly significant difference (HSD) post hoc test was used. There was an increase in the mean Motivation score from the MBTI – 16 INTP group (M = 2.60, SD = 1.012) to the ISFP group (M = 3.8, SD = 0.632), with a mean increase of 1.20 (SE = 0.467), which was not statistically significant (p = 0.462) with the Tukey HSD multiple-comparison correction applied.[3]

The formula for the number of pairwise comparisons is k*(k – 1)/2 (Malhotra, 2010). As the number of unique pairwise tests was 120 in this analysis (i.e. 120 = [16*(16 – 1)]/2), any multiple-correction factor applied would make it difficult to achieve significance. Therefore, a planned contrast was run comparing the highest and lowest Motivation scores. The Motivation score was statistically significantly higher in the ISFP group (M = 3.80, SD = 0.632) compared to the INTP group (M = 2.60, SD = 1.012), with a mean increase of 1.2 (SE = 0.467), p = 0.011 (t = 2.572, df = 187, equal variances assumed).

MBTI – 16 on Opportunity

Regarding Opportunity, six potential outliers were identified in the starting pool of sample respondents: one each for ENTP (ID = 238), ENFJ (ID = 178), ENFP (ID = 240), ESFP (ID = 183) and two for INTJ (IDs = 59, 157 [extreme]). Five outliers were omitted in the first round, with one still remaining for INTJ, and all six were omitted in the second round, showing no remaining outliers.

The one-way ANOVA test was then run on this reduced group. There was a lack of homogeneity of variances, as assessed by Levene's test for equality of variances (p <.0.0005). When considering the distribution characteristics and sample sizes, the Brown-Forsythe test was deemed to be the more appropriate non-equal variance test to use (Vallejo & Escudero, 2000).

A significant ANOVA result was found, with Opportunity statistically significantly different for the MBTI – 16 groups (n = 198), Brown-Forsythe's F(15, 67.294) = 1.843, p = 0.046[4], partial eta squared (η^2) = 0.117. This result suggests at least one of the MBTI – 16 group means was different from the others, with the MBTI – 16 factor explaining 11.7% of the variability in Opportunity for the sample, which would be considered a medium-to-large effect size (Cohen, 1988).

Follow-up pairwise comparisons were then conducted to identify where differences existed. As the homogeneity-of-variances assumption was violated, the Games-Howell post hoc test was used to check all potential pairwise comparisons. The closest pairwise comparison to approach any meaningful difference was an increase in the mean Motivation score from the MBTI – 16 ENFJ group (M = 2.60, SD = 1.012) to the ISFP group (M = 3.8, SD = 0.632), a mean increase of 0.746, SE = 0.207, which was not statistically significant (p = 0.206) with the Games-Howell multiple-comparison correction applied.

As noted before, as it was not expected to find a significant difference among 120 comparisons with a multiple-correction factor applied, a planned comparison between the highest and lowest scores was conducted using the 'equal variances not assumed' output. Due to two equal-highest scores, a complex contrast was run comparing the lowest Opportunity score (ESTJ, M = 3.4, SD = 1.3) with the two equal-highest groups, ISFP (*M* = 4.4, *SD* = 0.25) and ENTP (*M* = 4.4, *SD* = 0.48). The Opportunity score was statistically significantly higher in the (combined) ISFP and ENTP groups (*M* = 4.4) compared to the ESTJ group (*M* = 3.4), with a mean increase of 0.96 (*SE* = 0.41), $p = 0.034$ ($t = 2.357$, $df = 13.395$, equal variances not assumed).

MBTI – 16 on Ability

Regarding Ability, two potential outliers were identified in the starting pool of sample respondents: one in INTJ (ID = 157) and one in ESTJ (ID = 187). Both outliers were omitted in the first round, with a new one emerging for ESFJ (ID = 17). This third outlier was omitted for ESFJ, with a final check showing no remaining outliers.

The one-way ANOVA test was then run on this reduced group. There was homogeneity of variances, as assessed by Levene's test for equality of variances ($p = 0.246$). A significant ANOVA result was found, with Ability being statistically significantly for the different MBTI – 16 groups ($n = 203$), $F(15, 189) = 2.326$, $p = 0.005$, partial eta squared (η^2) = 0.156. This result suggests at least one of the MBTI – 16 group means was different from the others, with the MBTI – 16 factor explaining 15.6% of the variability in Ability for the sample, which would be considered a large effect size (Cohen, 1988).

Follow-up pairwise comparisons were then conducted to identify where differences existed. As the homogeneity-of-variances assumption was not violated, the Tukey HSD post hoc test was used. There was an increase in the mean Ability score from the MBTI – 16 ENTJ group (*M* = 2.6, *SD* = 0.56) to the ENFJ group (*M* = 3.7, *SD* = 1.01), with a mean increase of 1.15 (*SE* = 0.36), which was not statistically significant ($p = 0.119$) with the Tukey HSD multiple-comparison correction applied.

As before, a planned contrast was then conducted comparing the highest and lowest Ability scores. The Ability score was statistically significantly higher in the ENTP group (*M* = 4.0, *SD* = 0.79) compared to the ISTP group (*M* = 2.4, *SD* = 0.82), with a mean increase of 2.4 (*SE* = 0.52), $p < 0.0005$ ($t = 12.318$, $df = 189$, equal variances assumed).

Appendix B5: multiple regression analysis – MBTI – 4 on AMO

This appendix presents supplementary materials for the "Multiple regression analysis – MBTI – 4 on AMO" section. Multiple regression was used to determine the relationship between the MBTI – 4 (as the predictors) and HPWS (as the criterion or outcome), represented by Ability, Motivation and Opportunity. This was done by regressing the MBTI – 4 on each of the AMO elements using hierarchical regression, where the variables were entered in two sets (or steps). To control for respondent differences, age and gender were entered in step one of the regression. The four MBTI base pairs (MBTI – 4) were then entered in step two. Using this approach allows the incremental influence of the MBTI – 4 beyond that of the controls (age, gender) to be determined. Recommended settings were used, including excluding missing cases pairwise (Coakes, 2013).

In the initial run, the diagnostic information for each regression was reviewed. For the standardised residuals, outliers greater than ±3 standard deviations evaluated for removal with the aim of improving model fit. One respondent each was omitted from the sample for the Motivation and Opportunity regressions due to this requirement. No multicollinearity issues were identified, with all VIF values less than 1.2, which was well below the recommended threshold of 5 (Coakes, 2013; Yong & Pearce, 2013). Additionally, examination of the residuals suggested the relevant assumptions regarding the normality and independence were satisfied in the main.

Appendix B6: ANOVA – influence of MBTI – 16 on OCB and AOC

This appendix presents supplementary materials for the "ANOVA analysis – influence of MBTI – 16 on OCB and AOC" section.

MBTI – 16 on OCB

Regarding OCB, two potential outliers were identified in the starting pool of sample respondents: both in ESFJ (IDs = 146, 248). Both outliers were omitted in the first round, with a final check showing no remaining outliers.

The one-way ANOVA test was then run on this reduced group. There was homogeneity of variances, as assessed by Levene's test for equality of variances (p = 0.807). A non-significant ANOVA result was found, with OCB not statistically significantly different for different MBTI – 16 groups (n = 206), $F(15, 190)$ = 0.574, p = 0.893, with a partial eta squared (η^2) = 0.043, indicating a small-to-medium effect size.

To try to better understand the non-significant result, it was decided to run a planned comparison between the lowest and highest OCB groups as part of the analysis. The OCB score was marginally statistically significantly higher in the ISTJ group (M = 4.8, SD = 0.35) compared to the ISFP group (M = 4.3, SD = 0.50), with a mean increase of 0.50 (SE = 0.30), p = 0.10 (t = 1.653, df = 190, equal variances assumed).

MBTI – 16 on AOC

Regarding AOC, ten potential outliers were identified in the starting pool of sample respondents: INTJ (IDs = 157, 23, 236), ENTJ (ID = 213), ISFJ (ID = 2), ENTP (ID = 233), ESTJ (ID = 212) and ISTP (ID = 167) and ESFJ (IDs = 89, 75). Four outliers were omitted in the first run, four more in the second run and two in the third run, with a final check showing no remaining outliers. However, omitting the outliers for the ENTP and ISTP groups resulted in both groups having zero variance (as the remaining responses for ENTP and ISTP all had a value of 4, thus no variance for the two groups), which resulted in issues in running the ANOVA. Therefore, these two outliers were again included in the sample, thus resolving the zero-variance issue and resulting in a total of eight outliers being omitted.

The one-way ANOVA test was then run on this reduced group. There was homogeneity of variances, as assessed by Levene's test for equality of variances ($p = 0.209$). A non-significant ANOVA result was found, with AOC not statistically significantly different for the different MBTI – 16 groups ($n = 200$), $F(15, 184) = 0.344$, $p = 0.990$, with a partial eta squared (η^2) = 0.027, indicating a small effect size.

To try to better understand the non-significant result, it was decided to run a planned comparison between the lowest and highest AOC groups as part of the analysis. The AOC score was marginally statistically significantly higher in the ESFP group ($M = 4.4$, $SD = 0.63$) compared to the ISTP group ($M = 3.8$, $SD = 0.45$), with a mean increase of 0.64 ($SE = 0.33$), $p = 0.056$ ($t = 1.653$, $df = 190$, equal variances assumed).

Appendix B7: regression – MBTI – 4 on OCB and AOC

This appendix presents supplementary materials for the "Multiple regression analysis – MBTI – 4 on OCB and AOC" section. To assess the combined influence of the four MBTI – 4 base pairs (as the predictors) on OCB and AOC (the outcome), hierarchical regression was used, where the variables were entered in two sets (or steps). To control for respondent differences, age and gender were entered in step one, and the MBTI – 4 base pairs were then entered in step two. Recommended settings were used, including excluding missing cases pairwise, with the resulting sample size satisfying the recommended ratio of observations to variables.

In the initial run, the diagnostic information for each regression was reviewed. For the standardised residuals, outliers greater than ±3 standard deviations evaluated for removal with the aim of improving model fit, which meant two sample respondents were omitted from the sample for AOC due to this requirement. No multicollinearity issues were identified, with all VIF values less than 1.2, which was well below the recommended threshold of 5 (Coakes, 2013; Hair et al., 2014; Yong & Pearce, 2013). Additionally, examination of the residuals suggested the relevant assumptions regarding the normality and independence were satisfied in the main, though there was some banding evident for AOC, and the results for this regression should be viewed with some caution. The results are summarised in Table 4.7.

As presented in Table 4.7, the MBTI – 4 pair of Thinking/Feeling had the strongest influence of the four base pairs on both OCB and AOC, and this was the only base pair to achieve at least a marginally significant influence on OCB ($p = 0.09$), and just fall short of marginal significance in its influence on

AOC ($p = 0.102$), with the other relationships non-significant ($p > 0.20$). When looking at the results in Table 4.7, positive relationships can be seen relating to the Introvert vs Extrovert base pair when all of the variables are considered, in contrast, negative relationships are present in all variables associated with Intuition vs Sensing and Thinking vs Feeling, the rest of the relationship vary from positive to negative relationships. However, many of the relationships are very weak or negligible in magnitude, as well as non-significant.

Appendix B8: ANOVA analysis – influence of MBTI – 16 on Task Enjoyment

This appendix presents supplementary materials for the "ANOVA analysis – influence of MBTI – 16 on Task Enjoyment and Task Duration" section.

MBTI – 16 on Task Enjoyment

Regarding Task Enjoyment, three potential outliers were identified in the starting pool of sample respondents: two in ESTJ (IDs = 37, 154) and one in ENFP (ID = 273). Two outliers were omitted in the first round, with the third in a second round and a final check showing no remaining outliers.

The one-way ANOVA test was then run on this reduced group. There was a lack of homogeneity of variances, as assessed by Levene's test for equality of variances ($p = 0.03$). A marginally significant ANOVA result was found, with Task Enjoyment not statistically significantly different for different MBTI – 16 groups ($n = 206$), Welch's $F(15, 32.982) = 1.973$, $p = 0.051$,[5] partial eta squared (η^2) = 0.141, indicating a large effect size.

With the large effect size, inspection of the boxplots and the suggestion from the Welch test that something was happening in the data, it was decided to run a planned comparison between the lowest and highest Task Enjoyment groups as part of the analysis. The Task Enjoyment score was statistically significantly higher in the ENTP group ($M = 23.0$, $SD = 4.5$) compared to the INTP group ($M = 14.7$, $SD = 3.9$), with a mean difference of 8.3 ($SE = 2.6$), $p = 0.012$ ($t = 3.241$, $df = 8$, equal variances not assumed).

MBTI type and Task Duration

Table B5 shows the average Task Duration for completing different types of tasks undertaken by productivity experts. All of the means are in the 3–4 range, which covers durations ranging from 2–4 days (4) to one week (3).

MBTI – 16 on Task Duration

Regarding Task Duration (for all tasks), nine potential outliers were identified in the starting pool of sample respondents: INTP (IDs = 169), ENTP (ID = 238), INFJ (ID = 114, 191), ESFJ (ID = 77, 92, 142, 166), ISTP (ID = 119) and

Table B5 Mean Comparisons by MBTI Type and Task Duration

	All Tasks	*Soft Tasks*	*Hard Tasks*	*Routine Tasks*	*Non-routine Tasks*
Introvert	3.5	3.7	3.2	3.8	3.1
Extrovert	3.7	4.0	3.4	3.9	3.4
Intuition	3.5	3.7	3.2	3.7	3.2
Sensing	3.7	4.0	3.3	4.0	3.3
Feeling	3.6	3.9	3.2	3.9	3.2
Thinking	3.7	3.9	3.4	3.9	3.4
Judging	3.6	3.8	3.2	3.8	3.2
Perceiving	3.8	4.1	3.5	4.2	3.4

ESFP (IDs = 163). Seven outliers were omitted in the first round; however, case 169 was added back based on the resulting boxplot along with one more outlier identified for INFJ (114). In the second round, two more outliers were omitted and the last in the final round for a total of nine outliers omitted.

The one-way ANOVA test was then run on this reduced group. There was a lack of homogeneity of variances, as assessed by Levene's test for equality of variances (p = 0.012). A significant ANOVA result was found, with Task Duration statistically significantly different for different MBTI – 16 groups (n = 204), Welch's $F(15, 31.326) = 2.277$, $p = 0.025$,[6] partial eta squared (η^2) = 0.121, indicating a medium-to-large effect size (Vallejo & Escudero, 2000).

Follow-up pairwise comparisons were then conducted to identify where differences existed. It was decided to run a planned comparison between the lowest and highest Task Duration groups as part of the analysis. The Task Duration score was statistically significantly higher in the ESTP group (M = 4.6, SD = 0.54) compared to the INFP group (M = 2.9, SD = 0.65), with a mean difference of 1.7 (SE = 0.46), p = 0.023 (t = 3.649, df = 3.894, equal variances not assumed).

Appendix B9: regression analysis – influence of MBTI – 4 on Task Enjoyment and Task Duration

This appendix presents supplementary materials for the "Multiple regression analysis – MBTI – 4 on Task Enjoyment and Task Duration" section. To assess the combined influence of the four MBTI – 4 base pairs (as the predictors) on Task Enjoyment and Task Duration (the outcome), hierarchical regression was used, where the variables were entered in two sets (or steps). To control for respondent differences, age and gender were entered in step one, and the MBTI – 4 base pairs were then entered in step two. Recommended settings were used, including excluding missing cases pairwise, with the resulting sample size satisfying the recommended ratio of observations to variables.

In the initial run, the diagnostic information for each regression was reviewed. For the standardised residuals, outliers greater than ±3 standard deviations evaluated for removal with the aim of improving model fit, which meant one sample respondent was omitted from the sample for Task Enjoyment (for the Soft Tasks subgroup) due to this requirement. No multicollinearity issues were identified, with all VIF values less than 1.2, which was well below the recommended threshold of 5 (Coakes, 2013; Hair et al., 2014; Yong & Pearce, 2013). Additionally, examination of the residuals suggested the relevant assumptions regarding the normality and independence were satisfied in the main, though there was some possible grouping evident (two groups) in the residuals scatterplot for the Soft Tasks subgroup, and the results for the Soft Tasks subgroup regression should be viewed with some caution.

For Task Duration, after reviewing the standardised residuals, between three and five outliers were removed: three (all tasks), five (Soft Tasks), three (Hard Tasks), four (Routine Tasks) and four (Non-routine Tasks). No multicollinearity issues were identified, with all VIF values less than 1.2, which was well below the recommended threshold of 5 (Coakes, 2013; Hair et al., 2014; Yong & Pearce, 2013). Additionally, examination of the residuals suggested the relevant assumptions regarding the normality and independence were satisfied in the main.

The results are summarised in Table 4.10 for Task Enjoyment and Table 4.11 for Task Duration.

Appendix B10: regression analysis – moderation influence of MBTI – 4 on A-M-O → AOC, AOC + OCB → Task Duration and AOC + OCB → Task Enjoyment

This appendix presents supplementary materials for the "Exploring the moderator potential of the MBTI – 4 base pairs" section. To assess the moderating influence of the four MBTI – 4 base pairs, hierarchical regression was used, where the variables were entered in two sets (or steps). To control for respondent differences, age and gender were entered in step one, and the A-M-O variables were then entered in step two. Recommended settings were used, including excluding missing cases pairwise, with the resulting sample size satisfying the recommended ratio of observations to variables.

MBTI – 4 moderating influence on A-M-O → AOC

In the initial run, the diagnostic information for each regression was reviewed. For the standardised residuals, outliers greater than ±3 standard deviations evaluated for removal with the aim of improving model fit, which meant two sample respondents were omitted from the sample for each regression due to this requirement. No multicollinearity issues were identified, with all VIF values less than 1.8, which was well below the recommended threshold of 5 (Coakes, 2013; Hair et al., 2014; Yong & Pearce, 2013).

MBTI – 4 moderating influence on A-M-O → OCB

In the initial run, the diagnostic information for each regression was reviewed. For the standardised residuals, outliers greater than ±3 standard deviations evaluated for removal with the aim of improving model fit, which meant no (zero) sample respondents were omitted from the sample for each regression due to this requirement. No multicollinearity issues were identified, with all VIF values less than 1.8, which was well below the recommended threshold of 5 (Coakes, 2013; Hair et al., 2014; Yong & Pearce, 2013).

MBTI – 4 moderating influence on AOC + OCB → Task Duration

In the initial run, the diagnostic information for each regression was reviewed. For the standardised residuals, outliers greater than ±3 standard deviations evaluated for removal with the aim of improving model fit, which meant between three and four sample respondents were omitted from the sample for each regression due to this requirement. No multicollinearity issues were identified, with all VIF values less than 2.1, which was well below the recommended threshold of 5 (Coakes, 2013; Hair et al., 2014; Yong & Pearce, 2013).

MBTI – 4 moderating influence on AOC + OCB → Task Enjoyment

In the initial run, the diagnostic information for each regression was reviewed. For the standardised residuals, outliers greater than ±3 standard deviations evaluated for removal with the aim of improving model fit, which meant one sample respondent was omitted from the sample for each regression due to this requirement. No multicollinearity issues were identified, with all VIF values less than 2.1, which was well below the recommended threshold of 5 (Coakes, 2013; Hair et al., 2014; Yong & Pearce, 2013).

Appendix B11: Junior-Senior role analysis

This appendix presents supplementary materials for the "Differences in Junior and Senior roles" section. First, each group was tested to see if there was difference when equal proportions were specified for the 16 MBTI types. Significant differences were found for sample respondents in Junior roles (chi-square = 136.643, $df = 14$, $p < 0.001$[7]) and for those in Senior roles (chi-square = 91.077, $df = 15$, $p < 0.001$).

Second, the profile of the 16 MBTI types for each group of Junior or Senior sample respondents was then compared separately to the general population profile for the 16 MBTI types as reported by 16personalities.com (see Tables B6 and B7). A significant result was found for sample respondents in Senior roles (chi-square = 67.919, $df = 15$, $p < 0.001$). As the cell for ENTP types had a zero response for Junior roles (ENTP), this category was combined with an adjacent category (ENTJ) to facilitate the analysis. A significant result was found for sample respondents in Junior roles (chi-square = 137.252, $df = 14$, $p < 0.001$). Due to the number of cells having expected frequencies less than 5 for Senior roles

Table B6 MBTI – 16 Types and Junior Roles

MBTI Type	*Observed* N	*Expected* N	*Residual*
INTJ	11	2.1	8.9
INTP	5	3.5	1.5
ENTJ + ENTP	3	11.9	-8.9
INFJ	6	1.4	4.6
INFP	6	2.8	3.2
ENFJ	11	5.6	5.4
ENFP	4	9.8	-5.8
ISTJ	7	11.9	-4.9
ISFJ	19	9.8	9.2
ESTJ	9	18.2	-9.2
ESFJ	40	16.8	23.2
ISTP	3	8.4	-5.4
ISFP	3	8.4	-5.4
ESTP	3	14.0	-11.0
ESFP	10	15.4	-5.4
Total	140		

Note: The cell for ENTP types had zero responses for Junior roles (ENTP), so this category was combined with an adjacent category (ENTJ) to facilitate the analysis, resulting in 15 MBTI categories for analysis.

Table B7 MBTI – 16 Types and Senior Roles

MBTI Type	*Observed N*	*Expected N*	*Residual*
INTJ	7	1.6	5.4
INTP	1	2.6	-1.6
ENTJ	7	4.2	2.8
ENTP	5	4.7	.3
INFJ	3	1.0	2.0
INFP	2	2.1	-0.1
ENFJ	4	4.2	-0.2
ENFP	8	7.3	0.7
ISTJ	8	8.8	-0.8
ISFJ	15	7.3	7.7
ESTJ	6	13.5	-7.5
ESFJ	26	12.5	13.5
ISTP	2	6.2	-4.2
ISFP	1	6.2	-5.2
ESTP	3	10.4	-7.4
ESFP	6	11.4	-5.4
Total	104		

(seven cells, 43.8%) and Junior roles (four cells, 26.7%), these two results should be interpreted with caution.

In summary, the profile of MBTI – 16 types for each group of sample respondents in Junior or Senior roles were not similarly distributed for the financial services productivity specialists in this study as the general population reported by 16personalities.com. Specifically, the group of financial services productivity specialists in a Junior role in this study featured greater departures from the general population for ISFJ and ESFJ roles, which are over-represented, which may suggest that Organisation X has a preference towards these types of individuals for productivity-based work. Contrastingly, there appears to be an under-representation of ESTJ, ESTP, ISTP and ISFP roles, indicating there is a lesser representation of Extroverted individuals with a Sensing preference and Introverts with Perceiving preferences. Potential conclusions that can be drawn here include that perhaps there was a shortage of the above-mentioned types applying for productivity-based roles or simply Organisation X does not see these individuals as the best-fit for productivity-based work.

For those in Senior roles, greater departures from the general population were observed for ISFJ, with ESFJ roles being again over-represented and ESTP and ESTJ roles under-represented, meaning Organisation X again has a positive preference towards Sensing, Feeling, Judging individuals for productivity roles, whereas they have a negative association with Extroverted, Sensing, Thinking types. Again, these differences could be due to a lack of these individuals applying for these roles or the fact that the Organisation X does not see these roles as best-fit for productivity-based work.

Next, the Junior and Senior 16 MBTI profile groups were compared to each other using a chi-square test of homogeneity for Junior vs Senior for the profile of 16 MBTI types. Overall, no significant difference was found (chi-square = 19.168, $df = 15$, $p = 0.206$). However, due to the 14 cells (43.8%) that had an expected count less than 5, this result must be viewed with caution. Therefore, follow-up pairwise checks were conducted by dummy coding the MBTI variable into 16 new variables (Laerd Statistics, 2017), with differences noted for the following MBTI types: ENTJ (chi-square = 3.196, $df = 1$, $p = 0.074$), ENTP (chi-square = 6.872, $df = 1$, $p = 0.009$), ENFP (chi-square = 2.983, $df = 1$, $p = 0.084$) and ENFJ (chi-square = 1.664, $df = 1$, $p = 0.197$).

Lastly, the Junior and Senior roles were reviewed with the MBTI – 4 base-pair categories, using a binomial test for equal proportions for each base pair for each role category (see Table B8). The expected (tested) proportions for each category were set at 0.50 (50%). However, the actual numbers for those in Junior roles showed Extrovert being 57% vs Introvert 43%, Sensing 67% vs Intuition 33%, Thinking 29% and Feeling 71% and, lastly, Perceiving 24% and Judging 76%. For those in Senior roles, the results showed Extrovert being 63% vs Introvert 38%, Sensing 64% vs Intuition 36%, Thinking 38% and Feeling 63% and, lastly, Perceiving 27% and Judging 73%.

The proportions for each pair were significantly different from the 50% test proportion except for the Extrovert and Introvert category for Junior roles.

Next, the *phi* coefficient and point-biserial correlation coefficient were calculated to understand the strength and direction of the relationships between the MBTI – 4 and select individual organisational and performance variables. The *phi* coefficient is used for two dichotomous variables, while the point-biserial correlation is a special case of Pearson's correlation, where one variable is dichotomous (MBTI – 4 base pair) and the other continuous (interval or ratio scaled).

Table B8 Binomial Test for MBTI – 4 by Junior/Senior Roles

Binomial Test – Junior Roles

		Category	N	*Observed Proportion*	*Test Proportion*	*Exact Significance (Two-Tailed)*
MBTI: Introvert vs Extrovert	Group 1	Introvert	60	0.43	0.50	0.108
	Group 2	Extrovert	80	0.57		
	Total		140	1.00		
MBTI: Intuition vs Sensing	Group 1	Intuition	46	0.33	0.50	0.000
	Group 2	Sensing	94	0.67		
	Total		140	1.00		
MBTI: Thinking vs Feeling	Group 1	Thinking	41	0.29	0.50	0.000
	Group 2	Feeling	99	0.71		
	Total		140	1.00		
MBTI: Perceiving vs Judging	Group 1	Judging	106	0.76	0.50	0.000
	Group 2	Perceiving	34	0.24		
	Total		140	1.00		

Binomial Test – Senior Roles

		Category	N	*Observed Proportion*	*Test Proportion*	*Exact Significance (Two-Tailed)*
MBTI: Introvert vs Extrovert	Group 1	Introvert	39	0.38	0.50	0.014
	Group 2	Extrovert	65	0.63		
	Total	104	1.00			
MBTI: Intuition vs Sensing	Group 1	Intuition	37	0.36	0.50	0.004
	Group 2	Sensing	67	0.64		
	Total	104	1.00			
MBTI: Thinking vs Feeling	Group 1	Thinking	39	0.38	0.50	0.014
	Group 2	Feeling	65	0.63		
	Total	104	1.00			
MBTI: Perceiving vs Judging	Group 1	Judging	76	0.73	0.50	0.000
	Group 2	Perceiving	28	0.27		
	Total	104	1.00			

Table B9 MBTI – 4 Categories and Their Point-Biserial Correlation Coefficients

Category	*Tenure*	*Hours Worked*	*Productivity Experience*	*Projects Completed*	*Age*
MBTI Introvert vs Extrovert	$r_=$ 0.007 *p*-value = 0.915	0.062 0.324	0.037 0.567	0.097# 0.122	0.99# 0.163
Intuition vs Sensing	0.023 0.714	−0.133* 0.034	−0.074 0.255	−0.161* 0.011	0.016 0.828
Thinking vs Feeling	−0.172** 0.006	0.084# 0.183	0.132* 0.043	0.147* 0.019	−0.027 0.705
Perceiving vs Judging	−0.059 0.349	−0.051* 0.047	−0.051 0.440	0.097# 0.123	−0.001 0.988

Note: The point-biserial correlation coefficient (r_{pb}) is on the first row and *p*-value on the second row. # = $p \leq 0.20$, ^ = $p \leq 0.10$, * = $p \leq 0.05$ ** = $p \leq 0.01$, *** = $p \leq 0.001$.

Table B10 MBTI – 4 Categories and Their phi Coefficients

Category	*Gender*	*Productivity vs Non-productivity Role*	*Junior vs Senior*
MBTI Introvert vs Extrovert	*phi* = −0.018 *p*-value = 0.803	*phi* = 0.009 *p*-value = 0.884	*phi* = 0.054 *p*-value = 0.401
Intuition vs Sensing	0.059 0.407	−0.126* 0.050	−0.028 0.659
Thinking vs Feeling	−0.263 0.00	0.025 0.969	0.087# 0.178
Perceiving vs Judging	−0.141* 0.047	0.038 0.556	0.030 0.641

Note: the first number (top line) in the cell is the *phi* coefficient and the second (bottom line) is the *p*-value; # = $p \leq 0.20$, ^ = $p \leq 0.10$, * = $p \leq 0.05$ ** = $p \leq 0.01$, *** = $p \leq 0.001$.

These are presented in Table B9 (point biserial) and Table B10 (*phi*). Two MBTI – 4 types showed more significant point-biserial correlations – Intuition vs Sensing and Thinking vs Feeling – than the other types. The correlations ranged from moderate to weak in strength, with most associations not statistically significant.

In addition, the MBTI Introvert vs Extrovert category had a nearly perfect uphill positive linear relationship at 0.99, as the MBTI category increases the age category does too, though this figure is so strong that it must viewed with caution.

Notes

1 In the original sample, a marginally significant result was found ($n = 208$, $p = 0.08$), with a significant result found after the first round of omission, where only one extreme value was omitted from each category ($n = 205$, $p = 0.023$). This suggests that the omitted-outlier analysis is suitable.

2 For ANOVA, Cohen (1988) classifies 0.01 as a small effect, 0.06 as a medium effect and 0.14 as a large effect.

3 Without a multiple-comparison correction applied, the INTP-ISFP and INTP-EFFJ pairs would be significantly different (mean difference = 1.20, $p = 0.019$), along with many other pairwise comparisons.
4 There is a lack of agreement on which statistic is best in this situation. The other non-homogenous variances option is the Welch test, the result of which was Welch's $F(15, 32.549) = 1.603$, $p = 0.127$.
5 The alternative non-homogenous variance test result: Brown-Forsythe's $F(15, 16.426) = 1.760$, $p = 0.134$.
6 The alternative non-homogenous variance test result: Brown-Forsythe's $F(15, 70.825) = 1.764$, $p = 0.058$
7 Due to one of the 16 MBTI categories for Junior having zero responses, the test was calculated for 15 equal categories instead of 16.

References

Bryman, A., & Bell, E., (2011). *Business Research Methods.* Third Edition. Oxford University Press: Oxford, UK.

Coakes, S.J., (2013). SPSS Version 24 for MAC, Analysis without Anguish. John Wiley & Sons.

Fornell, C., & Larcker, D., (1981). Evaluating Structural Equation Models with Unobservable Variables and Measurement Error. *Journal of Marketing Research,* 18(1). 39–50.

Hair, J. J., Black, W. C., Babin, B. J., & Andersen, R. E. (2014). *Multivariate Data Analysis: Pearson New International Edition A Global Perspective* (7th ed.). Pearson Education Ltd: Harlow, UK.

Kumar, A., & Lawley, D., (2005). *Marketing Research.* The Pacific Rim Edition. John Wiley & Sons, Inc.

Malhotra, N. (2010). *Marketing Research: An Applied Orientation* (6th ed.). Pearson Education: Upper Saddle River, NJ.

Nunnally, J.C., & Bernstein, I.H., (1994). The Assessment of Reliability. *Psychometric Theory,* 3, 248–292.

O'Leary, Z., (2004). *The Essential Guide to Doing Research.* Sage Publications: London.

Pallant, J., (2007). *SPSS Survival Manual: A Step by Step Guide to Data Analysis using SPSS for Windows.* Third Edition. Open University Press: Maidenhead, UK.

Robbins, S.P., & Barnwell, N., (2002). *Organisational Theory.* Fourth Edition. Pearson Education Australia, Prentice Hall.

Sekaran, U., & Bougie, R., (2013). *Research Methods for Business: A Skill Building Approach.* Sixth Edition. Wiley & Sons Ltd.: New York.

VanVoorhis, C.R., & Morgan, L.B., (2007). Understanding Power and Rules of Thumb for Determining Sample Sizes. *Tutorials in Quantitative Methods for Psychology,* 3(2), 43–50.

Yong, A.G., & Pearce, S., (2013). A Beginner's Guide to Factor Analysis: Focusing on Exploratory Factor Analysis. *Tutorials in Quantitative Methods for Psychology,* 9(2), 74–94.

Index

For Product Safety Concerns and Information please contact our EU representative GPSR@taylorandfrancis.com
Taylor & Francis Verlag GmbH, Kaufingerstraße 24, 80331 München, Germany

www.ingramcontent.com/pod-product-compliance
Lightning Source LLC
LaVergne TN
LVHW021128300926
849160LV00010B/920
* 9 7 8 0 3 6 7 5 0 3 1 9 2 *